D1261881

# Clinician's Guide to Posttraumatic Stress Disorder

DREXEL UNIVERSITY
HEALTH SCIENCES LIBRARIES
HAHNEMANN LIBRARY

# Clinician's Guide to Posttraumatic Stress Disorder

Edited by

## Gerald M. Rosen
## B. Christopher Frueh

**WILEY**

John Wiley & Sons, Inc.

**WM
172
C642
2010**

This book is printed on acid-free paper. ♾

Copyright © 2010 by John Wiley & Sons, Inc. All rights reserved.

Published by John Wiley & Sons, Inc., Hoboken, New Jersey.
Published simultaneously in Canada.

No part of this publication may be reproduced, stored in a retrieval system, or transmitted in any form or by any means, electronic, mechanical, photocopying, recording, scanning, or otherwise, except as permitted under Section 107 or 108 of the 1976 United States Copyright Act, without either the prior written permission of the Publisher, or authorization through payment of the appropriate per-copy fee to the Copyright Clearance Center, Inc., 222 Rosewood Drive, Danvers, MA 01923, (978) 750-8400, fax (978) 646-8600, or on the web at www.copyright.com. Requests to the Publisher for permission should be addressed to the Permissions Department, John Wiley & Sons, Inc., 111 River Street, Hoboken, NJ 07030, (201) 748-6011, fax (201) 748-6008.

Limit of Liability/Disclaimer of Warranty: While the publisher and author have used their best efforts in preparing this book, they make no representations or warranties with respect to the accuracy or completeness of the contents of this book and specifically disclaim any implied warranties of merchantability or fitness for a particular purpose. No warranty may be created or extended by sales representatives or written sales materials. The advice and strategies contained herein may not be suitable for your situation. You should consult with a professional where appropriate. Neither the publisher nor author shall be liable for any loss of profit or any other commercial damages, including but not limited to special, incidental, consequential, or other damages.

This publication is designed to provide accurate and authoritative information in regard to the subject matter covered. It is sold with the understanding that the publisher is not engaged in rendering professional services. If legal, accounting, medical, psychological or any other expert assistance is required, the services of a competent professional person should be sought.

Designations used by companies to distinguish their products are often claimed as trademarks. In all instances where John Wiley & Sons, Inc. is aware of a claim, the product names appear in initial capital or all capital letters. Readers, however, should contact the appropriate companies for more complete information regarding trademarks and registration.

For general information on our other products and services please contact our Customer Care Department within the U.S. at (800) 762-2974, outside the United States at (317) 572-3993 or fax (317) 572-4002.

Wiley also publishes its books in a variety of electronic formats. Some content that appears in print may not be available in electronic books. For more information about Wiley products, visit our website at www.wiley.com.

*Library of Congress Cataloging-in-Publication Data:*

Clinician's guide to posttraumatic stress disorder / edited by Gerald M. Rosen, B. Christopher Frueh.
  p. cm.
  Includes index.
  ISBN 978-0-470-45095-6 (cloth); 978-0-470-64668-7 (e-book); 978-0-470-64691-5 (e-book); 978-0-470-64692-2 (e-book)
  1. Post-traumatic stress disorder. I. Rosen, Gerald M., 1945— II. Frueh, B. Christopher.
  RC552.P67C55   2010
  616.85'21—dc22

                                                                    2010000767

Printed in the United States of America

10 9 8 7 6 5 4 3 2 1

# Contents

# Author Biographies

RICHARD BRYANT, PhD, is Scientia Professor of Psychology at the University of New South Wales. Dr. Bryant also is director of the Traumatic Stress Clinic at Westmead Hospital, Sydney. He has published over 250 journal articles, with a research focus on biological and cognitive mechanisms in traumatic stress and the treatment of posttrauma disorders. Dr. Bryant has consulted with many civilian and military agencies around the world to advise on appropriate mental health responses in the aftermath of trauma.

JOHN COOPER, MBBS, MPM, FRANZCP is a psychiatrist who has worked clinically for over 20 years in the area of posttraumatic mental health. Dr. Cooper is an expert consultant to the Australian Centre for Posttraumatic Mental Health (ACPMH), and provides expert advice to state and federal government in the area of posttraumatic mental health. He has written a number of peer-reviewed papers examining best practice guidelines for treating posttraumatic stress disorder.

MARK CREAMER, PhD, is director of the Australian Centre for Posttraumatic Mental Health (ACPMH) and professor of psychology in the Department of Psychiatry at the University of Melbourne. Dr. Creamer has worked extensively with individuals, communities, and organizations following traumatic incidents of natural and human origin. He regularly consults with state and federal governments, has published over 100 journal publications, and serves on the Board of Directors of the International Society for Traumatic Stress Studies.

GRANT J. DEVILLY, PhD, is associate professor at Griffith University in Brisbane, Australia. Dr. Grant's research focus is predominantly on preventing long-term pathology following trauma. He has worked at the Institute of Psychiatry in London, England, and as a senior psychologist at both Queensland and Victorian psychiatric hospitals in Australia. Dr. Grant also has a part-time private practice in clinical psychology.

JON D. ELHAI, PhD, is assistant professor of psychology at the University of Toledo. Dr. Elhai has published numerous scientific articles and edited book chapters on posttraumatic stress disorder. His publications primarily focus on assessment, psychopathology, and health services issues. Dr. Elhai serves on the editorial boards of several journals, including the *Journal of Traumatic Stress, Journal of Trauma and Dissociation*, and *Psychological Trauma*.

EDNA B. FOA, PhD, is professor of clinical psychology in psychiatry at the University of Pennsylvania, and director of the Center for the Treatment and Study of Anxiety. Dr. Foa is internationally recognized for her studies on the psychopathology and treatment of anxiety disorders. She has published several books and over 350 articles; chaired the DSM-IV Subcommittee for OCD; co-chaired the DSM-IV Subcommittee for PTSD; and chaired the Treatment Guidelines Task Force of the International Society for Traumatic Stress Disorders. Dr. Foa's work has been recognized with numerous awards and honors including a Lifetime Achievement Award presented by the International Society for Traumatic Stress Studies.

JULIAN D. FORD, PhD, is associate professor of psychiatry at the University of Connecticut School of Medicine and director of the University's Health Center Child Trauma Clinic and Center for Trauma Response Recovery and Preparedness. Dr. Ford conducts research on psychotherapy and family therapy, health services utilization, psychometric screening and assessment, and psychiatric epidemiology. He serves on the Editorial Board of scientific and professional journals such as *Clinical Psychology: Science & Practice* and *Child Maltreatment*.

EVAN M. FORMAN, PhD, is associate professor of psychology at Drexel University, where he is the director of the doctoral program in clinical psychology. Dr. Evans' research interests include the development and evaluation of acceptance-based behavior interventions, mediators of psychotherapy outcome, and posttraumatic stress disorder. He is the author of numerous scholarly papers and chapters, as well as co-editor of a forthcoming book *Acceptance and Mindfulness in Cognitive-Behavior Therapy*.

B. CHRISTOPHER FRUEH, PhD, is a clinical psychologist and professor of psychology at the University of Hawaii, Hilo, HI, and McNair Scholar and director of Clinical Research at the Menninger Clinic, Houston, TX. Dr. Frueh has served as Principal Investigator (PI) on 13 federally funded research grants and authored over 170 scientific publications. His clinical and research focus has been on improving mental health services for trauma survivors, including veterans, civilians, and adults with severe mental illnesses. When work on this book was initiated, Dr. Frueh was a professor of psychiatry at Baylor College of Medicine.

ELKE GERAERTS, PhD, is assistant professor of clinical psychology and principal investigator of the Clinical Cognition Lab at the Erasmus University of Rotterdam in the Netherlands. Dr. Geraerts obtained her PhD degree at Maastricht University and was a postdoctoral fellow at Harvard University. Her research has focused on how people remember and forget traumatic events, and the cognitive functioning of those who report recovered memories of abuse. Dr. Geraerts has published over 30 peer-reviewed articles and has served as an expert witness on cases of childhood abuse.

RICHARD GIST, PhD, is a public health psychologist and principal assistant to the director of the Kansas City (Missouri) Fire Department. Dr. Gist holds research affiliations at Kansas City University of Medicine and Biosciences, and with the Department of Emergency Medicine at the University of Missouri (Kansas City). He has authored more than a hundred publications related to disaster response. Dr. Gist recently chaired for the National Fallen Firefighters Foundation a series of consensus meetings on occupational behavioral health in the fire service.

ANOUK L. GRUBAUGH, PhD, is associate professor in the Department of Psychiatry and Behavioral Sciences at the Medical University of South Carolina, and a research health scientist at Charleston VAMC.

Dr. Grubaugh has authored over 50 peer-reviewed publications, primarily on posttraumatic stress disorder, severe mental illness, and issues related to treatment adherence in public sector settings. She is the recipient of a VA Health Services Research and Development career development award.

ELIZABETH A. HEMBREE, PhD, is associate professor of psychology in the Department of Psychiatry, University of Pennsylvania. Dr. Hembree was director of clinical training in the Center for the Treatment & Study of Anxiety at University of Pennsylvania from 1999-2009. She is currently a member of the Board of Directors of the International Society of Traumatic Stress Studies. Dr. Hembree has consulted with the US Department of Veterans Affairs and the Department of Defense to train mental health workers in the provision of effective, evidence-based treatments.

JAMES D. HERBERT, PhD, is professor of psychology at Drexel University, where he directs the Anxiety Treatment and Research Program and serves as associate dean in the College of Arts and Sciences. Dr. Herbert's research focuses on acceptance-based behavior therapy, anxiety disorders, remote Internet-based clinical services, and the promotion of evidence-based practice in mental health. He is associate editor of the *Scientific Review of Mental Health Practice* and a fellow with several organizations including the Institute for Science in Medicine.

ALLAN V. HORWITZ, PhD, is currently dean of social and behavioral sciences at Rutgers University. He is a professor of sociology and has published numerous articles, chapters, and books on various aspects of mental illness. Dr. Horwitz's most recent books include *Diagnosis, Evidence, and Therapy: Conundrums of American Medicine* (with Gerald Grob; 2009) and *The Loss of Sadness: How Psychiatry Transformed Normal Sorrow into Depressive Disorder* (with Jerome Wakefield; 2007).

SCOTT O. LILIENFELD, PhD, is professor of psychology at Emory University and editor-in-chief of the *Scientific Review of Mental Health Practice*. His principal areas of interest are personality disorders, psychiatric diagnosis, and evidence-based practice in clinical psychology. Dr. Lilienfeld is past president of the Society for a Science of Clinical Psychology and a fellow with the Association for Psychological Science. He has authored and co-authored numerous books including *50 Great Myths of Popular Psychology* (2010).

PAUL R. MCHUGH, MD, was Henry Phipps Professor and Director of the Department of Psychiatry and Behavioral Sciences at the Johns Hopkins University School of Medicine and psychiatrist-in-chief at Johns Hopkins Hospital from 1975 through 2001. Dr. McHugh is now University Distinguished Service Professor of Psychiatry. He is author of *The Perspectives of Psychiatry* and *Try To Remember: Psychiatry's Clash Over Meaning, Memory, and Mind.*

JAMES A. NAIFEH, PhD, is research assistant professor in the Department of Psychiatry, Uniformed Services, University of the Health Sciences, and a scientist at the Center for the Study of Traumatic Stress. Previously, Dr. Naifeh was a postdoctoral fellow at the University of Mississippi Medical Center. His research focuses on issues related to the assessment of post-traumatic stress disorder (PTSD) and the role of cognitive-emotional vulnerabilities in PTSD and related disorders.

MEAGHAN O'DONNELL, PhD, is a clinical psychologist and acting research director at the Australian Centre for Posttraumatic Mental Health, University of Melbourne. Dr. O'Donnell has published over 40 peer-reviewed papers and book chapters in the area of posttraumatic mental health, and continues to conduct active research. She acts within a scientific advisory capacity for the Australian federal government, and is on the scientific panel for a number of research conferences including the Australian Conference for Traumatic Stress.

SCOTT P. ORR, PhD, is a medical research scientist at the Veterans Affairs Medical Center in Manchester, NH; psychologist (Psychiatry Service) at Massachusetts General Hospital; and associate professor of psychology in the Department of Psychiatry, Harvard Medical School. Dr. Orr also serves as the research and development coordinator at the

Manchester VA Medical Center. He has over 25 years of research experience focused on various aspects of posttraumatic stress disorder and serves as a member on national scientific review groups.

GERALD M. ROSEN, PhD, is a clinical psychologist in Seattle, Washington. He holds licenses in Washington, Alaska, and Oregon and is credentialed with the American Board of Professional Psychology. Dr. Rosen holds an appointment as clinical professor with the University of Washington's Department of Psychology, and with the medical school's Department of Psychiatry and Behavioral Sciences. He currently serves on the editorial board of the *Scientific Review of Mental Health Practice*, and is a fellow with the Association for Psychological Science.

ROBERT L. SPITZER, MD, is professor of psychiatry at Columbia University. Dr. Spitzer is most well known for his role in overseeing the development of psychiatry's *Diagnostic and Statistical Manual*, 3rd edition (DSM-III) and its revision (DSM-III-R). He has authored more than 200 publications, primarily dealing with issues of diagnosis and assessment. Dr. Spitzer also authored the Research Diagnostic Criteria and several assessment instruments in psychiatry such as the Structured Clinical Interview for DSM-IV (SCID) and the PHQ-9 (an instrument widely used in primary care research and clinical settings for the assessment of depression).

JEROME C. WAKEFIELD, PhD, DSW, is University Professor of Social Work and Professor of Psychiatry at New York University. He also is a licensed clinical social worker who has practiced both in community mental health and private practice. Dr. Wakefield has authored over 160 publications, primarily focused on the conceptual foundations of the mental health professions. He currently serves on editorial boards including the *Clinical Social Work Journal*. Dr. Wakefield co-authored with Allan Horwitz, *The Loss of Sadness: How Psychiatry Transformed Normal Sorrow into Depressive Disorder* (2007).

# Preface

Since its introduction in 1980, posttraumatic stress disorder (PTSD) has changed the landscape of stress studies and created an array of sociopolitical, conceptual, and clinical issues. For the better, research has grown exponentially over the years, providing clinicians, healthcare administrators, and policy makers with a better understanding of post-traumatic psychiatric morbidity. Despite this progress, controversies abound as to how clinicians should diagnose and treat psychiatric disorder in the aftermath of trauma. Further, a number of misconceptions and myths concerning PTSD have adversely influenced clinical practice and traumatic stress studies. This is of great concern, for it creates the risk of doing harm in our clinical work.

To address the core issues facing clinicians, we have brought together an international group of leading clinicians and clinical research-ers. Their scholarly reviews of the literature are joined with recom-mendations for clinical practice, thereby providing the clinician with insights and skills based on the best available evidence. In the first sec-tion (Chapters 1 through 5), the reader is provided with an overview of stress studies and core issues that concern the PTSD construct. The second section (Chapters 6 through 10) covers issues in the assessment and treatment of posttraumatic disorders. The Clinician's Guide con-cludes with an Afterword that considers future definitions of PTSD, and how changes may impact how we, as clinicians, conceptualize our patient's problems.

As the reader progresses through the chapters and learns more about recent research findings, several closely held beliefs are likely to be challenged. On those occasions, when a particular misconception or myth is examined, we ask that the reader remain open to new ideas. It is in this spirit that contributing authors have lent their time and expertise.

Gerald M. Rosen
B. Christopher Frueh

# Clinician's Guide to Posttraumatic Stress Disorder

# Core Issues

CHAPTER

# 1

# Posttraumatic Stress Disorder and General Stress Studies

GERALD M. ROSEN
B. CHRISTOPHER FRUEH
JON D. ELHAI
ANOUK L. GRUBAUGH
JULIAN D. FORD

In the relatively short span of three decades, posttraumatic stress disorder (PTSD) has captured the attention of mental health professionals, their patients, and the public at large. First introduced into the third edition of psychiatry's Diagnostic and Statistical Manual of Mental Disorders (DSM-III; APA, 1980), the diagnosis of PTSD has served as the focus of more than 12,000 studies in peer-review journals. Clinicians have found the diagnosis useful when conceptualizing patients' reactions to horrific and life-threatening events. Finding PTSD of benefit, clinicians have expanded its application in an effort to help patients with a variety of stress issues.

The general public has increasingly applied the "PTSD model" to their understanding of adjustment in the aftermath of trauma. Public awareness of psychiatric posttrauma tic issues has been furthered by extensive news coverage of events around the globe, including terrorist attacks in New York, London, and Madrid; Hurricane Katrina, earthquakes, and other natural disasters; widely publicized cases in America of child sexual abuse and international stories of child trafficking; mass genocides and other atrocities; and reports on the psychiatric casualties of war, including America's veterans who have fought in Iraq and Afghanistan.

To appreciate why PTSD was introduced in the DSM-III, and to understand the spiraling growth of research and clinical interest, it is instructive to step back and consider the origins from which the diagnosis emerged. By looking at PTSD's origins, its underlying assumptions, and the fruits of three decades of research, clinicians will better understand posttraumatic morbidity and issues surrounding patient care.

## HISTORICAL AND SOCIETAL PERSPECTIVES

The field of general stress studies was greatly influenced by the early work of Walter Cannon (e.g., Cannon, 1929) and his proposal that "critical stress" can disrupt the body's homeostatic mechanisms. Later, Hans Selye proposed a General Adaptation Syndrome (Selye, 1936), which conceived of stressors as "etiologically nonspecific." Selye's model held the view that any event of sufficient intensity (i.e., the stressor) was capable of producing a physiological adaptation response (i.e., the syndrome) whose features were constant regardless of event type.

By the mid-1970s, interest in the field of stress studies had grown substantially. This growth was demonstrated by Selye's (1975) estimate that he had more than 100,000 publications in his stress library. At that point in time, the literature had yielded several insights into the nature and effects of stressful life events (B. S. Dohrenwend & B. P. Dohrenwend, 1974a). Research demonstrated that "stressors" created a risk for subsequent illness, both physical and psychiatric. It also had been shown that severe stressors were more likely than mild ones to produce maladaptive responses (Brown, Sklair, Harris, & Birley, 1973; Wyler, Masuda, & Holmes, 1971), although the magnitude or severity of a stressful event was influenced by an individual's subjective appraisals (Lazarus & Alfert, 1964; Lazarus & Folkman, 1984). Research also suggested that the likelihood of a stressor producing psychopathological reactions was influenced by pre-incident risk factors, such as personality traits, as well as the buff-ering effects of social support (Andrews, Tennant, Hewson, & Vaillant, 1978; Cobb, 1976; Rabkin & Struening, 1976).

One issue long debated in the stress field concerned the specificity of effects. Selye's model of adaptation was non-specific: It postulated a gen-eral physiological response to a diverse set of events. In contrast, others believed that experimental findings brought into question the nonspeci-ficity concept. B. S. Dohrenwend and B. P. Dohrenwend (1974b) stated this alternative view:

> [The] question still to be answered is whether limited domains of possibly stressful life events will be found for some types of disorder, or whether the domain of possibly stressful life events encompasses all life changes for all or nearly all outcomes. The prospect of finding that relatively narrow domains of life events are related to specific disorders is an attractive one, either from a theoretical or a practical perspective that deserves systematic investigation (p. 321).

## Traumatic Stressors

The notion that a "narrow domain" of life events could be related to specific disorders is certainly not novel. Warriors' post-combat reac-tions have been noted throughout literature (e.g., "Epic of Gilgamesh;" writings of Homer and Shakespeare). Nineteenth century concepts of "railway spine" and "traumatic neuroses" were thought to result from high-impact accidents. Oftentimes, a term provided descriptive or explanatory elements for the noted reactions and behaviors. For exam-ple, after the U.S. Civil War, it was noted that many military veterans reported somatic symptoms related to chest pain and cardiac function-ing. These reactions included *fatigue, shortness of breath, heart palpita-tions, sweating,* and *chest pain*—yet physical examination revealed no physical abnormalities to explain the symptoms. The observed syn-drome was known as "soldier's heart." During and shortly after World War I, "shell shock" referred to a syndrome that was thought to be a neurological disorder caused by exposure to loud booming noises and

**Table 1.1  Posttraumatic Reactions: Historical Terms**

| | |
|---|---|
| Accident neurosis | Mediterranean back/disease |
| Accident victim syndrome | Postaccident anxiety syndrome |
| Aftermath neurosis | Postaccident syndrome |
| American disease | Posttraumatic syndrome |
| Attitudinal pathosis | Railway spine |
| Battered woman's syndrome | Rape trauma syndrome |
| Combat fatigue | Secondary gain neurosis |
| Compensation hysteria | Shell shock |
| Compensation/profit neurosis | Soldier's heart |
| Da Costa's syndrome | Traumatic hysteria |
| Fright neurosis | Traumatic neurasthenia |
| Greek disease | Traumatic neurosis |
| Greenback neurosis | Triggered neurosis |
| Gross stress reactions | Vietnam syndrome |
| Justice neurosis | Wharfie's back |
| Litigation neurosis | Whiplash neurosis |

bright flashes of sudden light associated with bursting artillery shells. "Combat fatigue" was a term used during World War II, when it was believed that combat reactions were caused by exposure to extreme stress and fatigue. In the 1970s, the concept of event specificity was applied to victims of sexual assault, with the creation of "rape trauma syndrome" (Burgess & Holmstrom, 1974) and "battered woman syndrome" (Walker, 1977). These historical terms and others applied to posttraumatic reactions are listed in Table 1.1. More detailed historical reviews on the precursors of what we now call PTSD have been provided elsewhere (e.g., Ford, 2008; Jones & Wessely, 2005; Satel & Frueh, 2009; Shephard, 2001).

## Posttraumatic Stress Disorder

The possible linkage of a specific class of events to psychiatric disorder was raised in 1952, when "Gross stress reaction" (GSR) was introduced in the first edition of the DSM. This condition was defined as a "transient situational personality disorder" that could occur when essentially "normal" individuals experienced severe physical demands or extreme emotional stress, such as in combat or civilian catastrophe. GSR had a relatively short life span: it was dropped from psychiatry's nosology in 1968, with publication of the DSM's second edition. It was 12 years later, in 1980, that the linkage of a specific class of events to a specific constellation of symptoms was formalized with the introduction of Posttraumatic Stress Disorder (PTSD).

The DSM-III defined traumatic events by Criterion A, and this criterion served a "gatekeeper" role for the diagnosis of PTSD. In other words, PTSD could not be diagnosed without the occurrence of a Criterion A event. Breslau and Davis (1987) observed how this conceptualization rendered PTSD distinct from other psychiatric diagnoses and from the general field of stress studies. Rather than all stressors creating an increased risk for a wide range of established conditions, there now was a distinct class of stressors that led to its own form of psychopathology. Thus, while any type of high stress could lead to increased risk of headaches, high blood pressure, or depression, only a Criterion A event such as combat, rape, or a life-threatening accident could lead to the distinct syndrome of PTSD. This assumption of a specific etiology, associated with a distinct clinical syndrome, provided the justification for a new field of "traumatology" to be carved out of general stress studies.

## Changing Criteria and Acute Stress Disorder

Criteria that defined PTSD were determined by a DSM-III subcommittee, who were influenced more by theory than empirical data. Committee members considered the observations of Horowitz (1978) on stress response syndromes, the writings of a self-described "psychohistorian" (Lifton, 1961), Kardiner's (1941) construct of a physioneurosis, and issues raised on behalf of the mental health needs of Vietnam veterans (see Scott, 1990; Young, 1995). Appreciating the origins of PTSD, Yehuda and McFarlane (1995) observed how the formulation of the diagnosis "addressed a social and political issue as well as a mental health one" (p. 1706).

With experience, and a growing empirical basis for defining PTSD, multiple changes have occurred in subsequent editions of the DSM (DSM-III-R, APA, 1987; DSM-IV, APA, 1994). For example, the original definition of Criterion A as provided in the DSM-III (APA, 1980) was a single sentence: "Existence of a recognizable stressor that would evoke significant symptoms of distress in almost everyone" (p. 238). By the time the DSM-IV was published (APA, 1994), Criterion A events were more clearly defined:

> The person has been exposed to a traumatic event in which both of the following were present: (1) the person experienced, witnessed, or was confronted with an event or events that involved actual or threatened death or serious injury, or a threat to the physical integrity of self or others; (2) the person's response involved intense fear, helplessness, or horror (p. 467).

Symptom criteria that defined the PTSD clinical syndrome also were revised in subsequent editions of the DSM. In the DSM-III, 12 symptom criteria were grouped into 3 clusters (Criteria B through D), representing reexperiencing, numbing of responsiveness, and hyperarousal reactions. With publication of the DSM-IV, 17 symptom criteria were specified, now covering reexperiencing, avoidance and numbing symptoms, and hyperarousal (see Table 1.2).

**Table 1.2  DSM-IV Diagnostic Criteria for Posttraumatic Stress Disorder**

A. The person has been exposed to a traumatic event in which both of the following were present:
  1. The person experienced, witnessed, or was confronted with an event or events that involved actual or threatened death or serious injury, or a threat to the physical integrity of self or others.
  2. The person's response involved intense fear, helplessness, or horror. Note: In children, this may be expressed instead by disorganized or agitated behavior.
B. The traumatic event is persistently reexperienced in one (or more) of the following ways:
  1. Recurrent and intrusive distressing recollections of the event, including images, thoughts, or perceptions. Note: In young children, repetitive play may occur in which themes or aspects of the trauma are expressed.
  2. Recurrent distressing dreams of the event. Note: In children, there may be frightening dreams without recognizable content.
  3. Acting or feeling as if the traumatic event were recurring (includes a sense of reliving the experience, illusions, hallucinations, and dissociative flashback episodes, including those that occur on awakening or when intoxicated). Note: In young children, trauma-specific reenactment may occur.

4. Intense psychological distress at exposure to internal or external cues that symbolize or resemble an aspect of the traumatic event.

5. Physiological reactivity on exposure to internal or external cues that symbolize or resemble an aspect of the traumatic event.

C. Persistent avoidance of stimuli associated with the trauma and numbing of general responsiveness (not present before the trauma), as indicated by three (or more) of the following:

1. Efforts to avoid thoughts, feelings, or conversations associated with the trauma.

2. Efforts to avoid activities, places, or people that arouse recollections of the trauma.

3. Inability to recall an important aspect of the trauma.

4. Markedly diminished interest or participation in significant activities.

5. Feeling of detachment or estrangement from others.

6. Restricted range of affect (e.g., unable to have loving feelings).

7. Sense of a foreshortened future (e.g., does not expect to have a career, marriage, children, or a normal life span).

D. Persistent symptoms of increased arousal (not present before the trauma), as indicated by two (or more) of the following:

1. Difficulty falling or staying asleep

2. Irritability or outbursts of anger

3. Difficulty concentrating

4. Hypervigilance

5. Exaggerated startle response

E. Duration of the disturbance (symptoms in Criteria B, C, and D) is more than 1 month.

F. The disturbance causes clinically significant distress or impairment in social, occupational, or other important areas of functioning.

*Specify* if

Acute: if duration of symptoms is less than three months.

Chronic: if duration of symptoms is three months or more.

With Delayed Onset: if onset of symptoms is at least six months after the Stressor.

*Source:* Reprinted with permission from the *American Psychiatric Association: Diagnostic and Statistical Manual of Mental Disorders*, 4th Edition, Text Revision (DSM-IV-TR). American Psychiatrics Association, 2000, pp. 467–468.

In DSM-III, a diagnosis of PTSD included Criterion E, which specified the course of posttraumatic reactions. The original form of Criterion E for acute PTSD stated: "Onset of symptoms within six months of the trauma" (p. 238). Over time, clinicians realized that this provision was problematic, because most people have significant reactions in the aftermath of trauma, even in the absence of any psychiatric disorder. To avoid widespread confusion between essentially normal reactions to adversity, and symptoms of psychiatric disorder, Criterion E was modified in the 1987 revision of the DSM (DSM-III-R; APA, 1987). At that time Criterion E specified, "Duration of the disturbance (symptoms B, C, and D) of at least one month" (p. 251).

Yet, the requirement that symptoms had to persist for at least one month raised its own concerns. This new statement of Criterion E left open the question of how to characterize individuals with unusually severe symptoms in the immediate aftermath of trauma. To address this concern, the fourth edition of the DSM introduced the diagnosis of Acute Stress Disorder (ASD; DSM-IV; APA, 1994). Like PTSD, the diagnosis of ASD required a Criterion A event, and it contained symptom criteria similar to those of PTSD. However, ASD included a separate criteria groupings for symptoms of dissociation (which were not included in PTSD) and emotional numbing (which was grouped with avoidance symptoms in PTSD's Criterion C). ASD cannot be diagnosed unless the symptoms and impairment last at least two days (to exclude immediate "peritraumatic" reactions which are relatively normative) and may not last beyond four weeks following exposure to a traumatic stressor (see Table 1.3). Thus, ASD serves as a means of identifying extreme traumatic stress reactions that occur too soon after trauma to be diagnosed as PTSD.

Changes in PTSD's defining criteria illustrate how various issues regarding posttraumatic reactions and psychiatric diagnoses remain in flux. Even now, there are numerous debates about how PTSD should be defined in the fifth edition of the DSM, whose publication is expected in or around 2013. There also are debates about whether ASD should be dropped in the DSM-V, because of empirical findings that fail to support its underlying assumptions (Bryant, 2004). That these kinds of debates continue should not be unexpected, as traumatology is a young field that emerged only three decades ago. Nevertheless, changes in PTSD criteria raise important issues that we will return to later.

## EPIDEMIOLOGY OF TRAUMATIC EVENTS AND POSTTRAUMATIC SYMPTOMS

Since the introduction of PTSD in the DSM-III, much has been learned about the nature and course of posttraumatic reactions. Consider that the DSM-III, back in 1980, had this to say about the important topic of

**Table 1.3  DSM-IV Diagnostic Criteria for Acute Stress Disorder**

A. Traumatic event exposure [As specified for PTSD]

B. Either while experiencing or after experiencing the distressing event, the individual has three (or more) of the following dissociative symptoms:

  1. A subjective sense of numbing, detachment, or absence of emotional responsiveness

  2. A reduction in awareness of his or her surroundings (e.g., "being in a daze")

  3. Derealization

  4. Depersonalization

  5. Dissociative amnesia (i.e., inability to recall an important aspect of the trauma)

C. The traumatic event is persistently reexperienced in at least one of the following ways: recurrent images, thoughts, dreams, illusions, flashback episodes, or a sense of reliving the experience; or distress on exposure to reminders of the traumatic event.

D. Marked avoidance of stimuli that arouse recollections of the trauma (e.g., thought, feelings, conversations, activities, places, people).

E. Marked symptoms of anxiety or increased arousal (e.g., difficulty sleeping, irritability, poor concentration, hypervigilance, exaggerated startle response, motor restlessness).

F. The disturbance causes clinically significant distress or impairment in social, occupational, or other important areas of functioning or impairs the individual's ability to pursue some necessary task, such as obtaining necessary assistance or mobilizing personal resources by telling family members about the traumatic experience.

G. The disturbance lasts for a minimum of two days and a maximum of four weeks and occurs within four weeks of the traumatic event.

H. The disturbance is not due to the direct physiological effects of a substance (e.g., a drug of abuse, a medication) or a general medical condition, is not better accounted for by Brief Psychotic Disorder, and is not merely an exacerbation of a preexisting Axis I or Axis II disorder.

*Source:* Reprinted with permission from the *American Psychiatric Association: Diagnostic and Statistical Manual of Mental Disorders,* 4th Edition, Text Revision (DSM-IV-TR). American Psychiatrics Association, 2000, pp. 467–468.

prevalence: "No information." These two words are a striking reminder that committee members back in 1980 framed PTSD's defining criteria without the benefit of empirical data.

By 1994 and publication of the DSM-IV, a large body of literature informed clinicians on posttraumatic reactions and the prevalence of PTSD (e.g., Breslau, Davis, Andreski, & Peterson, 1991; Davidson, Hughes, Blazer, & George, 1991; Norris, 1992). This is how the issue of prevalence is discussed in the most recent edition of the DSM (DSM-IV-TR; APA, 2000).

Community-based studies reveal a lifetime prevalence for Posttraumatic Stress Disorder of approximately 8% of the adult population in the United States. Information is not currently available with regard to the general population prevalence in other countries. Studies of at-risk individuals (i.e., groups exposed to specific traumatic incidents) yield variable findings, with the highest rates (ranging between one-third and more than half of those exposed) found among survivors of rape, military combat and captivity, and ethnically or politically motivated internment and genocide (p. 466).

Epidemiological studies also find that exposure to potentially traumatic events (Criterion A) is actually quite common, with 60 to 80% of the population reporting exposure to various types of traumatic events (e.g., Breslau et al., 1991; Kessler et al., 1995).

Studies find that people typically react in the immediate aftermath of trauma, with symptoms developing within days of the event (e.g., North, 2001). Among those individuals whose reactions are of sufficient severity and duration that they meet criteria for PTSD, upwards of 50% improve within three months without treatment (e.g., Galea et al., 2002; Rothbaum, Foa, Riggs, Murdock, & Walsh, 1992). This finding is so robust, across a variety of trauma types, that the DSM-IV specifically notes the pattern. Consequently, chronic PTSD (defined as symptoms lasting more than six months) is more uncommon than acute presentations (Yehuda & McFarlane, 1995). Of note, individuals who receive a diagnosis of PTSD are at three times greater risk of again meeting criteria if exposed to a later traumatic stressor, as compared with those who did not develop PTSD in the first instance (Breslau, Peterson, & Schultz, 2008). Thus, PTSD can be a recurrent disorder once it has first occurred, a finding that may be indicative of individual vulnerabilities and risk factors.

Epidemiological studies also have shown that PTSD symptoms are not the only, indeed not even the most likely, form of posttraumatic reactions. General reactions of fear, anxiety, sadness, dysphoria, anger, and guilt (among others) are common reactions to traumatic experiences. Other common reactions include the following: physical or somatic complaints (insomnia, gastrointestinal symptoms, headaches, sleep problems); social and relationship difficulties; and increased substance use (Breslau et al., 1991; Kessler et al., 1995).

## Posttraumatic Morbidity Versus Resilience

One of the most important lessons obtained from research is that most people who survive even the most harrowing of traumatic experiences do not develop PTSD or any other posttraumatic psychiatric disorder. This is not to suggest that people remain unaffected by traumatic experiences. To the contrary, most everyone is likely to experience at least short-term distress. Nevertheless, only a minority of individuals develop distress and functional impairment that rise to meet the criteria for one or more of the psychiatric disorders. Therefore, it is important scientifically and clinically to identify those characteristics of trauma-exposed people, and the stressors themselves, that contribute to adverse or positive outcomes.

## Individual Differences, Risk and Protective Factors

Research has demonstrated that individual vulnerabilities and risk factors serve as strong predictors of PTSD development. For example, one robust finding in both traumatic stress and general stress research is that social support can play an important buffering role: Lower social support is associated with increased risk of PTSD, and higher amounts or quality of social support is protective against the development of PTSD (Andrews, Brewin, & Rose, 2003).

Gender is an important risk factor, with females at increased risk of developing lifetime PTSD relative to men by a ratio of approximately 2:1 (Breslau et al., 1991; Breslau et al., 1998; Kilpatrick et al., 2003). In one study, 13% of women and 6.2% of men met criteria for lifetime PTSD based on a randomly selected event; and 17.7% of women and 9.5% of men met criteria for lifetime PTSD based on the study participant's self-identified worst event (Breslau et al., 1998). A gender difference in conditional risk has been observed, even when controlling for type of traumatic event (Breslau et al., 1998; Kessler et al., 1995). Possible factors contributing to the higher prevalence of PTSD among females have been reviewed by Tolin and Foa (2006).

Other factors generally associated, to varying degrees, with greater risk for PTSD are lower socioeconomic status, lower intelligence, lower educational attainment, prior history of poor social adjustment or psychiatric disorder, increased severity of initial (peritraumatic) stress reactions, increasing severity of traumatic exposure, and presence of other environmental stressors. Recent data also suggest the role of certain genetic phenotypes, which may interact with environmental variables to affect rates of PTSD in the aftermath of trauma, although no candidate genes have been identified definitively (Koenen, 2007).

## Comorbidity

Most individuals who have significant problems coping with trauma, and who meet the diagnostic criteria for PTSD, have additional problems. Consequently, comorbid depression, panic attacks, substance abuse, and other psychiatric issues can be common. In fact, there is good evidence to suggest that major depression is the most common form of posttraumatic psychopathology, even more prevalent than PTSD. In addition, PTSD patients frequently present with significant medical comorbidity (e.g., chronic pain) that requires increased health care (Elhai, North, & Frueh, 2005; Schnurr & Green, 2004).

## THEORIES UNDERLYING THE PTSD DIAGNOSIS

As previously discussed, the vast majority (i.e., 75 to 80%) of individuals exposed to traumatic stressors do not develop PTSD. Several theoretical models have been formulated to explain for whom, when, and why PTSD develops. Biological theories have focused on stress hormone responses (e.g., Yehuda, 2002), neuroanatomy (e.g., Gilbertson et al., 2002), neurocircuitry (e.g., Shin & Handwerger, 2009), and genetic predispositions (e.g., Koenen, 2007). Psychosocial theories focus on exposure to life threat and interpersonal violence, histories of childhood abuse or other severe childhood adversities, and recent life stressors (Brewin, Andrews, & Valentine, 2000; Ozer, Best, Lipsey, & Weiss, 2008; Schnurr, Lunney, & Sengupta, 2004). Psychosocial theories also posit beneficial or buffering effects of protective factors including socioeconomic resources, education, intelligence, and social support. Cognitive theories of PTSD identify patterns of altered beliefs and information processing consistent with persistent fear and hypervigilance (Dalgleish, 2004; Ehlers & Clark, 2000). Janoff-Bulman (1992) has suggested that "shattered assumptions" about self and the world are the basis for PTSD. Learning theories posit fear networks (Foa & Kozak, 1986) whereby trauma will condition associations and cognitions associated with hyperreactivity to reminders of the original event and behavioral avoidance. Emotional processing theories extend earlier fear network models, with additional emphasis on cognitive processing (Foa & Riggs, 1993; Foa & Rothbaum, 1998). Finally, there are theories that account for PTSD as a function of how traumatic memories are stored and processed (e.g., Brewin, Dalgeish, & Joseph, 1996).

Anyone reading this list of theories probably wants to know which one is correct. Unfortunately, there is no simple answer (Brewin & Holmes, 2003). The current situation may be likened to the proverbial blind men, each of whom describes a part of an elephant while missing the whole. So it may be that posttraumatic morbidity is a function of multiple factors including stress hormones, altered neural activity in the brain, cognitive appraisals, shattered beliefs, fear conditioning, intrusive memories, and biological and psychosocial risk and protective factors.

## ISSUES AND CONTROVERSIES

Despite PTSD's success in spurring research, assisting clinicians, and providing a framework widely understood by the public, there are multiple issues and controversies that remain unresolved. Robert Spitzer, who served as chair of the DSM-III, observed with his colleagues (Spitzer, First, & Wakefield, 2007): "Since its introduction into the DSM-III in 1980, no other DSM diagnosis, with the exception of Dissociative Identify Disorder, has generated so much controversy in the field as to the boundaries of the disorder, diagnostic criteria, central assumptions, clinical utility, and prevalence in various populations" (p. 233).

In the sections that follow, we review the major issues and controversies that have arisen with regard to the PTSD diagnosis. We will then consider the implications of these concerns for the practicing clinician.

## Challenges to the Assumption of a Specific Etiology

As previously discussed, the assumption of a specific etiology was fundamental to the origins of PTSD, and provided justification to separate a particular class of stressors from the general field of stress studies. If this assumption is correct, then individuals who do not experience a Criterion A traumatic event should not suffer from PTSD symptoms. Unfortunately for the "PTSD model," this has not turned out to be the case (Long & Elhai, 2009: Rosen & Lilienfeld, 2008). Instead, multiple studies have demonstrated that non-Criterion A events (e.g., not traumatic) can result in equivalent rates of PTSD (e.g., Long et al., 2008). Case reports have documented clinical presentations of PTSD among individuals who have suffered such non-life threatening events as financial strains, loss of friendships, marital infidelity, and collapse of adoption arrangements (e.g., Scott & Stradling, 1994). When loss of livestock on a ranch was reportedly associated with PTSD, commentators asked, "What is a traumatic event?" (Elhai, Kashdan, & Frueh, 2005).

It turns out that the assumption of a specific etiology for PTSD is so fraught with difficulties that a recent paper spoke of "the Criterion A problem" (Weathers & Keane, 2007). Most recently, analysts have considered the issue with proposals ranging from tighter definitions of traumatic events (Kilpatrick, Resnick, & Acierno, 2009) to the other extreme of totally doing away with the gatekeeper function of Criterion A (Brewin, Lanius, Novac, Schnyder, & Galea, 2009). Totally abandoning the PTSD "notion" of a qualitatively unique type of stressor could be premature in light of evidence from both animal and human studies that certain stressors which threaten survival of the organism elicit biological and behavioral reactions that are particularly extreme and persistent (Magnea & Lanius, 2008; Ronan & Summers, 2008). Whether "traumatic" stressors are in fact qualitatively different than other stressors, or better understood as extreme types on a continuum of stressors, remains unclear. Also, notice that if we eliminate Criterion A completely, then the T in PTSD must logically be dropped. In effect, we will have returned to the general field of stress studies and the nature of post-stress disorders.

## The Symptom Criteria

PTSD is highly comorbid with other mental disorders—especially major depressive disorder, substance use and other anxiety disorders (Kessler et al., 1995). Moreover, several of PTSD's symptoms are shared by other mood and anxiety disorders' criteria. In fact, criteria for diagnosing PTSD can be completely fulfilled with the diagnoses of depression and specific phobia. Consider, for example, the PTSD reexperiencing symptoms B4 and B5. Criterion B4 reads "intense psychological distress at exposure to internal or external cues that symbolize or resemble an aspect of the traumatic event." Criterion B5 reads "physiological reactivity on exposure to internal or external cues that symbolize or resemble an aspect of the traumatic event." A comparison of these definitions with Criteria A and B for specific phobia shows them to be essentially the same. Thus, Criterion A for specific phobia states, "marked and persistent fear that is excessive or unreasonable, cued by the presence or anticipation of a specific object or situation." Criterion B for specific phobia states, "exposure to the phobic stimulus almost invariably provokes an immediate anxiety response, which may take the form of a situationally bound or situationally predisposed Panic Attack." Criterion C2 for PTSD reads, "efforts to avoid activities, places, or people that arouse recollections of the trauma," while Criterion D for specific phobia reads, "The phobic situation(s) is avoided or else is endured with intense anxiety or distress." Criterion C4 for PTSD reads, "markedly diminished interest or participation in significant activities," while Criterion 2A for major depression reads, "markedly diminished interest or pleasure in all, or almost all, activities most of the day, nearly every day." The interested clinician can find other examples of symptom overlap by comparing the criteria of these varied disorders.

In light of the similarity in defining criteria among different disorders, some have questioned if PTSD's high rates of comorbidity with depression, panic attack, and other anxiety problems results from the artifact of overlapping symptoms. Such considerations also have raised the question of whether PTSD (as currently defined in DSM-IV) is actually a unique disorder or merely an amalgam of other mood and anxiety disorders (Rosen, Spitzer, & McHugh, 2008; Spitzer & Wakefield, 2007). Adding to these concerns, some researchers have demonstrated that a core set of PTSD's symptoms are best conceptualized as general dysphoria or distress, most common to other mood and anxiety disorders (Simms, Watson, & Doebbelling, 2002; Watson, 2005). Further, Bodkin, Pope, Detke, and Hudson (2007) demonstrated a high incidence of PTSD symptoms (78%) among depressed patients who had not reported a Criterion A event. Such findings suggest that PTSD symptoms may have been previously ignored (e.g., nightmares) among other patient groups, even though these stress reactions are part of the alternate clinical presentations. While initial studies on criteria sets that remove PTSD's overlapping symptoms find similar rates of prevalence and comorbidity, (Elhai, Grubaugh, Kashdan, & Frueh, 2008; Ford, Elhai, Ruggiero, & Frueh, 2009), these findings do not resolve all concerns.

A case example that illustrates the issues was presented by Rosen, Spitzer, and McHugh (2008). A captain of a fishing boat that was lost at sea, in an incident that resulted in the death of several crew members, returned home with anxiety reactions that prevented him from continuing in his usual career. As a result of these new and unfamiliar anxiety problems, loss of career, resulting financial pressures, and associated adjustment issues, the captain developed severe situationally-based depression. Prior to the DSM-III, and introduction of a PTSD diagnosis, the captain's clinical problems would have been conceptualized as a conditioned phobic reaction resulting from the maritime accident, grief reactions related to loss of crew and friends, and a reactive depression resulting from situational stress. Clinicians and researchers alike can ask how our understanding of the captain's psychiatric problems has been furthered with the diagnosis of PTSD. To the extent PTSD merely duplicates precursor diagnoses and does not lead to increasingly efficient and effective treatment strategies, its construct validity and clinical utility are called into question (McHugh & Treisman, 2007).

## Criterion Creep

Application of PTSD by clinicians, and public interest in the diagnosis, has not been tempered by challenges to the construct's validity. Instead, what can be thought of as the "PTSD model," has been extended to an ever-increasing array of events and to an expanding set of stress reactions. Consider how the concept of a specific set of stressors associated with PTSD (Criterion A), once reserved for those who experienced or witnessed a traumatic event, can now be applied to individuals who simply hear of misfortunes befalling others. This change occurred when the definition of Criterion A was changed in the DSM-IV (APA, 1994). Now, with the new definition of what constitutes trauma, peer-reviewed journal articles have reported on cases of PTSD resulting from viewing television (Ahern, Galea, Resnick, & Vlahov, 2004; Bernstein et al., 2007; Eth, 2002; Simons & Silveira, 1994). It also has been argued that non-traumatic events can lead to PTSD by creating a worry or anticipation of future trauma. For example, if an individual makes an inappropriate sexual comment in the workplace, might that create PTSD in a co-worker who becomes concerned over what other transgressions might occur. This creates the conceptual equivalent of "pre-traumatic" stress disorder, leading one commentator to observe: "Any unit of classification that simultaneously encompasses the experience of surviving Auschwitz and that of being told rude jokes at work must, by any reasonable lay standard, be a nonsense, a patent absurdity" (Shephard, 2004, p. 57).

Expansion of the PTSD model, a phenomenon referred to as "criterion creep" (Rosen, 2004a), also has occurred with the symptom criteria. Normal and even expected reactions to a traumatic event, such as anger or uncertainties about the future, are now referred to as "symptoms." This labeling is encouraged by terms such as "subsyndromal," "subthreshold," or "partial" PTSD. In these cases, individuals who exhibit *some* PTSD symptoms after an adverse event, but who do not meet full PTSD criteria, can still be said to be having symptoms of that disorder. While there is empirical evidence that "subthreshold PTSD" is associated with some psychosocial impairment (Breslau, Lucia, & Davis, 2004; Stein, Walker, Hazen, & Forde, 1997), "full PTSD" is associated with "higher magnitude" (more severe) traumatic stressors and greater impairment. Such distinctions support the construct validity of full PTSD as distinct from partial or subthreshold variants. It follows, therefore, that the notion of partial PTSD may be no more meaningful diagnostically than saying that someone with a bad cold has the symptoms of tuberculosis or lung cancer. This logical fallacy becomes more extreme if the individual is coughing only because they are in a smoky tavern (Rosen & Lilienfeld, 2008).

Once again, clinicians are reminded of the essential need to distinguish between normal reactions to a particular situation, and the symptoms of disorder (Horwitz & Wakefield, 2007).

## Delayed Onset PTSD

Although included in DSM-IV as a possible subcategory of the disorder, there is little in the way of empirical data to support the existence of delayed-onset PTSD. Large-scale epidemiological studies have reported zero or extremely low rates of delayed-onset PTSD in civilians and veterans (Breslau, Davis, Andreski, & Peterson, 1991; Frueh, Grubaugh, Yeager, & Magruder, 2009; Helzer, Robins, & McEvoy, 1987). On the other hand, if "delayed-onset" is redefined and conceptualized as a delay in seeking treatment, or subsequent exacerbation of prior symptoms years after an event, then the phenomenon may be relatively common (Andrews, Brewin, Philpott, & Stewart, 2007). Such findings encourage clinicians to take careful histories regarding a patient's course of symptoms and possible delays in seeking treatment, before applying the diagnostic qualifier of delayed-onset.

## PTSD in the Courtroom

The assumption of a specific etiology (Criterion A) that is distinctive of the PTSD diagnosis also creates special concerns when patients are involved in claims of compensation or personal injury lawsuits. Slovenko (1994) observed:

> In tort litigation, PTSD is a favored diagnosis in cases of emotional distress because it is incident specific. It tends to rule out other factors important to the determination of causation. Thus plaintiffs can argue that all of their psychological problems issue from the alleged traumatic event and not from myriad other sources encountered in life. A diagnosis of depression, in contrast, opens the issue of causation to many factors other than the stated cause of action (p. 441).

An awareness of PTSD's attractiveness in court cases likely contributed to the DSM-IV including a specific cautionary guideline for clinicians: "Malingering should be ruled out in those situations in which financial remuneration, benefit eligibility, and forensic determinations play a role" (p. 467; APA, 1994). Unfortunately, the task of ruling out malingering is easier said than done. In one study (Hickling, Blanchard, Mundy, & Galovski, 2002), six actors presented false claims of PTSD at a clinic that specialized in the assessment of motor vehicle accident victims. After clinical assessment interviews, psychological tests, and a psychophysiologic assessment of responses to trauma relevant stimuli, all six "patients" received a diagnosis of PTSD. This study demonstrates the ability of individuals to feign both an event (the non-existent accident) and subjective symptoms (intrusive thoughts, nightmares). Other studies on malingering confirm that clinicians are not lie detectors (Slovenko, 2002)—a reality that does not change even with years of clinical experience.

Clinicians who find themselves performing a forensic role and serving as an expert for the courts, should acquaint themselves with the large literature on malingering and the proper conduct of forensic assessments (e.g., Simon, 2003). When clinicians are treating patients involved in litigation, they should remain aware of their advocacy role and reliance on self-report. A clinician who testifies at trial can tell a jury that their patient reported problems with nightmares and appropriate treatment was provided. At the same time, the clinician should not tell a jury that they independently determined the existence of nightmares or the truthfulness of their patient's reporting. Strategies for dealing with these complex issues have been discussed in several publications (e.g., Taylor, Frueh, & Asmundson, 2007; Pankratz, 1998; Rosen, 2004b).

## Traumatic Memory

There has long been a wide-held belief that memory for traumatic events works differently from memory for other, more common, aspects of the human experience. Dating back to the work of Sigmund Freud right on through to contemporary writers, and popularized in Hollywood movies, there has been the claim that highly traumatic experiences, especially those occurring in childhood, are susceptible to being repressed into the unconscious mind. That is, certain events are so horrific that the human mind cannot tolerate them, and therefore banishes them to some hidden place deep in the unconscious, from which they may emerge to cause psychopathology and interpersonal maladjustment. This phenomenon has been used to explain putative "multiple personalities," borderline personality disorder, and delayed PTSD.

As it turns out, a large body of research (McNally, 2003) has failed to support this notion of a special mechanism for traumatic memory, and there is no valid scientific evidence to support the claims of "body memory" or "recovered memory" made by a small number of adherents. A number of provocative lawsuits based on claims of "recovered memory" have made the news, and some still linger in U.S. courts. In some cases, huge awards have been obtained by patients who recanted a therapeutically "recovered" memory and then sued their therapist for improperly implanting the falsely held belief (e.g., Gustafson, 1995). Although debates continue, with an occasional call for middle ground (Ost, 2003), it is important that clinicians appreciate the dangers, clinically and legally, of attempting to help or encourage patients to recall "repressed" trauma memories. Clinicians are strongly advised to avoid the use of such "recovered memory" techniques (e.g., Brandon et al., 1997).

## Failed Treatments and Exaggerated Claims

Clinicians hold to the singular purpose of helping others. A corollary to this therapeutic goal is "Primum Non Nocere," or "first do no harm." Unfortunately, in the short history of traumatology's three decades, a number of well-intentioned treatments have produced questionable, if not outright harmful results. Research indicates that early interventions in the form of critical incident stress debriefings (CISD) can impede the natural recovery and resilience that is characteristic of most individuals after trauma (e.g., Rose, Bisson, & Wessely, 2001). More damaging are previously referenced techniques that can lead to false trauma memories, unfounded accusations, and the tearing apart of families (Hagen, 1997). These controversial areas of clinical concern are discussed elsewhere in this text.

In other instances, inadequately tested therapies have been promoted with exaggerated and even extreme claims of success. In the 1990s, a group of such treatments came to be known as the "Power Therapies." When these therapies were introduced, it was claimed (without empirical support) that they were more effective, efficient, or in some other way more powerful than other empirically established procedures. Perhaps not surprisingly, when research was conducted on the power therapies, it was found that nothing miraculous or special was occurring. Instead, known principles of behavior change appeared to operate, at a level of efficacy and efficiency already known to accepted clinical practice (Rosen, Lohr, McNally, & Herbert, 1998). Ill-conceived treatments and exaggerated claims remind clinicians that they can best serve patients, and avoid doing harm, by relying on empirically supported methods and practices (Cukor, Spitalnik, Difede, Rizzo, & Rothbaum, 2009).

## PTSD, STRESS STUDIES, AND THE NEED FOR EVIDENCE-BASED PRACTICE

There is little doubt that mental health clinicians are in a stronger position to conceptualize, assess, and treat posttraumatic disorders as compared to three decades ago. When PTSD was introduced in 1980, little was known about the prevalence and course of posttraumatic symptoms, nor was there an appreciation for the important issue of comorbidity. We now know that the majority of individuals face trauma at one or more points in their lifetime. While all individuals may be expected to have reactions in the immediate aftermath of adversity, this does not necessarily constitute psychiatric disorder. In fact, most individuals demonstrate resilience and cope successfully over time. Nevertheless, a minority of those who experience a traumatic event have reactions of sufficient severity and duration to warrant psychiatric diagnosis. In such cases, the appropriate diagnosis may be PTSD, although this diagnosis should not be reflexively provided to all patients presenting in the aftermath of trauma. Instead, clinicians should take a broad view (e.g., considering all viable and evidence-supported hypotheses) when formulating a diagnosis and planning appropriate treatment interventions.

Research findings also have challenged most every assumption upon which PTSD is based. Studies have shown that symptom criteria for diagnosing PTSD can occur in the absence of traumatic events, even presenting at high rates in non-traumatized patients. Such findings raise the question of whether PTSD is a distinct disorder, or if instead it was constituted by artificially joining already extant problems (e.g., phobia and depression). Additional challenges to the construct validity of PTSD have been raised and remain in active debate. To some extent, these issues have been reflected in changing criteria through various editions of the DSM. How the issues will be resolved, and how PTSD should be defined in future editions of the DSM, remains uncertain. Clearly, an informed clinician who works with traumatized patients has a full plate of issues on which to stay current.

It is important to note that when issues are raised concerning how best to understand and apply the PTSD diagnosis, we are not questioning the emotional pain of those who have survived traumatic events or suffered horrific loss. That pain and suffering exists no matter what label a clinician chooses to use. When we strive to apply assessment and treatment practices that are evidenced based, and when we debate controversial issues, the reality of our patients and their problems is always foremost in our minds. It is in this spirit that every clinician can and should question if the introduction of PTSD, on balance, has advanced our assessment, diagnosis, and treatment of posttraumatic psychiatric disorders. Only through this active process of questioning and exploring will we come to know if PTSD is a valid and clinically informative diagnosis that was appropriately carved out of general stress studies.

## REFERENCES

Ahern, J., Galea, S., Resnick, H., & Vlahov, D. (2004). Television images and probable posttraumatic stress disorder after September 11: The role of background characteristics, event exposures, and peri-event panic. *Journal of Nervous and Mental Disease, 192,* 217–226.

American Psychiatric Association. (1980). *Diagnostic and statistical manual of mental disorder* (3rd ed.). Washington, D.C.: Author.

American Psychiatric Association. (1987). *Diagnostic and statistical manual of mental disorders* (3rd ed., revised). Washington, D.C.: Author.

American Psychiatric Association. (1994). *Diagnostic and statistical manual of mental disorders* (4th ed.). Washington, D.C.: Author.

American Psychiatric Association. (2000). *Diagnostic and statistical manual of mental disorders* (4th ed., text revision). Washington, D.C.: Author.

Andrews, B., Brewin, C. R., Philpott, R., & Stewart, L. (2007). Delayed-onset posttraumatic stress disorder: A systematic review of the evidence. *The American Journal of Psychiatry, 164,* 1319–1326.

Andrews, B., Brewin, C.R., & Rose, S. (2003). Gender, social support, and PTSD in victims of violent crime. *Journal of Traumatic Stress, 16*, 421–427.

Andrews, G., Tennant, C., Hewson, D. M., & Vaillant, G. E. (1978). Life event stress, social support, coping style, and risk of psychological impairment. *Journal of Nervous and Mental Disease, 166*, 307–316.

Bernstein, K. T., Ahern, J., Tracy, M., Boscarino, J. A., Vlahov, D., & Galea, S. (2007). Television watching and the risk of incident probable posttraumatic stress disorder: A prospective evaluation. *Journal of Nervous and Mental Disease, 195*, 41–47.

Bodkin, J.A., Pope, H. G., Detke, M. J., & Hudson, J. I. (2007). Is PTSD caused by traumatic stress? *Journal of Anxiety Disorders, 21*, 176–182.

Brandon, S., Boakes, J., Glaser, D., Green, R., MacKeith, J., & Whewell, P. (1997). Reported recovered memories of child sexual abuse: Recommendations for good practice and implications for training, continuing professional development and research. *Psychiatric Bulletin, 21*, 663–665.

Breslau, N., & Davis, G. C. (1987). Posttraumatic stress disorder: The stressor criterion. *The Journal of Nervous and Mental Disease, 175*, 255–264.

Breslau, N., Davis, G. C., Andreski, P., & Peterson, E. (1991). Traumatic events and posttraumatic stress disorder in an urban population of young adults. *Archives of General Psychiatry, 48*, 216–222.

Breslau, N., Kessler, R. C., Chilcoat, H. D., Schultz, L. R., Davis, G. C., & Andreski, P. (1998). Trauma and posttraumatic stress disorder in the community: The 1996 Detroit area survey of trauma. *Archives of General Psychiatry, 55*, 626–632.

Breslau, N., Lucia, V. C., & Davis, G. C. (2004). Partial PTSD versus full PTSD: An empirical examination of associated impairment. *Psychological Medicine, 34*, 1205–1214.

Breslau, N., Peterson, E. L., & Schultz, L. R. (2008). A second look at prior trauma and the posttraumatic stress disorder effects of subsequent trauma: A prospective epidemiological study. *Archives of General Psychiatry, 65*, 431–437.

Brewin, C. R., Andrews, B., & Valentine, J.D., (2000). Meta-analysis of risk factors for posttraumatic stress disorder in trauma-exposed adults. *Journal of Consulting and Clinical Psychology, 68*, 748–766.

Brewin, C. R., Dalgleish, T., & Joseph, S. (1996). A dual representation theory of posttraumatic stress disorder. *Psychological Review, 103*, 670–686.

Brewin, C. R., & Holmes, E. A. (2003). Psychological theories of posttraumatic stress disorder. *Clinical Psychology Review, 23*, 339–376.

Brewin, C. R., Lanius, R. A., Novac, A., Schnyder, U., & Galea, S. (2009). Reformulating PTSD for DSM-V: Life after Criterion A. *Journal of Traumatic Stress, 22*, 366–373.

Brown, G.W., Sklair, F., Harris, T. O., & Birley, J. L. T. (1973). Life events and psychiatric disorders: Part I. Some methodological issues. *Psychological Medicine, 3*, 74–87.

Bryant, R. A. (2004). In the aftermath of trauma: Normative reactions and early interventions. In G. M. Rosen (Ed.), *Posttraumatic stress disorder: Issues and controversies* (pp. 187–211). Chichester, England: John Wiley & Sons.

Burgess, A. W., & Holmstrom, L. L. (1974). Rape trauma syndrome. *American Journal of Psychiatry, 131*, 981–986.

Cannon, W. B. (1929). *Bodily changes in pain, hunger, fear and rage*. New York: D. Appleton & Company.

Cobb, S. (1976). Social support as a moderator of life stress. *Psychosomatic Medicine, 38*, 300–314.

Cukor, J., Spitalnick, J., Difede, J., Rizzo, A., & Rothbaum, B. O. (2009). Emerging treatments for PTSD. *Clinical Psychology Review, 29*, 715–726.

Dalgleish, T. (2004). Cognitive approaches to posttraumatic stress disorder: The evolution of multirepresentational theorizing. *Psychological Bulletin, 130*, 228–260.

Davidson, J. R. T., Hughes, D., Blazer, D. G., & George, L. K. (1991). Posttraumatic stress disorder in the community: An epidemiological study. *Psychological Medicine, 21*, 713–721.

Dohrenwend, B. S., & Dohrenwend, B. P. (Eds.) (1974a). *Stress life events: Their nature and effects*. New York: John Wiley & Sons.

Dohrenwend, B. S., & Dohrenwend, B. P. (1974b). Overview and prospects for research on stressful life events (pp. 313–331). In B.S. Dohrenwend & B.P. Dohrenwend (Eds.), *Stress life events: Their nature and effects*. New York: John Wiley & Sons.

Ehlers, A., & Clark, D. (2000). A cognitive model of posttraumatic stress disorder. *Behaviour Research and Therapy, 38*, 319–345.

Elhai, J. D., Grubaugh, A. L., Kashdan, T. B., & Frueh, B. C. (2008). Empirical examination of a proposed refinement to *DSM-IV* posttraumatic stress disorder symptom criteria using the National Comorbidity Survey Replication data. *Journal of Clinical Psychiatry, 69*, 597–602.

Elhai, J. D., Kashdan, T. B., & Frueh, B. C. (2005). What is a traumatic event? *British Journal of Psychiatry, 187*, 189–190.

Elhai, J. D., North, T. C., & Frueh, B. C. (2005). Health service use predictors among trauma survivors: A critical review. *Psychological Services, 2*, 3–19.

Eth, S. (2002). Television viewing as a risk factor. *Psychiatry, 65*, 301–303.

Foa, E. B., & Kozak, M. J. (1986). Emotional processing of fear: Exposure to corrective information. *Psychological Bulletin, 99*, 20–35.

Foa, E. B., & Riggs, D. S. (1993). Post-traumatic stress disorder in rape victims. In J. Oldham, M.B. Riba, & A. Tasman (Eds.), *American Psychiatric Press Review of Psychiatry, 12,* 273–303. Washington, DC: American Psychiatric Press.

Foa, E. B., & Rothbaum, B. O. (1998). *Treating the trauma of rape: Cognitive behavioral therapy for PTSD.* New York: Guilford Press.

Ford, J. D. (2008). History of psychological trauma. In G. Reyes, J. D. Elhai, & J. D. Ford (Eds.), *Encyclopedia of psychological trauma* (pp. 315–319). Hoboken, NJ: John Wiley & Sons.

Ford, J. D., Elhai, J. D., Ruggiero, K. J., & Frueh, B. C. (2009). Refining the posttraumatic stress disorder diagnosis: Evaluation of symptom criteria with the National Survey of Adolescents. *Journal of Clinical Psychiatry, 70,* 748–755.

Frueh, B. C., Grubaugh, A. L., Yeager, D. E., & Magruder, K. M. (2009). Delayed-onset posttraumatic stress disorder among veterans in primary care clinics. *British Journal of Psychiatry, 194,* 515–520.

Galea, S., Ahern, J., Resnick, H., Kilpatrick, D., Bucuvalas, M., Gold, J., et al. (2002). Psychological sequelae of the September 11 terrorist attacks in New York City. *New England Journal of Medicine, 346,* 982–987.

Gilbertson, M. W., Shenton, M. E., Ciszewski, A., Kasai, K., Lasko, N. B., Orr, S. P., et al. (2002). Smaller hippocampal volume predicts pathologic vulnerability to psychological trauma. *Nature Neuroscience, 5,* 1242–1247.

Gustafson, Paul. (August 1995). Jury awards patient $2.6 million: Verdict finds therapist Humenansky liable in repressed memory trial. *Minneapolis St. Paul Tribune.*

Hagen, M. A. (1997). *Whores of the court: The fraud of psychiatric testimony and the rape of American justice.* New York: Harper-Collins.

Helzer, J. E., Robins, L., & McEvoy, L. (1987). Post-traumatic stress disorder in the general population: Findings of the epidemiologic catchment area survey. *New England Journal of Medicine, 317,* 1630–1634.

Hickling, E. J., Blanchard, E. B., Mundy, E., & Galovski, T. E. (2002). Detection of malingered MVA related posttraumatic stress disorder: An investigation of the ability to detect professional actors by experienced clinicians, psychological tests, and psychophysiological assessment. *Journal of Forensic Psychology Practice, 2,* 33–54.

Horowitz, M. J. (1978). *Stress response syndromes.* Northvale, N.J.: Jason Aronson, Inc.

Horwitz, A. V., & Wakefield, J. C. (2007). *The loss of sadness: How psychiatry transformed normal sorrow into depressive disorder.* Oxford: Oxford University Press.

Janoff-Bulman, R. (1992). *Shattered assumptions: Towards a new psychology of trauma.* New York: Free Press.

Jones, E., & Wessely, S. (2005). *Shell shock to PTSD: Military psychiatry from 1900 to the Gulf War.* New York: Psychology Press.

Kardiner, A. (1941). *The traumatic neurosis of war.* New York: Paul Hoeber.

Kessler, R. C., Sonnega, A., Bromet, E., Hughes, M., & Nelson, C.B. (1995). Posttraumatic stress disorder in the National Comorbidity Survey. *Archives of General Psychiatry, 52,* 1048–1060.

Kilpatrick, D. G., Resnick, H. S., & Acierno, R. (2009). Should PTSD criterion A be retained? *Journal of Traumatic Stress, 22,* 374–383.

Koenen, K. C. (2007). Genetics of posttraumatic stress disorder: Review and recommendations for future studies. *Journal of Traumatic Stress, 20,* 737–750.

Lazarus, R. S., & Alfert, E. (1964). Short–circuiting of threat by experimentally altering cognitive appraisal. *Journal of Abnormal and Social Psychology, 59,* 195–205.

Lazarus, R. S., & Folkman, S. (1984). *Stress, appraisal, and coping.* New York: Springer.

Lifton, R. J. (1961). *History and human survival.* New York: Random House.

Long, M. E., & Elhai, J. D. (2009). Posttraumatic stress disorder's traumatic stressor criterion: History, controversy, clinical and legal implications. *Psychological Injury and Law, 2,* 167–178.

Long, M. E., Elhai, J. D., Schweinle, A., Gray, M. J., Grubaugh, A. L., & Frueh, B. C. (2008). Differences in posttraumatic stress disorder diagnostic rates and symptoms severity between Criterion A1 and non-Criterion A1 stressors. *Journal of Anxiety Disorders, 22,* 1255–1263.

Magnea, G., & Lanius, R. (2008). Biology, brain structure, and function, adult. In G. Reyes, J. D. Elhai & J. D. Ford (Eds.), *Encyclopedia of psychological trauma* (pp. 84–90). Hoboken, New Jersey: John Wiley & Sons.

McHugh, P. R., & Treisman, G. (2007). PTSD: A problematic diagnostic category. *Journal of Anxiety Disorders, 21,* 211–222.

McNally, R. J. (2003). *Remembering trauma.* Cambridge, MA: The Belknap Press of Harvard University Press.

Norris, F. H. (1992). Epidemiology of trauma: Frequency and impact of different potentially traumatic events on different demographic groups. *Journal of Consulting and Clinical Psychology, 60,* 409–418.

North, C. S. (2001). The course of post-traumatic stress disorder after the Oklahoma City bombing. *Military Medicine, 166* (Suppl. 2), 51–52.

Ost, J. (2003). Seeking the middle ground in the 'memory wars.' *British Journal of Psychology, 94,* 125–139.

Ozer, E. J., Best, S. R., Lipsey, T. L., & Weiss, D. S. (2008). Predictors of posttraumatic stress disorder and symptoms in adults: A meta-analysis. *Psychological Trauma: Theory, Research, Practice, and Policy, S*(1), 3–36.

Pankratz, L. (1998). *Patients who deceive: Assessment and management of risk in providing health care and financial benefits.* Springfield: Charles C. Thomas Publisher.

Rabkin, J. G., & Struening, E. L. (1976). Life events, stress, and illness. *Science, 194,* 1013–1021.

Ronan, P., & Summers, C. (2008). Biology, animal models. In G. Reyes, J. D. Elhai, & J.D. Ford (Eds.), *Encyclopedia of psychological trauma* (pp. 80–83). Hoboken, New Jersey: John Wiley & Sons.

Rose, S., Bisson, J., & Wessely, S. (2001). Psychological debriefing for preventing posttraumatic stress disorder (PTSD) (Cochrane Review) *The Cochrane Library* (3rd ed.). Oxford: Update Software.

Rosen G. M. (2004a). Traumatic events, criterion creep, and the creation of pretraumatic stress disorder. *The Scientific Review of Mental Health Practice, 3,* 39–42.

Rosen, G.M. (2004b). Malingering and the PTSD data base. In G. M. Rosen (Ed.), *Posttraumatic Stress Disorder: Issues and Controversies* (pp. 85–99). Chichester, England: John Wiley & Sons.

Rosen, G. M., & Lilienfeld, S. O. (2008). Posttraumatic stress disorder: An empirical analysis of core assumptions. *Clinical Psychology Review, 28,* 837–868.

Rosen, G. M., Lohr, J. M., McNally, R. J., & Herbert, J. D. (1998). Power Therapies: Evidence vs miraculous claims. *Behavioural and Cognitive Psychotherapy, 27,* 9–12.

Rosen, G. M., Spitzer, R. L., & McHugh, P. R. (2008). Problems with the posttraumatic stress disorder diagnosis and its future in DSM-V. *British Journal of Psychiatry, 192,* 3–4.

Rothbaum, B. O., Foa, E. B., Riggs, D. S., Murdock, T., & Walsh, W. (1992). A prospective examination of post-traumatic stress disorder in rape victims. *Journal of Traumatic Stress, 5,* 455–475.

Satel, S. L., & Frueh, B. C. (2009). Sociopolitical aspects of psychiatry: Posttraumatic stress disorder. In B. J. Sadock, V. A. Sadock, & P. Ruiz (Eds.), *Comprehensive textbook of Psychiatry* (9th ed.; pp. 728–733). Baltimore, MD: Lippincott, Williams, & Wilkins.

Schnurr, P. P., & Green, B. L. (2004, Eds). *Trauma and health: Physical health consequences of exposure to extreme stress.* Washington DC: American Psychological Association.

Schnurr, P. P., Lunney, C. A., & Sengupta, A. (2004). Risk factors for the development versus maintenance of posttraumatic stress disorder. *Journal of Traumatic Stress, 17,* 85–95.

Scott, M. J., & Stradling, S. G. (1994). Post-traumatic stress disorder without the trauma. *British Journal of Clinical Psychology, 33,* 71–74.

Scott, W. (1990). PTSD in DSM-III: A case in the politics of diagnosis and disease. *Social Problems, 37,* 294–310.

Selye, H. (1936). A syndrome produced by diverse nocuous agents. *Nature (Lond.), 138,* 32.

Selye, H. (1975). Confusion and controversy in the stress field. *Journal of Human Stress, 1,* 37–44.

Shephard, B. (2001). *A war of nerves: Soldiers and psychiatrists in the twentieth century.* Cambridge, MA: Harvard University Press.

Shephard, B. (2004). Risk factors and PTSD: A historian's perspective. In G. M. Rosen (Ed.), *Posttraumatic stress disorder: Issues and controversies* (pp. 39–61). Chichester: John Wiley & Sons.

Shin, L. M., & Handwerger, K. (2009). Is posttraumatic stress disorder a stress-induced fear circuitry disorder? *Journal of Traumatic Stress, 22,* 409–415.

Simon, R. I. (2003). *Posttraumatic stress disorder in litigation: Guidelines for forensic assessment* (2nd ed.). Washington, DC: American Psychiatric Publishing, Inc.

Simons, D., & Silveira, W. R. (1994). Post-traumatic stress disorder in children after television programmes. *British Medical Journal, 308,* 389–390.

Simms, L. J., Watson, D., & Doebbelling, B. N. (2002). Confirmatory factor analyses of posttraumatic stress symptoms in deployed and nondeployed veterans of the Gulf War. *Journal of Abnormal Psychology, 111,* 637–647.

Slovenko, R. (1994). Legal aspects of post-traumatic stress disorder. In D.A. Tomb (Ed.), *The Psychiatric Clinics of North America: Post-traumatic stress disorder, 17*(2), 439–446.

Slovenko, R. (2002). *Psychiatry in Law/Law in Psychiatry.* New York: Brunner-Routledge.

Spitzer, R. L., First, M. B., & Wakefield, J.C. (2007). Saving PTSD from itself in DSM-V. *Journal of Anxiety Disorders, 21,* 233–241.

Stein, M. B., Walker, J. R., Hazen, A. L., & Forde, D. R. (1997). Full and partial posttraumatic stress disorder: Findings from a community survey. *American Journal of Psychiatry, 154,* 1114–1119.

Taylor, S., Frueh, B. C., & Asmundson, G. J. G. (2007). Detection and management of malingering in people presenting for treatment of posttraumatic stress disorder: Methods, obstacles, and recommendations. *Journal of Anxiety Disorders, 21,* 22–41.

Tolin, D. F., & Foa, E. B. (2006). Sex differences in trauma and posttraumatic stress disorder: A quantitative review of 25 years of research. *Psychological Bulletin, 132,* 959–992.

Walker, L. E. (1977). Battered women and learned helplessness. *Victimology, 2,* 525–534.

Watson, D. (2005). Rethinking the mood and anxiety disorders: A quantitative hierarchical model for DSM-V. *Journal of Abnormal Psychology, 114,* 522–536.

Weathers, F.W., & Keane, T. M. (2007). The criterion A problem revisited: Controversies and challenges in defining and measuring psychological trauma. *Journal of Traumatic Stress, 20,* 107–121.

Williams, C. W., Lees-Haley, P. R., & Djanogly, S. E. (1999). Clinical scrutiny of litigants' self-reports. *Professional Psychology: Research and Practice, 30,* 361–367.

Wyler, A. R., Masuda, M., & Holmes, T. H. (1971). Magnitude of life events and seriousness of illness. *Psychosomatic Medicine, 33,* 115–122.

Yehuda, R. (2002). Current status of cortisol findings in post-traumatic stress disorder. *Psychiatric Clinics of North America, 25,* 341–368.

Yehuda, R., & McFarlane, A. C. (1995). Conflict between current knowledge about posttraumatic stress disorder and its original conceptual basis. *American Journal of Psychiatry, 152,* 1705–1713.

Young, A. (1995). *The harmony of illusions: Inventing post-traumatic stress disorder.* Princeton, New Jersey: Princeton University Press.

CHAPTER

# 2

⮞◆⮜

# Normal Reactions to Adversity or Symptoms of Disorder?

Jerome C. Wakefield
Allan V. Horwitz

Posttraumatic stress disorder (PTSD) is a young diagnosis, only entering psychiatric nosology in 1980. Nevertheless it has become an emblematic diagnosis of our time, pervading not only professional practice and research but also media discussions and lay descriptions of responses to trauma. In this chapter, we explore some of the ways that the PTSD diagnosis appears to have spread beyond the strict confines of mental disorder to encompass what is likely normal intense human suffering from disturbing and shocking experiences.

## OVERVIEW AND CAVEATS

The mental health professions have several functions in our society. Their primary function is to recognize and treat, as well as prevent, mental disorders in the medical sense—that is, harmful mental dysfunctions in which mental processes are not performing as they were biologically designed to do (Wakefield, 1992). This is analogous to the primary task of physical medicine to treat and prevent physical disorders. However, both the physical and mental health professions are mandated to extend the application of their knowledge and skills beyond prevention and treatment of this disorder to include the treatment of a variety of problematic non-disordered conditions. In physical medicine, for example, this distinction allows fertility, pregnancy, the pain experienced during childbirth, and cosmetic anomalies (all challenging normal conditions) to be targeted for medical intervention.

Analogously, the mental health professions often address a variety of problems that are not mental disorders but that arise from normal human reactions to extreme or changing environments or from socially or personally undesirable normal variation. These include, for example: (a) The DSM's "V-Codes," which encompass non-disordered conditions that are nonetheless commonly the target of psychiatric intervention, such as relationship problems and problems in selecting a career; (b) reduction of mental suffering and social role impairment accompanying normal distress (e.g., grief, performance anxiety); (c) control and treatment of normal but socially undesirable trait variations in individuals whose traits do not fit our social needs and opportunities (e.g., lack of assertiveness; fear of public speaking; lack of resilience); and (d) enhancement of individuals' normal mental function in "cosmetically" desirable ways that serve the personal happiness of the individual (e.g., heightening relationship intimacy; positive psychology; leadership training).

Thus, the fact that a condition is not a disorder is no obstacle to its being a target of mental health intervention, and the issue we discuss does not concern intervention per se. Rather, the issue that concerns us is that the "disorder" category can sometimes get confused with the "painful and intense normal suffering" category. Confusion over this can pose an obstacle to understanding the nature of a patient's problem. It also can constrict a clinician's attention to the range of intervention options that should be considered.[1]

---

1 The group at which the PTSD diagnosis was primarily aimed and which remains prominent in PTSD discussion is military personnel subjected to horrific wartime experiences. Respect for the enormous sacrifices and consequent needs for psychological support of our military personnel demands mention of several important caveats to our discussion. Horrific experiences do sometimes cause genuine disorders: We are not denying that there really are some disorders that fall under the current "PTSD" category. Moreover, the real human suffering that follows such experiences, even if not a mental disorder,

## HISTORICAL COMMENTS

Although the PTSD diagnosis entered the DSM relatively recently, it should be kept in mind that what we call "PTSD" is not at all new. For example, in the Second World War, nearly a million American soldiers were diagnosed with "neuropsychiatric breakdowns." About one-fourth of all soldiers in combat divisions were hospitalized at one point or another for psychiatric reasons: for those exposed to longer periods of combat on the front lines, the figure reached 70% (Grob, 1991). According to one projected estimate of psychiatric casualties, the average soldier would suffer a breakdown after 88 days of continuous combat; by 260 days, the psychiatric casualty rate would reach 95% (Appel & Beebe, 1946). Similar projections of almost universal eventual breakdown were calculated for fighter pilots doing many sorties a day, each highly stressful and a grave threat to life and limb. Clearly, just as a bone snaps when there is sufficient stress placed on it, so the human mind is not designed to handle stress over a certain threshold.

Kutchins and Kirk (1997) observed that the introduction of PTSD in DSM-III was not the creation but "the *reinvention* of a psychiatric diagnosis.... The diagnosis War Neurosis had disappeared from DSM until the Vietnam veterans pressured the American Psychiatric Association" (p. 18; emphasis added). Gunderson and Sabo (1993) noted that "awareness of posttraumatic psychiatric consequences has been present since the Civil War" (p. 19), when it was referred to as "Soldier's Heart."

Traditionally, combat fatigue was an acute condition in the vast majority of cases: Only a small proportion of affected soldiers continued to have mental symptoms once they were outside the combat zone. Indeed, the most effective treatment for combat fatigue was simply to take an individual away from the front lines for a period of a few days

---

demands social response, so treatment when desired or needed to improve important role functioning is certainly appropriate. This is even more the case when the experiences causing the individual's distress result from the individual having been placed in harm's way to serve society's purposes. Indeed, our view suggests that support and intervention should likely be more routine components of military personnel's reentry into society after serving in war because of the extraordinary psychological challenges involved. However, the appropriateness of providing psychological support to traumatized individuals, and the moral urgency of providing adequate mechanisms for adjustment upon return from warfare, are not the same as saying that the individual who suffers a trauma has a mental disorder.

to a few weeks. In most cases individuals would recover enough to warrant their return to combat, a consideration that may have provided an incentive for some to remain "ill" (Grob, 1991). More chronic reactions of the kind characterizing PTSD—including "railroad neurosis" (the original form of posttraumatic disorder) and "war neurosis"—were recognized as disorders.

## NATURAL AND PATHOLOGICAL RESPONSES TO TRAUMA

When people's basic sense of values or reality is challenged, it can be a difficult and lengthy process to reconstruct their meaning systems to suit the new circumstances. Experiences that we call "trauma" are experiences that call into question the assumptions upon which daily activities in our culture are built, such as belief in personal safety, expectation of continued existence and denial of mortality, a just world, and other basic assumptions. Extreme distress and lengthy grappling with such events is not unexpected. Even less extreme stressors that involve changes in one's meaning system, such as dissolution of a marriage, romantic betrayal or loss of a job can trigger lengthy and highly painful psychological processes. Eventually, there is a return to homeostasis and a revised meaning system that allows the individual to live with changed circumstances.

Although the clinician is likely familiar with the DSM criteria for defining PTSD, it may be useful to review the diagnostic criteria for PTSD (see Chapter 1, Table 1.2), which make an intrinsic connection between trauma exposure and particular symptoms assumed to be pathological. These include intrusive memories and upsetting dreams about the traumatic event, feeling upset about reminders of the event, re-experiencing the event, unpleasant somatic sensations and heightened arousal, irritability, difficulty concentrating, sleep difficulties, and awareness of danger when reminded of the event. Yet, these symptoms can be products of the inherent cognitive bias of fear mechanisms that promote the reinforcement and recollection (rather than forgetting) of past traumatic experiences (Mineka, 1992). Moreover, symptoms of intrusion, avoidance, and hyperarousal that trauma researchers assume are intrinsically connected to *traumatic* events are not inherently pathological but also characterize responses to non-traumatic stressors.

A central question for clinicians to consider when evaluating if PTSD criteria identify only mental disorders or encompass normal responses as well is: Do these symptoms occur only in the case of extreme stressors such as those mentioned in Criterion A, or can they be seen as a more general response to a range of stressors? The evidence suggests that PTSD symptoms often constitute a common way that people respond to a broad range of challenging new meanings.

Typical scales that measure PTSD ask respondents questions about their responses to traumatic events, such as "I thought about it when I didn't mean to" or "I tried to remove it from memory." One study used such a scale to ask college students questions about how often they relived or avoided thinking about *the worst movie (or worst television program)* they had seen in the last few months (Lees-Haley Price, Williams, & Betz, 2001). Forty-one percent of respondents scored in the high range, 31% in the medium range, and 28% in the low range of scores obtained from victims of events that are commonly viewed as traumatic (e.g., survivors of an airplane crash). Another study (Mol et al., 2005), compared PTSD symptoms in the general population that followed from traumatic events with those that followed from non-traumatic stressors (e.g., a variety of interpersonal, academic, and occupational problems). There were no statistically significant differences between the two groups: Average PTSD scores were actually higher for those reporting non-traumatic events. Similar findings emerged in a study asking American college students about traumatic and non-traumatic stressors. Students who experienced non-traumatic stressors reported more PTSD symptoms than those who had experienced trauma (Gold, Marz, Soler-Baillo, & Sloan, 2005).

These findings indicate how typical questions used to assess an individual's adjustment after trauma do not necessarily capture *disordered* responses. Instead, these questions address the occurrence of intrusive thoughts, feelings, and images that apply equally well to any disturbing but non-traumatic experience. Such "symptoms" occur as normal responses to a wide variety of experiences, from humiliation to betrayal. For example, responses to a romantic partner's unfaithfulness typically involve intrusive and recurrent thoughts of sexual activities, avoidance of reminders of the affair, and symptoms of sleep difficulties, anger, and hypervigilance (Datillio, 2004). Because adverse events happen to most people at some point in their life, PTSD criteria create the potential for a massive pathologization of natural responses to recollections of disturbing experiences. Indeed, anyone who has tried to stop thinking about a song they cannot get out of their head might receive a substantial score on a checklist of "trauma" symptoms.

Consider comments by Donna Brazile, an Al Gore presidential campaign aide, who expressed how she felt after Gore lost the presidency:

> Campaigns are not for the fainthearted. They are tough—mentally, physically and spiritually. Once a campaign ends, an emptiness comes over you. You find yourself struggling to figure out how to become human again. . . . you're in a state of emotional disrepair . . . No matter how hard you try to contain it, you're both angry and sad. . . . I remember feeling lost and disillusioned. I was empty inside. . . . I had no idea what to do with my life. . . . I had no energy to start looking for work. I was obsessed with those chads: hanging, swinging and, my favorite, pregnant. Above all else, I did not want to quit fighting. . . . It will take you weeks to readjust and for the world to appear normal.

Keep in mind that this is from a *political*, not a military, campaign. Brazile's comments remind us how difficult re-entry to usual roles may be after immersion in a different sort of life, but the kind of reactions she describes does not represent mental disorder.

It is not necessarily pathological to try and avoid thinking about stressful experiences (whether traumatic or not), minimize exposure to them, and become physiologically aroused when thinking about them (Spitzer, First, & Wakefield, 2007). No less than traumatic events, ordinary stressors such as the death of a loved one, interpersonal problems, or embarrassing and humiliating events can lead to rumination, re-experiencing, pondering, avoidance of reminders of the stressor, and selective attention (Marks & Nesse, 1994). Symptoms such as intrusive thoughts, emotional numbing, increased arousal, or acting or feeling as if an event were happening again are not specific to recollections of trauma. These reactions can typify normal recollections, not only to stressful experiences, but even to intense positive experiences. Consider the following report from a young woman:

I was walking along Broadway, and I was suddenly overcome by a vivid "flashback" to an intense lovemaking session a few days earlier with someone with whom I am very much in love. The memory and bodily sensations were sufficiently intense and "real" that I look around in embarrassment, wondering if others could tell the sort of experience I am reliving.

## ADAPTIVE RESPONSES

A clinician's need to distinguish between "adaptive responses" and symptoms of mental disorder is illustrated by the symptom of hypervigilance, as presented in a case of PTSD widely reported in the news media:

> BELLMORE, New York (CNN)—Walking through a crowded shopping mall can bring back memories of war. The shifting crowds, the jostle of passers-by and the din can all trigger Army Sgt. Kristofer Goldsmith's post-traumatic stress disorder. "You get used to scanning what everybody's doing. Your brain just starts working so fast and it's purely instinctual because you want to know what everyone's intent is around you," said Goldsmith, who served four years in active duty. "You want to know if anyone has the intent to harm you or the capabilities to harm you."
>
> (Gajilan, 2008)

This sort of hypervigilance triggered by perceptual experiences even when the danger is long past is not uncommon in everyday life. It is the result of strongly learned survival techniques that are resistant to extinction. Behavioral psychologists have demonstrated that there are what they call "prepared responses" that are biologically easy to learn and extremely difficult to extinguish. The classic case is when a rat is fed something at a given location in his cage that makes the rat nauseated; no matter how many times one feeds the rat good food at that location, the rat will resist and will not voluntarily go there to collect available food. In effect, the rat is "hypervigilant." The same response in humans is sometimes seen in the refusal to ever again eat at a restaurant where one has gotten ill, despite low odds of it ever happening again. It is possible that certain behaviors and experiences trigger deeply programmed responses that are biologically prepared, and are very difficult to extinguish once one returns to usual roles.

The previously discussed case of Sgt. Goldsmith illustrates another issue, as the sergeant also engaged in violent behavior. Here it is useful to remember what the DSM-IV itself has to say about the diagnosis of conduct disorder in adolescents. A textual commentary insists that the clinician should not diagnose conduct disorder on the basis of antisocial behavior alone, if there is a better explanation in terms of a normal response to an extreme environment (as when an inner city child joins a gang for self-protection). The DSM goes on to mention the possibility that a child may have been immersed in an environment where violence and other forms of what we consider to be antisocial behavior is the norm, thus creating future difficulties when adapting to the norms of a new environment:

> Concerns have been raised that the Conduct Disorder diagnosis may at times be misapplied to individuals in settings where patterns of undesirable behavior are sometimes viewed as protective (e.g., threatening, impoverished, high-crime). Consistent with the DSM-IV definition of mental disorder, the Conduct Disorder diagnosis should be applied only when the behavior in question is symptomatic of an underlying dysfunction within the individual and not simply a reaction to the immediate social context. **Moreover, immigrant youth from war-ravaged countries who have a history of aggressive behaviors that may have been necessary for their survival in that context would not necessarily warrant a diagnosis of Conduct Disorder.** It may be helpful for the clinician to consider the social and economic context in which the undesirable behaviors have occurred.
>
> (APA, 2000, p. 88; *emphasis added*)

This qualification to the diagnostic criteria for conduct disorder essentially says that an individual's difficulty adjusting to a new environment (e.g., when one is conditioned to a more violent environment) does not necessarily constitute disorder. Extending the same idea to PTSD criteria suggests a new way to look at what is now classified as mental disorder in returning veterans like Sgt. Goldsmith.

## DIFFICULTY OF DEFINING THE BOUNDARY OF PTSD

For various reasons, the boundaries of PTSD are "fuzzy" and use of the diagnosis has been expanded to an ever-increasing array of events and an ever-increasing range of symptoms. One reason for the expansion is the previously discussed difficulty of distinguishing normal recollections of a trauma from pathological symptoms. This issue is especially hard to resolve for PTSD because extreme stressors naturally entail intensely disturbing memories and other consequences. It is particularly difficult to establish how people are naturally designed to recollect traumatic experiences and thus how natural reactions differ from disordered ones.

Second, the boundaries of PTSD pathology can also grow by expanding the definition of what counts as a trauma. This phenomenon has been termed "criterion creep" (Rosen, 2004), and is especially problematic because sharp boundaries between traumatic and non-traumatic stressors do not exist in nature. Therefore, demarcations can be drawn in many places. The borders of traumatic exposure are porous and can easily be manipulated with the result of changing rates of putative PTSD.

A third boundary issue is that the symptoms of PTSD and those of other disorders are especially permeable. Traumatic events are associated with numerous pathological conditions including a variety of anxiety disorders, depression, and substance use. These other conditions need not entail a traumatic cause. Yet, it is difficult to distinguish what symptoms are *unique* to PTSD. For example, studies of psychiatric outpatients with depression show that levels of PTSD symptoms are equivalent among those who have and have not experienced traumatic events (Bodkin, Pope, Derke, & Hudson, 2007). Moreover, the same people typically experience a range of disorders including mood and other anxiety disorders as well as PTSD after traumatic events making the distinctiveness of a PTSD diagnosis questionable (Breslau, Davis, Peterson, & Schultz, 2000).

A fourth consideration is that people have incentives to define any post-traumatic condition as PTSD because this diagnosis can bring about benefits that do not accrue from other conditions (Frueh, Grubaugh, Elhai, & Buckley, 2007). Most psychiatric diagnoses are either stigmatizing or have some degree of stigma attached to them. A PTSD diagnosis, in contrast, is often sought after. "It is rare to find a psychiatric diagnosis that anyone likes to have," notes psychiatrist Nancy Andreasen, "but PTSD seems to be one of them" (1995, p. 964). By clearly rooting symptoms in an environmental cause, PTSD can deflect blame from the individual, lead to therapeutic help, and, often, to monetary compensation and other rewards. No other psychiatric diagnosis involves issues where drawing boundaries is not just a matter of diagnostic convenience but also of justice and injustice.

As a consequence of the above considerations, PTSD, a diagnosis originally conceived to capture the effects of wartime trauma and other horrific life-threatening experiences, has become widespread in our culture and applied to all manner of negative experiences.

## PTSD AS A CHALLENGE TO THE WEB OF BELIEF

Consider the sort of experiences described on an anonymous web submission, but of the kind that clinicians treating PTSD in veterans all too commonly come across:

> The individual had been unexpectedly deployed, and virtually simultaneously with arrival in Iraq, his beloved grandfather had died and his marriage had run into trouble. He was already coping with major challenges to his meaning system. Then, a young boy whom he had befriended, and who helped out the soldiers at a guard point, learned broken English from them and relieved them of cokes and food for his family, and eventually worked for them as a translator, was suddenly killed in a cross-fire by a rocket-propelled grenade on his way home from the new school he had been attending—and this was revealed when his mother wandered past them dragging a heavy bag behind her, and when they examined the bag the boy's body was inside.
>
> (Anonymous, 2007)

The sort of experiences described in this vignette challenge an individual's basic assumptions—continuity of life, continued existence of an object of his affection, sanctity of a child's life, the ability to have pleasure in a simple human relationship. As often happens, earlier experiences prepared the way for the impact of the boy's death, an impact that can best be understood as the second of a one-two punch to the meaning system. In this individual's case, he reported that he had lost his beloved grandfather just when he arrived in Iraq and was having marital problems. Thus, the soldier was already processing changed meanings about mortality, solace, and primary relationships when the incident with the boy occurred. The inability to process so many central meanings without a prolonged struggle emotionally—and the enduring residue of suffering associated with those experiences—does not always require the attribution of a medical disorder.

## WHY DOES IT MATTER?

Two questions arise immediately. First: Why does it matter whether we label PTSD-type conditions disorders or non-disorders, irrespective of what they really are? Second, what about the benefits of being labeled as medically disordered and thus the harm that reclassification might cause?

It would seem that three benefits of conceiving the PTSD syndrome as a disorder stand out. First, such a conception has enabled individuals suffering from PTSD symptoms to more readily get treatment when they want it. Second, the "disorder" label has sometimes enabled sufferers to qualify for medical or veterans' disability payments when the symptoms interfered with their ability to work. Third, to some extent, understanding PTSD symptoms as a disorder relieves the individual of moral responsibility as part of the "sick role."

At the same time, it should be borne in mind that disorder diagnoses carry with them certain potentially negative consequences, especially if no disorder in fact exists. First, those with disorders are subject to what sociologists call "stigma"—they tend to be seen as "damaged" and to some extent judged negatively and shunned or perhaps even feared (Link, 1987). Mental disorders by definition are abnormalities in one's mind, and the mind is the organ of social interaction and reasoning, so those with mental disorders can easily come to be seen as defective in fundamental ways that undermine their equal status within society. This stigmatization may explain why there is no evidence that treatment helps soldiers who are screened as mental health risks. Remarkably, in a major study of this issue it was reported that: "an inverse relationship existed between receiving mental health services and improvement in symptoms" (Milliken, Auchterlonie, & Hoge, 2007, p. 2143). That is, among all soldiers that screened positively for PTSD, those who did not enter mental health treatment had higher improvement rates than those who were treated. Moreover, soldiers who received referrals to mental health treatment but did not attend any therapeutic sessions had better outcomes than referred soldiers who did go into treatment, even though the severity measured by comorbidity was the same in the two groups. These findings document real-life consequences, and highlight why it does matter when clinicians label reactions as disorder.

Another downside to diagnosing normal reactions to adverse circumstances as disorder is that the person's experiences tend to be delegitimated and seen as the mechanical outcome of some sort of pathology. Any truth or illumination that lies in the experiences may be lost. The individual becomes an object of medical technology, rather than a person who is responding with nuanced meanings to horrific experiences. In addition, relief from social expectations tends to be limited to disorders, leading to a narrowing of the acceptable scope of intense negative human emotions. Broadening the scope of such relief would seem to be a better strategy than mislabeling painful but normal human reactions as disorders.

There are other reasons why the disorder versus non-disorder distinction matters. Certainly, clinicians want to understand the nature of each patient's condition in order to approach treatment appropriately and with informed consent—and without preconceived labels getting in the way of as broad and as flexible an understanding as possible. Different kinds of conditions may well have different optimal treatment options. Indeed, if PTSD symptoms can be identified as normal variants of biologically designed responses, then one can think about treatment in new ways and link into broader knowledge about normal processes. Rather than a cure for a disordered mental condition, patients may need support in successfully grappling with the challenges an experience has posed to their meaning systems (as can happen to all of us at times). In such cases, prognosis might be much more positive. Indeed, recent research suggests that rumination and other depressive and PTSD symptomatic processes may be part of a problem-solving process. In this context, support of successful problem solving rather than cessation of the process may be a useful strategy (Andrews & Thomson, 2009). Distinguishing intense normal suffering from disorder potentially opens up new avenues of theoretical speculation and treatment approaches, and provides a framework for a more universal and humanitarian response.

Another reason the "disorder" versus "non-disorder" question matters is that there is a huge research establishment focused on studying PTSD. Indeed, at present, PTSD generates by far more research than any other anxiety disorder. If current trends continue, by 2015 it will spawn more than twice as many articles as the next most studied anxiety disorder (Boschen, 2009). Articles about PTSD in the medical literature doubled between 1985 and 1995 and then doubled again between 1995 and 2005. However, to do effective research, one must study individuals who are as homogeneous as possible in terms of their underlying condition. If one mixes together individuals who are disordered with individuals who are experiencing intense and enduring versions of biologically normal adaptive processes, then research may yield findings that are muddied and not illuminating. Making appropriate distinctions within the current PTSD category between disordered versus intense normal responses may further the fruitfulness of PTSD research.

Finally, it matters because it is important in the long run to get these conceptual issues right, rather than doing whatever is expedient at a given moment in time. The problem is that in our instant-communication society, a decision anywhere has repercussions for decisions everywhere. If an overly encompassing definition of PTSD is allowed to be applied where we might like it applied—say, to military service personnel—then the same definition can be used by other individuals in other situations who want to claim victim status. This is just what has been happening with PTSD: A disorder category that was originally conceived to apply to a relatively small number of individuals after very extreme experiences has been stretched and expanded in various ways so that it now pervades social discussion of harm, victimization, and justice. In this broader realm of what is an inherently fuzzy domain, it matters all the more that we try to think clearly about the disorder/non-disorder divide.

## Increasing the Specificity of a PTSD Diagnosis

A central concern in our discussion is that even symptoms most distinctive of PTSD appear to have normal analogs. Accordingly, PTSD "symptoms" must be made as specific as possible to distinguish pathology from normal stress responses. Otherwise, the possibility exists that even criteria-satisfying responses to truly traumatic stressors (in the Criterion-A sense) may be false positive normal responses.

One part of the solution to this problem is to "tighten" symptom descriptors with higher thresholds that are more indicative of pathology, rather than normal reactions to highly negative life events. This approach will not fully address the problem because normal responses can be quite intense, but it is a place to start. While we refrain from a detailed proposal here, the clinician may find it useful to ponder what symptom definitions could more clearly indicate disorder rather than normal processing of radically altered meanings (for further discussion see Spitzer, First, & Wakefield, 2007). For example, any extremely negative or worrisome event may be recalled, reviewed, and worked through repeatedly in the memory of a non-disordered individual. Similarly, many non-disordered people generally try to avoid thinking about a highly stressful event and minimize their exposure to reminders. Individuals also may find themselves physiologically aroused when memories of an event trigger negative emotions. Thus, symptoms such as "recurrent and intrusive distressing recollections of the event," "intense psychological distress at exposure to internal or external cues that symbolize or resemble an aspect of the traumatic event," and "physiological reactivity on exposure to internal or external cues that symbolize or resemble an aspect of that traumatic event" are not sufficiently specific to define disordered responses.

Threshold qualifiers pose challenges for operationalizing criteria. One approach is to conceptually aim to set symptom descriptor thresholds higher, requiring recurrent and intrusive distressing recollections of the event "of an intensity, frequency, and/or duration beyond that associated with the expectable emotional pain and lengthy working through of intensely negative life events." One might require "excessively intense, frequent, or enduring" psychological distress at reminders of the event "beyond the negative emotions expectably associated with recalling such negative life events within the normal range of emotional intensity." Comparable threshold changes might be made for physiological reactivity to distinguish it from arousal due to normal negative emotions upon recalling the event. Similarly, other symptom descriptors might be aimed at capturing a higher threshold of excessive arousal or excessive avoidance associated with pathology. In all cases, descriptors would take into account the fact that occasional arousal and avoidance at substantial levels over a long period of time, as well as estrangement from certain other people associated with the event, can be part of a normal response to intensely negative experiences.

We are hopeful that future editions of the DSM will do a better job when it comes to defining PTSD's symptom criteria. In the meantime, clinicians do not need to wait for text changes to think critically about threshold qualifiers, and to make important distinctions between normal reactions to adversity and the symptoms of disorder.

## REFERENCES

American Psychiatric Association. (2000). *Diagnostic and Statistical Manual of Mental Disorders* (4th ed., text rev.). Washington, DC: American Psychiatric Association.

Andreasen, N. (1995). Posttraumatic stress disorder: Psychology, biology, and the Manichean warfare between false dichotomies." *American Journal of Psychiatry, 1523,* 963–965.

Andrews, P. W., & Thomson, J. A. Jr. (2009). The bright side of being blue: Depression as an adaptation for analyzing complex problems. *Psychological Review, 116,* 620–654.

Anonymous. (2007). *IED's and PTSD: Interview with an Iraq war vet.* Associated Content, updated February 27, 2007. Accessed 1-10-09 at: http://www .associatedcontent.com/article/154485/ieds_and_ptsd_interview_with_an _iraq.html?page=2&cat=47

Appel, J. W., & Beebe, G. W. (1946). Preventive psychiatry. *Journal of the American Medical Association, 131,* 1469–1475.

Blake, J. (2008). *Miraculous survivors: Why they live while others die.* CNN, updated September 8, 2008. Accessed 1-10-09 at: http://www.cnn.com/2008/ US/09/08/survive/index.html

Bodkin, A., Pope, H. G., Detke, M. J., & Hudson, J. I. (2007). Is PTSD caused by traumatic stress? *Journal of Anxiety Disorders, 21*, 176–182.

Boschen, M. J. (2009). Publication trends in individual anxiety disorders: 1980-2015. *Journal of Anxiety Disorders*, in press.

Breslau, N., Davis, G. C., Peterson, E. L., & Schultz, L. R. (2000). A second look at comorbidity in victims of trauma: The posttraumatic stress disorder–major depression connection. *Biological Psychiatry, 48*, 902–909.

Dattilio, F. M. (2004). Extramarital affairs: The much overlooked PTSD. *The Behavior Therapist, 27*, 76–78.

Frueh, B. C., Grubaugh, A. L., Elhai, J. D., & Buckley, T. C. (2007). U.S. Department of Veterans Affairs disability policies for PTSD: Administrative trends and implications for treatment, rehabilitation, and research. *American Journal of Public Health, 97*, 2143–2145.

Gajilan, C. (2008). *Iraq vets and post-traumatic stress: No easy answers.* CNN updated October 24, 2008; accessed 1-10-09 at: http://www.cnn.com/2008/HEALTH/conditions/10/24/ptsd.struggle/index.html?iref=newssearch

Gold, S. D., Marx, B. P., Soler-Baillo, J. M., & Sloan, D. M. (2005). Is life stress more traumatic than traumatic stress? *Journal of Anxiety Disorders, 19*, 687–698.

Grob, G. N. (1991). *From asylum to community: Mental health policy in modern America.* Princeton: Princeton University Press.

Gunderson, J. G., & Sabo, A. N. (1993). The phenomenological and conceptual interface between borderline personality disorder and PTSD. *American Journal of Psychiatry, 150*, 19–27

Kutchins, H., & Kirk, S. (1997). *Making us crazy: DSM: The psychiatric bible and the creation of mental disorders.* New York: Free Press.

Lees-Haley, P., Price, J. R., Williams, C. W., & Betz, B. P. (2001). Use of the impact of events scale in the assessment of emotional distress and PTSD may produce misleading results. *Journal of Forensic Neuropsychology, 2*, 45–52.

Link, B. (1987). Understanding labeling effects in the area of mental disorders: An assessment of the effects of the expectation of rejection. *American Sociological Review, 52*, 96–112.

Marks, I. M., & Nesse, R. (1994). Fear and fitness: An evolutionary analysis of anxiety disorders. *Ethnology and Sociobiology, 15*, 247–261.

Milliken, C. S., Auchterlonie, J. L., & Hoge, C. W. (2007). Longitudinal assessment of mental health problems among active and reserve component soldiers returning rrom the Iraq war. *JAMA, 298*, 2141–2148.

Mineka, S. (1992). Evolutionary memories, emotional processing, and the emotional disorders. *Psychology Learning Motivation, 28*, 161–206.

Mol, S. S. L., Arntz, A., Metsemakers, F. M., Dinant, G.-J., Vilters-Van Montfort, P., & Knottnerus, J. A. (2005). Symptoms of post-traumatic stress disorder after non-traumatic events: Evidence from an open population study. *British Journal of Psychiatry, 186,* 494–499.

Rosen, G. M. (2004). Traumatic events, criterion creep, and the creation of pretraumatic stress disorder. *The Scientific Review of Mental Health Practice, 3,* 39–42.

Spitzer, R. L., First, M. B., & Wakefield, J. C. (2007). Saving PTSD from itself in DSM-V. *Journal of Anxiety Disorders, 21,* 233–241.

Wakefield, J. C. (1992). The concept of mental disorder: On the boundary between biological facts and social values. *American Psychologist, 47,* 373–388.

# 3

# Criterion A: Controversies and Clinical Implications

MEAGHAN L. O'DONNELL

MARK CREAMER

JOHN COOPER

Marsha, a 45-year-old woman, was working in a residential care unit for behaviorally disturbed adolescents. One afternoon, a 12-year-old boy entered the room where she was talking with another child, raised a gun, and pointed it at her head. She experienced intense fear, along with thoughts that she was going to die and would never see her children again. She started to cry. The boy suddenly laughed and revealed that the gun was plastic—a cheap and very poor replica of a real gun. Soon after the incident, Marsha developed symptoms associated with the diagnosis of PTSD.

Bob, a 38-year-old non-combatant cook in the armed forces, developed PTSD symptoms following an incident in which he witnessed the transfer of six bodies from a helipad to the morgue. Although the bodies were in bags, he knew they were young civilian boys and girls killed in an insurgent bomb blast. He became very distressed. Vivid pictures of what he imagined the bodies would look like began to dominate his waking hours and haunt him in nightmares.

Bill, a 45-year-old traffic policeman, developed PTSD after attending a relatively minor motor vehicle accident in which a small child had been injured. Although he had attended a large number of incidents, including many gruesome fatalities, during his 25-year career he had never before experienced any powerful emotional reactions to those events. On the contrary, he would "put it out of his mind and get on with the job." Following this latest incident, he experienced multiple distressing images of several fatal accidents he had attended over the years. He tried to avoid anything connected with his work and became unable to function.

Marie, a 34-year-old woman, developed PTSD symptoms after being hit in the back of the head by a sheet of metal that blew off a building site. She experienced a brief loss of consciousness and was amnesic to the event and the immediate aftermath. She reported powerful distressing memories of waking up on the ground and not knowing what had happened to her. She experienced repeated nightmares that she was in danger but did not know why. She avoided building sites and had become phobic of wind.

In our examples, Marsha's life was never in danger; Bob did not actually see anything particularly unpleasant; Bill was unaffected for many years by the incidents that now haunt him, and Marie had no memory of her accident. Can all these individuals be diagnosed with PTSD? Do they pass the first crucial hurdle for a diagnosis: Criterion A?

## CRITERION A

The diagnosis of PTSD requires that a person experience a traumatic event. In DSM-IV, it is Criterion A that defines a traumatic stressor for the purpose of a diagnosis. Defining what constitutes a traumatic event, however, is not an easy task and much heated debate has revolved around Criterion A and its role in the genesis of PTSD. With the development of DSM-V, due for release in 2013, the question of defining trauma in PTSD has been reignited and several excellent papers have appeared in recent years discussing the many complex issues associated with Criterion A (e.g., Long & Elhai, 2009; North, Suris, Davis, & Smith, 2009; Weathers & Keane, 2007). This chapter aims to distill the key issues raised by other commentators, so as to help the clinician negotiate the complex debates over what constitutes a traumatic stressor. We will return to our case examples at the end of the chapter to help clinicians understand the application of these issues in their own practice.

In the course of our discussions it may help to keep in mind that the word trauma essentially means wound. Thus, in this context, we are talking about an event that results in a "psychic wound" or psychological injury. It is useful to distinguish between potentially traumatic events, which have the *potential* to precipitate psychological injury, and traumatic events, which actually do result in psychological injury. While this injury may be a brief and relatively minor adjustment reaction, it may also be a serious condition such as PTSD or another psychiatric disorder. Underpinning the concept of PTSD is the hypothesis that these traumatic events are qualitatively and/or quantitatively different from other types of stressors. That is, traumatic events differ from other stressors in their nature (quality) and intensity (quantity).

## Qualitative Differences

Those who have proposed that traumatic events are qualitatively different from other life stressors suggest that broad "traumatogenic" aspects underpin certain types of events. Bonnie Green (1990) was one of the first authors to identify the qualities of an event that make it traumatic. She proposed that such events typically involve an encounter with death or serious physical threat to the self or important others. Thus, traumatic events may be characterized by such aspects as threat to one's life or bodily integrity, severe physical harm or injury, exposure to the grotesque in the form of death or suffering of others, violent or sudden loss of a loved one, witnessing or learning of violence to a loved one, learning of exposure to a noxious agent, and causing death or severe harm to another.

More recently, Shalev (2002) proposed that events that violate the bio-social habit of humans distinguish a traumatic event from stressful events. For example, *loss* interferes with attachment to significant others, coping resources and social networks. *Relocation* impacts the territorial nature of humans. *Isolation* violates the social needs of a person. *Dehumanization, humiliation,* and *degradation* violate the need to belong to the social group. Other authors have proposed further aspects for consideration. For example, traumatic events differ from other stressors in that they are unexpected, uncontrollable, and/or inescapable (Foa, Zinbarg, & Rothbaum, 1992).

## Quantitative Differences

The idea that trauma represents a quantitative difference from stressful events can be best summarized by the "dose-response model." This model proposes that it is the magnitude of the stressor that makes it traumatic; the more severe the exposure (along, for example, the aspects discussed above) the more likely it is to cause traumatic injury. In an early review of the literature, March (1993) concluded that stressor magnitude was directly proportional to the subsequent risk of developing PTSD. More recent meta-analyses (e.g., Brewin, Andrews, & Valentine, 2000; Ozer, Best, Lipsey, & Weiss, 2003) have confirmed the important contribution of event severity—and particularly threat to life—as one of a number of important risk factors for PTSD. While this model has much to recommend it in terms of face validity, it is not without its limits. Thus, the very meta-analyses that affirm the contribution of event severity, also find that other factors contribute more to the development of psychiatric morbidity. Factors such as psychiatric history, a history of childhood abuse, or family history are consistently identified as factors that increase vulnerability to PTSD (Bowman & Yehuda, 2004).

## THE EVOLUTION OF CRITERION A

The DSM psychiatric nomenclature has always included some kind of category for pathological response to extreme stress. DSM-I described maladaptive responses to trauma as "gross stress reaction." This was replaced in DSM-II by the somewhat weaker diagnostic category of an "adjustment reaction of adult life." In both cases, it was assumed that most people recovered once the stressor had passed. For those who suffered long-term psychiatric effects following a traumatic event, it was assumed they were highly vulnerable and constitutionally predisposed to developing mental illness. That is, the etiology for the posttrauma psychopathology was to be found in the individual's prior vulnerability, while the event acted only as a trigger. When the diagnosis of PTSD entered the diagnostic nomenclature in DSM-III in 1980, it represented a major paradigm shift (Jones & Wessely, 2007). The role of the traumatic event became central. Correspondingly, less emphasis was placed on individual vulnerability.

When PTSD was introduced, Criterion A was included to provide guidance regarding what constituted a traumatic stressor. In many ways, Criterion A was designed to act as a gatekeeper of the diagnosis (Davidson & Foa, 1991). That is, if the person did not experience an event that met this definition of traumatic stressor, then that person could not be diagnosed with PTSD regardless of whether other criteria (e.g., the symptoms that comprise the PTSD clinical syndrome) are met. Each version of DSM since DSM-III has seen a modification of Criterion A, reflecting the inherent difficulty in defining what constitutes a traumatic event.

## DSM-III

Criterion A was first defined in DSM-III in this manner:

> Existence of a recognizable stressor that would evoke significant symptoms of distress in almost everyone (American Psychiatric Association, 1980, p. 238).

The descriptive text identified that the traumatic event was generally outside the range of usual human experience and included natural disasters, accidental man-made disasters, or deliberate man-made disasters. DSM-III explicitly stated that bereavement, chronic illness, business losses, or marital conflict were not included under Criterion A because they were not regarded as outside the range of usual experience. By defining a traumatic event as one in which almost everyone would experience distress, the emphasis was clearly placed on the role of the event in the development of PTSD, rather than on individual vulnerability. In this sense, Criterion A in DSM-III reflected its social and political origins, having been developed in the context of the anti-Vietnam war movement (McHugh & Treisman, 2007) and increased concern for sexual assault victims. Within this cultural context, discussion of pre-existing risk factors—the idea that an individual may have specific vulnerabilities that predisposed him/her to PTSD—was seen as "victim blaming." Therefore, emphasis was placed on the traumatic event itself as the primary contributing factor in the development of PTSD.

The 1980 definition of Criterion A in DSM-III was criticized for several reasons. It did not provide much guidance as to what constituted "outside the range of usual experience" or "causing high levels of distress in almost everyone" (Davidson & Foa, 1991). Furthermore, examples provided in the text (e.g., 'accidental man-made disasters') were descriptive categories that failed to address the common traumatogenic aspects that underpin traumatic events. Finally, the definition also failed to separate objective stressor characteristics (e.g., threat of injury) from subjective perceptions of threat (e.g., fear, helplessness, or horror) (Weathers & Keane, 2007).

## DSM-III-R

DSM-III was revised in 1987, and Criterion A received a makeover. The idea of traumatic events being "outside the range of usual human experience" and "markedly distressing to almost everyone" was retained. DSM-III-R added, however, a list of qualifying events that reflected some of the underlying aspects characteristic of traumatic experiences:

> The person has experienced an event that is outside the range of usual human experience and that would be markedly distress-ing to almost everyone, e.g., serious threat to one's life or physi-cal integrity; serious threat or harm to one's children, spouse or other close relatives and friends; sudden destruction of one's home or community; or seeing another person who has recently been or is being seriously injured or killed as the result of an accident or physical violence (p. 250).

By the time of the 1987 revision, it was increasingly recognized that even the most extreme stressors did not lead to the development of PTSD in all, or even most, of those exposed to trauma. Consistent with this finding, consideration was given to paying more attention to the role of an individual's subjective experience, defining it as one of "intense fear, terror and helplessness." Also embedded in the descrip-tive text was identification of a new category of qualifying events. Up until this point, all traumatic events meeting Criterion A had to be directly experienced. DSM-III-R introduced the idea of indirect expo-sure, that is, "learning about a serious threat or harm to a close friend or relative."

Despite efforts to better define Criterion A in the DSM-III-R, the new text, like its predecessors, was criticized, particularly in the context of epidemiological studies that provided new information on the frequency of traumatic events. It increasingly became evident that Criterion A events, far from being "outside the range of usual human experience," actually occurred relatively frequently (Creamer, Burgess, & McFarlane, 2001; Kessler, Sonnega, Hughes, & Nelson, 1995).

## DSM-IV

In DSM-IV, Criterion A was split into two parts. Criterion A1 represented the objective elements of the event while Criterion A2 highlighted the importance of the subjective experience. DSM-IV recognized that traumatic events occur frequently and the requirement that a traumatic event had to be "outside the range of usual human experience" was dropped. The descriptor now identified the traumatogenic aspects of physical injury as a central theme.

> The person experienced, witnessed, or was confronted with an event or events that involved actual or threatened death or serious injury, or a threat to the physical integrity of self or others (p. 427).

The descriptive component of DSM-IV PTSD emphasized that events after which PTSD develops are "extreme traumatic stressors," although they no longer needed to be directly experienced:

> . . . direct personal experience of an event that involves actual or threatened death or serious injury, or other threat to ones physical integrity; or witnessing an event that involves death, injury, or threat to the physical integrity of another person; or learning about unexpected or violent death, serious harm, or threat of death or injury experienced by a family member or other close associate (p. 424).

The DSM-IV text further clarified A1 by providing examples of traumatic events:

> Traumatic events that are experienced directly include, but are not limited to, military combat, violent personal assault (sexual assault, physical attack, robbery, mugging), being kidnapped, being taken hostage, terrorist attack, torture, incarceration as prisoner of war or in a concentration camp, natural or manmade disasters, severe automobile accidents, or being diagnosed with a life-threatening illness. For children, sexually traumatic events may include developmentally inappropriate sexual experiences without threatened or actual violence or injury.

Witnessed events include, but are not limited to, observing the serious injury or unnatural death of another person due to violent assault, accident, war, or disaster or unexpectedly witnessing a dead body or body parts. Events experienced by others that are learned about include, but are not limited to, violent personal assault, serious accident, or serious injury experienced by a family member or a close friend, learning about the sudden, unexpected death of a family member or a close friend; or learning that one's child has a life-threatening disease (p. 424).

Although this description covers a broad range of events, emphasis remained on a single event causing PTSD. Thus, there is little explicit recognition of the potential role that multiple events might play in contributing to psychopathology—the cumulative effects that may be experienced, for example, by emergency services workers, military personnel following multiple deployments, or even repeated child maltreatment. In practice, this probably does not alter application of the diagnosis—any one of those events alone would probably meet criterion A1—but it does not recognize the fact that, in all likelihood, the person would not have developed a psychiatric disorder if he/she had been exposed to only a single occurrence.

Although it has been argued that DSM-IV broadened the definition of traumatic events by allowing them to be directly or indirectly experienced, this concept had already been introduced in DSM-III-R. Nevertheless, it may be that the broad scope of Criterion A has resulted in events being identified as traumatic in ways that had not initially been anticipated (Andreasen, 2004; Spitzer, First, & Wakefield, 2007). The idea that PTSD can develop as a result of indirectly learning that a traumatic event occurred to another person, in particular, has lead to considerable controversy. It has been suggested that, under this broadened definition, a person watching the terrorist attacks of 9/11 on television can go on to develop PTSD (Marshall et al., 2007). It is likely that such an approach is not consistent with the intent behind the DSM-IV wording since it (presumably) would not be a close family member or friend seen on television. Nevertheless, Marshall et al.'s data indicate that some people may develop a symptom pattern consistent with PTSD following such an experience, regardless of whether it meets Criterion A1. This conundrum is addressed further below.

In DSM-IV, the person's subjective experience was elevated from being embedded in the text (as in DSM-III-R) to being an actual criterion (Criterion A2).

> The person's response involved intense fear, helplessness, or horror. Note: In children, this may be expressed instead by disorganised or agitated behaviour (p. 428).

The elevation of the emotional response of an individual to an essential criterion is the center of much debate that we will address shortly. The key thing to note here is that the subjective experience becomes the key to defining a traumatic event. While two people may experience exactly the same event, it will only be traumatic for the person who experiences a powerful emotional reaction: in this case, intense fear, helplessness, or horror. Stated another way, A1 events represent *potentially traumatic events* (PTE). A positive A2 criterion (intense fear, helplessness, or horror) is what moves an event from being a PTE to an actual *traumatic event* (TE) (Weathers & Keane, 2007). The question of whether either A1 or A2 are actually necessary for the development of PTSD is the subject of the next section.

## CONTENTIOUS ASPECTS OF CRITERION A

There are two broad aspects of Criterion A that make it contentious. First, it implies that a traumatic event is etiologically involved in PTSD. That is, Criterion A is necessary, if not sufficient, for development of the disorder. We will refer to this as the Etiological Debate. The second contentious aspect of the definition is the attempt to place boundaries on what constitutes a traumatic event. This has resulted in the Narrow versus Broad Definition Debate. That is, some commentators think the current definition is too limiting, while others think it is too broad. While we will address these debates separately, they do overlap.

## The Etiological Debate: Is a Traumatic Event Necessary for PTSD?

Underpinning the current definition of PTSD according to DSM-IV is the assumption that a Criterion A level stressor is necessary (albeit not sufficient) for the development of the remaining PTSD criteria (B-F criteria). That is, it is assumed that PTSD cannot develop without experience of a traumatic event. In examining whether Criterion A is necessary for the development of the remaining PTSD symptoms, we will consider Criterion A1 and A2 separately.

## Criterion A1?

Large epidemiological studies clearly indicate that Criterion A1 events are associated with PTSD (Creamer, Morris, Biddle, & Elliott, 1999; Kessler, Sonnega, Hughes, & Nelson, 1995). Both these studies—and many others—indicate that certain events such as rape, sexual molestation, and combat are consistently associated with the highest levels of PTSD. Furthermore, as described earlier, the evidence suggests a relationship between the magnitude of the stressor and the risk of developing PTSD. For example, being injured during the attacks on the World Trade Center on September 11, 2001, was associated with higher levels of PTSD than being caught in the dust cloud of the collapsing buildings which, in turn, resulted in higher rates than witnessing horrific events during the terrorist attacks (Digrande et al., 2008). That is, as the intensity of the stressor increases so does the risk for developing PTSD. This is good evidence to support the etiological role of the traumatic event.

There are, however, some studies that have identified PTSD criteria B-F in people who did not meet Criterion A1 but, rather, had experienced other types of stressful life event. Gold, Marx, Soler-Baillo, and Sloan (2005), for example, found that university students with "non A1 level" stressors were actually more likely to meet the remaining symptom criteria for PTSD than those with A1 level stressors. Experiences identified as most traumatic for those in the non A1 group included death or serious illness of a close person, relationship problems, and medical problems. Similar results were obtained by Mol et al. (2005) in a large community survey. It is worth noting that both these studies used self-report questionnaires to assess PTSD, so the results need to be interpreted cautiously. Specifically, self-report questionnaires may incorrectly identify normal reactions as PTSD symptoms (e.g., ruminative thoughts about the trauma incorrectly identified as intrusive thoughts about the event).

Bodkin, Pope, Detke, and Hudson (2007) found that, in a sample of treatment seeking depressed patients, criteria defining the clinical syndrome of PTSD were just as likely to be met regardless of whether or not the patient had experienced an A1 level stressor. Other studies have identified PTSD following such non-criterion A1 level events as farmers dealing with cattle lost to foot and mouth outbreak (Olff, Koeter, Van Haaften, Kersten, & Gersons, 2005), work-related stressors (Scott & Stradling, 1994), and non-serious physical assault (Seidler & Wagner, 2006). A number of recent studies have found that stressors classified as non-traumatic were more likely to be associated with PTSD relative to stressors that met the A1 criterion (Long et al., 2008; Van Hooff, McFarlane, Baur, Abraham, & Barnes, 2009). Thus, it would appear that Criterion A1—at least as it is currently worded—may not be a necessary condition for developing the PTSD clinical syndrome.

## Criterion A2?

There is good evidence that Criterion A2 is associated with the development of PTSD. Brewin, Andrews, and Rose (2000), for example, found that victims of violent crime who developed PTSD were significantly more likely to report intense levels of fear, helplessness, or horror than those who did not. Creamer, Burgess, and McFarlane (2001) reported that only 4 people in a community sample of 6,104 individuals who had experienced an A1 event, but who did not meet criterion A2, went on to develop the remaining symptoms of PTSD. Several other studies show that an absence of A2 predicts the absence of PTSD (Bedard-Gilligan & Zoellner, 2008; Breslau & Kessler, 2001; Brewin, Andrews, & Rose, 2000). Thus, in terms of diagnostic accuracy, criterion A2 has a high level of sensitivity; that is, the majority of those who develop PTSD have high levels of fear, helplessness, or horror during or just after the trauma. At the same time, A2 also has a low positive predictive power. That is, of all those who experience intense fear, helplessness, or horror, only a small proportion will go on to develop PTSD (Bedard-Gilligan & Zoellner, 2008).

Some studies suggest that intense negative emotional experiences other than fear, helplessness, or horror can be associated with the development of PTSD. Brewin et al. (2000), for example, found that feelings of guilt or shame were associated with the development of PTSD in victims of violent crime. Adler, Wright, Bliese, Eckford, and Hoge (2008) found PTSD criteria in soldiers returning from Iraq who did not meet A2 criteria but did have high levels of anger at the time of their A1 event(s). These findings suggest that fear, helplessness, or horror, as required by the current A2 criteria, may not be the only powerful emotional reactions associated with subsequent development of PTSD. A final consideration before leaving A2 concerns the timing of this response. The question is sometimes raised regarding those who do not experience a powerful emotional reaction at the time of an event, but who do so some time later when they reflect upon their experience. This may apply, for example, to emergency services personnel or combat troops who are required to remain focused in order to function at a high level during and immediately following a traumatic event. These people may have the capacity to put powerful emotional reactions "on hold" until the danger has passed, even if that is some months later (as in the case of military deployment). Most clinicians would deem A2 to have been met in circumstances such as these, even if the fear, helplessness, or horror appeared some time after the exposure.

## The Narrow Versus Broad Definition Debate

If Criterion A is not necessary for the development of PTSD, then is this an argument for abolishing the requirement? One consideration supporting this stance is that making a diagnosis solely on the basis of symptom severity and duration, with no reference to an etiological event, would bring PTSD in line with most other DSM disorders (McNally, 2004). Few psychiatric diagnoses, with the exception of the adjustment disorders, actually specify causality in their diagnostic criteria.

The main argument against complete removal of Criterion A is that it would be a significant departure from the original conception of PTSD (Weathers & Keane, 2007). As we have described earlier, PTSD was introduced into DSM nomenclature in recognition that terrifying events could produce a persistent and impairing psychological state. Taking the terrifying event from the diagnosis, some would argue, would be missing the point—after all, PTSD is, by definition, a "post-trauma" condition.

## Broadening Criterion A

Rather than removing Criterion A altogether from the definition of PTSD, others have proposed that the definition be broadened. Many have argued that Criterion A as it currently stands fails to include many dimensions of trauma and, as a consequence, many people who develop the symptoms of PTSD in the context of a non-Criterion A level trauma cannot receive the diagnosis. As noted above, this exclusion is not always consistent with clinical realities. It might be argued, for example, that peer rejection during adolescence is traumatic because it represents a major loss of social resources (Lev-Wiesel, Nuttman-Shwartz, & Sternberg, 2006), or sexual harassment is traumatic because it threatens physical boundaries and personal control (Avina & O'Donohue, 2002). Other stressful life events that have been related to PTSD symptoms, such as divorce or chronic disease, may also be "threatening" on levels other than threat to life or physical integrity (Mol et al., 2005). Broadening Criterion A to include a greater range of life events might make it easier for individuals who meet PTSD symptom criteria after highly distressing experiences to access effective mental health care and, possibly, legal recourse (Olff & Gersons, 2005).

Many arguments have been proposed as to why a broadening of Criterion A would be problematic. These arguments tend to center around the assumption that, as Criterion A broadens, the number of PTSD cases being diagnosed will increase. Indeed, there is some data to support the notion that an inclusive definition of trauma increases the rates of diagnosable PTSD. For example, Breslau and Kessler (2001) examined the prevalence of PTSD diagnosed using the DSM-III-R criterion and compared it with those diagnosed under the more inclusive DSM-IV Criterion A. They found that the wider variety of stressors allowed in DSM-IV increased the rates of PTSD by 38%. It should be noted, however, that this is in contrast to several other studies, including the original DSM-IV field trials, that found virtually no impact on PTSD prevalence using various definitions for Criterion A (Kilpatrick et al., 1997).

One key question that broadening the A criteria may raise is this: If the prevalence of PTSD were to rise, would that be a problem? One possible danger is that a broader definition of Criterion A may increase the risk of PTSD being incorrectly diagnosed. The risk then becomes one of inappropriate treatment; the trauma-focused psychological approaches that are the treatment of choice for PTSD (Forbes et al., 2007; National Collaborating Centre for Mental Health, 2005) are not the treatment of choice for other diagnosable conditions. It is well established that PTSD is not the only psychiatric disorder to develop following a traumatic stressor (O'Donnell, Creamer, Pattison, & Atkin, 2004). Depression, generalized anxiety disorder, simple phobias, substance use disorders, and complicated grief commonly develop. In many cases, symptoms that appear following a traumatic stressor may be better described as, for example, a depressive disorder, an anxiety disorder, or adjustment disorder rather than PTSD (Rosen, Spitzer, & McHugh, 2008). Health care providers who lack experience with trauma may try to fit the PTSD diagnosis to the patient simply because Criterion A has been met. Importantly this may result in inappropriate treatments being administered.

This, in turn, has implications for litigation, a topic about which clinicians need to be aware even if medico-legal work is not the mainstay of their practice. It is not unusual for treating clinicians to be required to give evidence in cases of mental injury where compensation may be an issue. As previously pointed out, PTSD is "the preferred" psychiatric disorder for litigants (Slovenko, 2004). This is because, if the court accepts the diagnosis of PTSD, then the question of causation is effectively settled by the application of Criterion A. If the diagnosis is, for example, depression, not only must the court be convinced of the presence of a psychiatric disorder, but the relationship between that disorder and the stressor in question must also be demonstrated. Many argue that broadening the definition of trauma will result in the courts being crippled with unnecessary PTSD litigation (Elhai, Kashdan, & Frueh, 2005), with the result that genuine PTSD cases may not receive the consideration they deserve.

Another argument against broadening Criterion A is that this may increase the heterogeneity among PTSD symptoms, further blurring an already complex picture of how the disorder overlaps with other conditions such as depression. This, of course, again harks back to the idea of etiology—the notion that there is something qualitatively different about the biopsychosocial reactions that humans experience in response to very high magnitude stressors. The idea, for example, that PTSD developing in the context of a person hearing that a friend has been raped is the same as development of the condition in a person who has actually been raped has been questioned (McNally, 2003). McNally argues that grouping these diverse events under the same stressor rubric will impede research that aims to identify the unique psychobiological mechanisms underlying this symptomatic expression.

Finally, the extensive broadening of the definition of a traumatic stressor leads to a type of "criterion creep" (Rosen, 2004) that may be the functional equivalent of eliminating Criterion A all together. After all, having no gatekeeper to limit what qualifies as a traumatic stressor yields the same result as including every stressor (Rosen & Lilienfeld, 2008).

Clearly, there is no simple solution to the "Criterion A problem" (Weathers & Keane, 2007). The empirical literature at this point is unable to clarify whether there is any truly distinct subset of high-magnitude stressors that produces an equally distinct clinical syndrome known as PTSD.

## UNDERSTANDING WHY PTSD SYMPTOMS MAY OCCUR AFTER NON CRITERION A EVENTS

One way of informing this debate is to consider the proposed mechanisms at work in the development of PTSD. Drawing on a range of existing theories, Olff, Langeland, and Gersons (2005) present a model of the development of PTSD that suggests that PTSD results from a psychobiological dysregulation of the fear system. Like many cognitive models, they propose that this psychobiological stress response is dependent on the subjective appraisal of the event—that is, the event is appraised as being highly threatening or aversive. They argue that loosening the definition of trauma would not result in the misdiagnosis of PTSD because the proposed psychobiological mechanisms are tied to the extreme threat appraisal of the event. Implicit within this argument is that low-magnitude stressors would not be appraised as highly threatening, the psychobiological dysregulation of the fear system would not occur and, therefore, symptoms that are associated with the PTSD clinical syndrome would not develop. As noted above, this hypothesis is inconsistent with some research that has reported high rates of PTSD after low-magnitude stressors. Several other methodologically tight studies, however, support the notion that lower-magnitude stressors (e.g., indirect traumas such as learning about harm occurring to a family member) were less likely to be associated with PTSD than higher-magnitude stressors (Bedard-Gilligan & Zoellner, 2008; Breslau & Kessler, 2001). McNally (2004) rightly points out that this is, indeed, the case when appraisal closely tracks reality (i.e., an event that is perceived to be highly threatening *is* objectively threatening). However, when the threat appraisal is overestimated there is potential for lower-magnitude stressors to be associated with PTSD. This, of course, raises the vexing question of vulnerability: Are some people more likely than others to appraise a given event as threatening? It is well established that many factors increase vulnerability to PTSD (Brewin, Andrews, & Valentine, 2000; Ozer et al., 2003). It may be that, among other things, vulnerability factors mediate the relationship between the objective stressor and the threat appraisal. As such, someone with high levels of vulnerability may only require a low-magnitude stressor to develop symptoms associated with PTSD criteria.

## IMPLICATIONS FOR THE CLINICIAN

These complex and often conflicting issues that surround Criterion A provide a confusing context for the clinician treating patients with PTSD. The key message we wish clinicians to take from the preceding discussion is that the relationship between Criterion A and PTSD is very gray. As a result the clinician has to cope with a certain level of ambiguity. Of course, the bottom line is that our patients do not really care how we define Criterion A in the DSM; they are concerned only with the distress they experience and the impact this distress is having on their social and occupational functioning. Certain stressor events may produce PTSD (or other posttraumatic mental health problems) regardless of the specific wording generated by the DSM committee. It is reasonable to assume that if a person meets the remaining criteria for PTSD, but does not meet the strict wording of Criterion A, they would still benefit from treatment (Davidson & Foa, 1991; Olff et al., 2005). Further, there is little to suggest that the evidence-based treatment of choice would be substantially different regardless of whether A was met.

On the other hand, the development of PTSD symptoms in someone exposed to a low-level stressor should alert the clinician to the possibility of a more complex etiology. Clinicians should use their judgment regarding Criterion A to guide their assessment, with particular reference to other risk and vulnerability factors that may help to explain the development of PTSD-type symptoms in the absence of a severe physical threat. The outcome of this assessment may have implications for intervention with, for example, increased attention paid to enhancing broader symptom management and coping skills in those for whom the event may have served as a trigger activating other pre-existing psychological problems. For example, a person who develops PTSD in the context of a low-level stressor may have a history of childhood abuse. This individual may then require emotional regulation skills training before commencing treatment on the current trauma. In the next section, we return to our case examples to highlight particular issues with Criterion A that may have implications for clinical assessment and treatment.

## The Assessment of Criterion A

In clinical practice, we suggest that assessment of Criterion A should be informed by the remainder of the PTSD symptom cluster, notably the re-experiencing phenomena (B Criteria) and symptoms C1 and C2. That is, if the patient is being haunted by powerful and distressing sensory memories (images, smells, sounds, etc.) of an event, it is reasonable to assume that the event was traumatic for that person regardless of whether it met the strict wording of Criterion A. (Of course, some of the current B criteria, such as psychological distress when reminded of the event, are less specific and may not carry the same weight in evaluating the subjective experience of the incident). Similarly, if the person is avoiding reminders of the trauma (C1 and C2) because they may activate painful recollections of the experience (rather than through fear of future danger), it is reasonable to assume that the event caused a psychological injury. Careful assessment of the B Criteria and symptoms C1 and C2, conducted in the context of Criterion A assessment, will help the clinician to decide whether PTSD provides a better formulation of the clinical picture than another disorder such as depression, simple phobia, or generalized anxiety disorder.

## PTSD Symptoms Following Non A-Criterion Stressors

If a patient has clear PTSD symptoms following an event that does not meet the A criteria, it is important to explore the patient's perception of the event: What did they think was happening? In some circumstances, a patient may perceive an event as life threatening when in reality it was not. Intense emotional experiences at the time of the event may provide the starting point for therapeutic exploration.

This was the situation for Marsha, our first case example at the start of this chapter; although the situation was not actually life threatening—it was a toy gun—Marsha believed at the time that her life was in danger and she responded as if the threat was real. When asked what went through her mind at the time, she said, "I thought I was going to die; I thought I would never see my children again." Importantly for our discussion, those appraisals were fundamental to the powerful memory of the event that was formed at the time of the threat. The problem for Marsha was her difficulty incorporating the new correct information into this memory network to modify it into something that did not lead to ongoing distress. In this type of situation, the clinician should investigate their patient's perceptions. Questions such as "What did you think was going to happen? What was going through your mind at the time?" are useful to elicit perceptions of threat and to elucidate mechanisms through which posttraumatic symptoms may have developed.

A second area for consideration by clinicians when presented with a patient who does not meet Criterion A1, but who does have PTSD symptoms, is the person's pretrauma risk and vulnerability profile. As discussed earlier, vulnerability may mediate the relationship between a low-magnitude stressor and the development of PTSD symptoms. This consideration, and others, applies to Bob, the second case example presented in the chapter's introduction.

While Bob's experience may, in theory, meet DSM-IV's Criterion A1, there is no doubt that it represents a low-magnitude stressor. A thorough assessment undertaken with Bob revealed several risk factors that helped to explain the development of PTSD, not least of which was the death of his son in a car accident several years earlier. In his intrusive images, his dead son's face was often transposed onto the (imagined) bomb victims' faces. Bob also had a history of alcohol abuse, relationship problems, and other current life stress that a therapist would want to take into account when formulating a treatment plan. Although PTSD remained an initial focus, treatment for Bob required attention to a range of other psychosocial issues. Failure to adequately address these other vulnerability factors would have left him at high risk of relapse in response to another stressor.

As noted above, Criterion A in the DSM is geared toward a single traumatic stressor and does not deal well with the cumulative effects of multiple exposures. This is particularly relevant to people such as Bill, our third case example, who like many emergency services workers was exposed to repeated exposures. Bill's situation illustrated an individual who responded to each highly stressful event by remaining detached during the incident and by putting it out of his mind as soon as the event was over. Sometimes the consumption of alcohol ("a few drinks with the boys") facilitated the process. This strategy served him well for many years until one event—in this case, a relatively minor exposure—triggered the vivid memories and powerful emotional reactions associated with earlier experiences that had been put aside. We may never be entirely sure why that particular event triggered Bill's deterioration, although he did report several life stressors including significant financial and family problems. In Bill's case, the management plan included trauma-focused psychological interventions targeted at each individual Criterion A event, as well as social problem solving to address his ongoing life stressors.

For clinicians working with patients who have sustained a head injury, resulting in loss of consciousness, the question arises as to whether PTSD can occur when the person has no memory of the event itself (A1), and/or no emotional reaction during the event (A2). In Marie's case, for example, are we justified in diagnosing PTSD? She certainly experienced an A1 event, despite having no clear memory of being hit. She did not experience "fear, helplessness, or horror" at the time of the impact because she was unconscious, but she did report these powerful emotions later when she realized what had happened to her. There is much literature to show that PTSD can develop in the context of memory loss and traumatic brain injury (e.g., Creamer, O'Donnell, & Pattison, 2005). Patients may have islands of memory that are re-experienced, or they may "reconstruct" vivid and distressing memories from photos, verbal descriptions, or their imagination. Phenomenologically and functionally, these re-experiencing symptoms appear to be no different to those described by people without head injury. As described earlier, thorough assessment of relevant symptom criteria will help inform the clinician's understanding of Criterion A. Again, however, it is important not to assume that PTSD is the only possibility. Amnesic patients often have a symptom profile that more closely resembles a phobic response; they are avoiding anticipated future danger rather than stimuli that trigger memories of the trauma. In those cases, simple phobia may be a more appropriate diagnosis than PTSD.

Although the best diagnosis for Marie turned out to be simple phobia rather than PTSD, most clinicians would argue that she, as well as Marsha, Bob, and Bill, met the spirit of Criterion A even if they did not meet a literal interpretation. If the remaining symptoms are present, a formulation of PTSD in these cases makes most sense in terms of driving an intervention plan.

## CONCLUSION

There is no doubt that Criterion A will continue to be the center of discussion and disagreement as we move towards DSM-V and beyond. Central to this discussion is the stipulation that a diagnosis of PTSD cannot be made in the absence of Criterion A—a fundamental assumption given our current conceptualization of the disorder. Broadening or narrowing the definition of Criterion A has implications for the identification of patients, the allocation of scarce treatment resources, litigation, and the scope of traumatic stress research. Although there are no simple answers, clinicians need to be aware of these complex issues in order to meaningfully formulate trauma presentations and to construct appropriate treatment plans.

## REFERENCES

Adler, A. B., Wright, K. M., Bliese, P. D., Eckford, R., & Hoge, C. W. (2008). A2 diagnostic criterion for combat-related posttraumatic stress disorder. *Journal of Traumatic Stress, 21*(3), 301–308.

American Psychiatric Association. (1980). *Diagnostic and Statistical Manual of Mental Disorders, 3rd Edition.* Washington, DC: American Psychiatric Association.

Andreasen, N. C. (2004). Acute and delayed posttraumatic stress disorder: A history and some issues. *American Journal of Psychiatry, 161*(8), 1321–1323.

Avina, C., & O'Donohue, W. (2002). Sexual harassment and PTSD: Is sexual harassment diagnosable trauma? *Journal of Traumatic Stress, 15*(1), 69–75.

Bedard-Gilligan, M., & Zoellner, L. A. (2008). The utility of the A1 and A2 criteria in the diagnosis of PTSD. *Behaviour Research and Therapy, 46*(9), 1062–1069.

Bodkin, J. A., Pope, H. G., Detke, M. J., & Hudson, J. I. (2007). Is PTSD caused by traumatic stress? *Journal of Anxiety Disorders, 21*(2), 176–182.

Bowman, M. L., & Yehuda, R. (2004). Risk factors and the adversity-stress model. In G.M. Rosen (Ed.), *Posttraumatic stress disorder: Issues and controversies* (pp. 39–61). Chichester: John Wiley & Sons.

Breslau, N., & Kessler, R. C. (2001). The stressor criterion in DSM-IV posttraumatic stress disorder: An empirical investigation. *Biological Psychiatry, 50*(9), 699–704.

Brewin, C. R., Andrews, B., & Rose, S. (2000). Fear, helplessness, and horror in posttraumatic stress disorder: Investigating DSM-IV criterion A2 in victims of violent crime. *Journal of Traumatic Stress, 13*(3), 499–509.

Brewin, C. R., Andrews, B., & Valentine, J. D. (2000). Meta-analysis of risk factors for posttraumatic stress disorder in trauma-exposed adults. *Journal of Consulting and Clinical Psychology, 68*(5), 748–766.

Creamer, M., Burgess, P., & McFarlane, A. C. (2001). Post-traumatic stress disorder: Findings from the Australian National Survey of Mental Health and Well-being. *Psychological Medicine, 31*(7), 1237–1247.

Creamer, M., Morris, P., Biddle, D., & Elliott, P. (1999). Treatment outcome in Australian veterans with combat-related posttraumatic stress disorder: A cause for cautious optimism? *Journal of Traumatic Stress, 12*(4), 545–558.

Creamer, M., O'Donnell, M. L., & Pattison, P. (2005). Amnesia, traumatic brain injury, and posttraumatic stress disorder: A methodological inquiry. *Behaviour Research and Therapy, 43*(10), 1383–1389.

Davidson, J., & Foa, E. B. (1991). Diagnostic issues in posttraumatic stress disorder: Considerations for the DSM-IV. *Journal of Abnormal Psychology, 100*(3), 346–355.

Digrande, L., Perrin, M. A., Thorpe, L. E., Thalji, L., Murphy, J., Wu, D., et al. (2008). Posttraumatic stress symptoms, PTSD, and risk factors among lower Manhattan residents 2–3 years after the September 11, 2001 terrorist attacks. *Journal of Traumatic Stress, 21*(3), 264–273.

Elhai, J. D., Kashdan, T. B., & Frueh, B. C. (2005). What is a traumatic event? Comment. *British Journal of Psychiatry, 187*, 189–190.

Foa, E. B., Zinbarg, R., & Rothbaum, B. O. (1992). Uncontrollability and unpredictability in post-traumatic stress disorder: An animal model. *Psychological Bulletin, 112*(2), 218–238.

Forbes, D., Creamer, M., Phelps, A., Bryant, R., McFarlane, A., Devilly, G. J., et al. (2007). Australian guidelines for the treatment of adults with acute stress disorder and post-traumatic stress disorder. *Australian and New Zealand Journal of Psychiatry, 41*(8), 637–648.

Gold, S. D., Marx, B. P., Soler-Baillo, J. M., & Sloan, D. M. (2005). Is life stress more traumatic than traumatic stress? *Journal of Anxiety Disorders, 19*(6), 687–698.

Green, B. L. (1990). Defining trauma: Terminology and generic stressor dimensions. *Journal of Applied Social Psychology, 20*(20, Pt 2), 1632–1642.

Jones, E., & Wessely, S. (2007). A paradigm shift in the conceptualization of psychological trauma in the 20th century. *Journal of Anxiety Disorders, 21*(2), 164–175.

Kessler, R. C., Sonnega, A., Hughes, M., & Nelson, C. B. (1995). Posttraumatic stress disorder in the national comorbidity survey. *Archives of General Psychiatry, 52*, 1048–1060.

Kilpatrick, D. G., Resnick, H. S., Freedy, J. R., Pelcovitz, D., Resick, P., Roth, S., et al. (1997). The posttraumatic stress disorder field trial: Evaluation of the PTSD construct: Criteria A through E. In T. A. Widiger, A. J. Frances, H. A. Pincus, M. B. First, R. Ross & W. Davis (Eds.), *DSM-IV Sourcebook (Volume IV)*. Washington DC: American Psychiatric Press.

Lev-Wiesel, R., Nuttman-Shwartz, O., & Sternberg, R. (2006). Peer rejection during adolescence: Psychological long-term effects—A brief report. *Journal of Loss & Trauma, 11*(2), 131–142.

Long, M. E., & Elhai, J. (2009). Posttraumatic stress disorder's traumatic stressor criterion: history, controversy, clinical and legal implications. *Psychological Injury and Law*, *2*, 167–178.

Long, M. E., Elhai, J. D., Schweinle, A., Gray, M. J., Grubaugh, A. L., & Frueh, B. C. (2008). Differences in posttraumatic stress disorder diagnostic rates and symptom severity between criterion A1 and non-criterion A1 stressors. *Journal of Anxiety Disorders*, *22*(7), 1255–1263.

March, J. S. (1993). What constitutes a stressor? The criterion A issue. In J. R. Davidson & E. B. Foa (Eds.), *Posttraumatic Stress Disorder: DSM-IV and Beyond* (pp. 37–54). Washington DC: American Psychiatric Press.

Marshall, R. D., Bryant, R. A., Amsel, L., Suh, E. J., Cook, J. M., & Neria, Y. (2007). The psychology of ongoing threat: Relative risk appraisal, the September 11 attacks, and terrorism-related fears. *American Psychologist*, *62*(4), 304–316.

McHugh, P. R., & Treisman, G. (2007). PTSD: A problematic diagnostic category. *Journal of Anxiety Disorders*, *21*(2), 211–222.

McNally, R. J. (2003). Progress and controversy in the study of posttraumatic stress disorder. *Annual Review of Psychology*, *54*, 229–252.

McNally, R. J. (2004). Conceptual problems with the *DSV-IV* criteria for posttraumatic stress disorder. In G. M. Rosen (Ed.), *Posttraumatic stress disorder: Issues and controversies*. Chichester: John Wiley & Sons.

Mol, S. S., Arntz, A., Metsemakers, J. F., Dinant, G. J., Vilters-van Montfort, P. A., & Knottnerus, J. A. (2005). Symptoms of post-traumatic stress disorder after non-traumatic events: Evidence from an open population study. *British Journal of Psychiatry*, *186*, 494–499.

National Collaborating Centre for Mental Health. (2005). *Posttraumatic stress disorder: The management of PTSD in adults and children in primary and secondary care* (Vol. Clinical guideline 26). London: National Centre for Clinical Excellence.

North, C. S., Suris, A. M., Davis, M., & Smith, R. P. (2009). Toward validation of the diagnosis of posttraumatic stress disorder. *American Journal of Psychiatry*, *166*, 34–41.

O'Donnell, M. L., Creamer, M., Pattison, P., & Atkin, C. (2004). Psychiatric morbidity following injury. *American Journal of Psychiatry*, *161*(3), 507–514.

Olff, M., & Gersons, B. (2005). What is a traumatic event? Reply. *British Journal of Psychiatry*, *187*, 190–190.

Olff, M., Koeter, M. W., Van Haaften, E. H., Kersten, P. H., & Gersons, B. P. (2005, February). Impact of a foot and mouth disease crisis on post-traumatic stress symptoms in farmers. *British Journal of Psychiatry*, *186*, 165–166.

Olff, M., Langeland, W., & Gersons, B. P. (2005). Effects of appraisal and coping on the neuroendocrine response to extreme stress. *Neuroscience & Biobehavioral Reviews, 29*(3), 457–467.

Ozer, E. J., Best, S. R., Lipsey, T. L., & Weiss, D. S. (2003). Predictors of posttraumatic stress disorder and symptoms in adults: A meta-analysis. *Psychological Bulletin, 129*(1), 52–73.

Rosen, G. M. (2004). Traumatic events, criterion creep, and the creation of pre-traumatic stress disorder. *The Scientific Review of Mental Health Practice, 3*, 39–42.

Rosen, G. M., & Lilienfeld S. O. (2008). Posttraumatic stress disorder: An empirical analysis of core assumptions. *Clinical Psychology Review, 28*, 837–868.

Rosen, G. M., Spitzer, R. L., & McHugh, P. R. (2008). Problems with the posttraumatic stress disorder diagnosis and its future in DSM-V. *British Journal of Psychiatry, 192*(1), 3–4.

Scott, M. J., & Stradling, S. G. (1994). Post-traumatic stress disorder without the trauma. *British Journal of Clinical Psychology, 33*(1), 71–74.

Seidler, G. H., & Wagner, F. E. (2006). The stressor criterion in PTSD: Notes on the genealogy of a problematic construct. *American Journal of Psychotherapy, 60*(3), 261–270.

Shalev, A. Y. (2002). Acute stress reactions in adults. *Biological Psychiatry, 51*(7), 532–543.

Slovenko, R. (2004). The watering down of PTSD in criminal law. *Journal of Psychiatry & Law, 32*(3), 411–437.

Spitzer, R. L., First, M. B., & Wakefield, J. C. (2007). Saving PTSD from itself in DSM-V. *Journal of Anxiety Disorders, 21*(2), 233–241.

Van Hooff, M., McFarlane, A. C., Baur, J., Abraham, M., & Barnes, D. J. (2009). The stressor criterion-A1 and PTSD: A matter of opinion? *Journal of Anxiety Disorders, 23*(1), 77–86.

Weathers, F. W., & Keane, T. M. (2007). The Criterion A problem revisited: Controversies and challenges in defining and measuring psychological trauma. *Journal of Traumatic Stress, 20*(2), 107–121.

# 4

# Posttraumatic Memory

ELKE GERAERTS

Imagine remembering each little thing that ever happened to you. Although no such person has yet been found, there are some people with incredible autobiographical memory. Consider the example of AJ, a 42-year-old woman from California (Parker, Cahill, & McGaugh, 2006). AJ remembers every day of her life, since her teens, in astonishing detail. For example, when you refer to any date over a span of several decades, she mentally travels back to that day, thinking about where she was and what she was doing. AJ reports that her personal memories are vivid, like "a running movie that never stops" (p. 35). One might feel that having such an outstanding memory would be wonderful. AJ, however, says it comes with a price. For example, when unpleasant things happen to her, AJ wants to forget, but she cannot. The continuous reminders are very distracting and "seem to rule her life" (p. 35).

Would you prefer AJ's memory over your own? Or might it be that normal processes of forgetting are not all that negative? For many years now, researchers have been pointing out that forgetting may actually serve a useful function. Schacter (2001), for example, argues that forgetting has an adaptive purpose, preventing us from storing mundane, confusing or out-of-date memories. We want to remember our current phone number, not an old one, and where we parked our car today, not yesterday.

A topic of great clinical interest concerns how we remember and how we forget more emotional and even *traumatic* experiences. How does memory work when people have experienced combat, childhood abuse, or other horrifying events? This chapter addresses the issues that bear on this question. First, theories on posttraumatic memory will be considered. Second, some common misunderstandings about the occurrence of traumatic amnesia will be summarized. Next, it will be explored whether people can also create false memories for autobiographical events. Finally, we will examine whether people can forget and later remember traumatic events. The issues are important to clinicians, because how we conceptualize posttraumatic stress disorder, and its underlying pathogenic mechanisms, is likely to influence how we approach treatment.

## THE "INNER LOGIC" OF PTSD

The history of PTSD is rooted in theories that place special emphasis on the distinct, if not unique nature of traumatic memory. Theories propose that memories related to severe life-threatening events are somehow stored differently than "regular" memories. In this context several proposals have been put forward though all share common elements (Brewin, Dalgleish & Joseph, 1996; Ehlers & Clark, 2000; van der Kolk, 1994). Hence, according to this view, there are *qualitative* differences between traumatic memories and ordinary memories. Most notably, traumatic memories are unique because they are mainly perceptually processed, causing fragmentary storage of the trauma memories. This leaves survivors with memories that are not readily accessible (i.e., dissociative or psychogenic amnesia) and/or flashbacks that possess strong sensory qualities. This dissociative style of processing also creates a substantial overlap between dissociative and PTSD symptoms. So the core assumption these theories have in common is that trauma has a special impact on the way in which memories of the traumatic event are organized. Young (2004) has analyzed this viewpoint, and referred to the trauma memory hypothesis as providing an "inner logic" for PTSD. Within the context of these theories, trauma memories are not just another symptom of a disorder. Instead, it is the very nature of how trauma memories are assumed to be stored that accounts for the syndrome's other symptoms.

To the clinician, memory fragmentation becomes apparent when a trauma victim during psychotherapy has to describe the traumatic experience. It is then that the clinician notices that a patient's recounting of a trauma is often far from perfect, with missing details, many repetitions, and a chaotic recollection of the exact temporal order of events. Moreover, trauma victims often experience these fragmentary qualities in the form of intrusive re-experiences of the trauma, flashbacks, nightmares, and bodily sensations. It is these intrusive and re-experiencing symptoms that trauma victims often find highly distressing and are thought by some to lie at the heart of PTSD (APA, 2000).

If these theories are correct, and PTSD is a disorder resulting from fragmented memory, then the clinical implications are profound. Such theories suggest that treatment of PTSD should focus on the elaborating, organizing, and integrating of fragmented, non-verbal aspects of memory. In that way, a verbal, integrated form of the trauma narrative can be attained.

## Are Trauma Memories Unique?

Although trauma memory theories have been influential in clinical literature and practice, supporting empirical evidence is limited. Studies that have analyzed trauma narratives and interpreted the data in support of a memory hypothesis, have been questioned on methodological grounds (for comprehensive reviews, see Berntsen, Willert, & Rubin, 2003; McNally, 2003; Zoellner & Bittinger, 2004). Consider, for example, that high levels of intelligence in general, and greater verbal skills in particular, act as buffers against pathological responses to trauma exposure (e.g., Vasterling, Brailey, Constans, Borges, & Sutker, 1997). Consequently, attempts to measure memory fragmentation in PTSD patients by inspecting the verbal coherence of their trauma narratives is utterly confounded by deficiencies in verbal skills among PTSD patients. Moreover, memory fragmentation is not consistently associated with recovery following psychotherapeutic treatment. Another methodological weakness in most studies is that they fail to compare trauma narratives with the recall of other highly distressing memories (Zoellner & Bittinger, 2004). Studies that directly address this issue and incorporate these comparisons have shown that memory fragmentation does not reliably discriminate either within or between individuals with and without PTSD (e.g., Gray & Lombardo, 2001). Collectively, the available empirical evidence raises concerns about whether memory fragmentation can continue to be seen as a valid marker of qualitative differences between trauma memories in PTSD and ordinary or non-PTSD distressing memories.

Related areas of research have challenged other crucial aspects of theories that postulate the uniqueness of trauma memories. Dissociative processes, such as in acute stress disorder, have been found to be neither necessary for nor predictive of PTSD onset (e.g., Bryant, 2007). Involuntary memories triggered by environmental cues are not limited to memories for traumatic experiences but pertain to a large variety of autobiographical memories (Berntsen, 2001). Traumatic memories also do not invariably produce "flashbacks," a finding demonstrated with British war veterans (Jones et al., 2003), Dutch concentration camp survivors (Merckelbach, Dekkers, Wessel, & Roefs, 2003), and Croatian war veterans (Geraerts, Kozaric-Kovacic, Merckelbach, Peraica, Jelicic, & Candel, 2007). Hence, intrusive recollections in the form of sudden flashbacks cannot be seen as a hallmark feature of PTSD. Similar concerns apply to the alleged extraordinary perceptual qualities of the flashbacks experienced by PTSD patients. That is, these sensory qualities are not specific to trauma memories but also apply to autobiographical memories in general, regardless of their affective content.

Summing up, theories that stress the uniqueness of trauma memories have a *prima facie* logic to them, a consideration that may explain their popularity among many clinicians. Nevertheless, experimental evidence that has accumulated over recent years strongly refutes the underlying assumptions of these theories.

## Normal Memory Processes

An alternative view to theories on the uniqueness of traumatic memory comes from the work of Berntsen and co-workers (2003; see also Berntsen & Rubin, 2007). These authors argue that trauma memories are processed and stored according to normal mechanisms that apply to all autobiographical memories. That is, traumatic memories are not unique. A plethora of research has supported this view, and further has shown that emotional events are actually better remembered than neutral ones (LaBar & Cabeza, 2006). Thus, instead of leading to disintegration, trauma memories become particularly well processed and integrated into autobiographical memory. Because they are so distinctive and have an immense emotional impact, traumatic memories can form a "cognitive reference point" for the organization of autobiographical knowledge. By cognitive reference point, Berntsen et al., 2003 mean that the traumatic event forms a central component of the autobiographical self (i.e., a vivid landmark) or is considered to be a turning point in one's life that might even become relied upon to attribute meaning to other experiences. It is in this context that traumatic memories are seen as having a permanent impact on the processing, integration, and interpretation of forthcoming non-traumatic experiences. These impacts occur, not because traumatic memories are fragmented or different from "normal" memories, but because they are extremely salient to the individual's view of the world and self.

Of course, such memory processing mechanisms are functional in the case of highly important yet non-traumatic events (e.g., wedding day, birth of a child). Unfortunately, these same mechanisms may become dysfunctional when traumatic experiences lead to strongly elaborated memories that serve as autobiographical landmarks against which all subsequent experiences are compared. Thus, according to Berntsen et al. (2003), trauma-exposed individuals with PTSD and those without PTSD differ with regard to whether the trauma memory has formed a landmark in the organization of autobiographical memory. Experimental evidence for this position comes from recent studies showing that the degree to which traumatic experiences are integrated into autobiographical memory is positively related to severity of PTSD symptomatology and may even predict PTSD symptoms irrespective of the degree to which dissociative experiences were present (e.g., Berntsen & Rubin, 2007). These studies suggest that enhanced rather than poor integration of trauma memories may be crucial in promoting PTSD symptoms.

On a related note, Rubin, Berntsen, and Bohni (2008) have developed a mnemonic model of PTSD, highlighting that the interaction between characteristics of the event and the processes of remembering determines whether someone develops PTSD. They postulate that the pathogenic *memory* of the event, rather than exposure to the traumatic event itself, is crucial in understanding PTSD.

## Implications for Clinicians

One must wonder how a new emerging theory on trauma memory can be so diametrically opposed to the original notions of fragmentation and dissociation. The best explanation for this turn of events probably lies in an oft repeated phenomenon, wherein "intuitively" appealing hypotheses are corrected by the findings of systematic research programs. This history provides a striking demonstration of why it is important that clinicians rely on theories and implement treatments that are empirically informed.

The clinician must ask what such a radical shift in thinking means for their understanding of PTSD and accordingly, their approach to treatment. One clear implication of current research findings is that a clinical emphasis on identifying narrative fragmentation and subsequent efforts at "integration" may be ill advised. Our current understanding of traumatic memory processes strongly argues that such efforts involve a misplaced and incorrect focus on mechanisms that do not, in fact, underlie posttraumatic memory. Instead, a clinician is advised to concentrate treatment efforts on a patient's memory as it exists, while working to reduce anxiety and alter dysfunctional cognitions.

## TRAUMATIC AMNESIA

It is possible to conclude with confidence, on the basis of current research, that victims remember traumatic experiences rather well. Some clinical theorists, however, believe that a significant minority of individuals dissociate or repress their traumatic experiences, thereby failing to have clear memory for important parts of an event. Unfortunately, several studies cited in support of the existence of traumatic amnesia are misunderstood (for a detailed review of such misunderstandings, see Geraerts & McNally, 2009; McNally, 2003).

### Normal Encoding and Forgetting

The DSM-IV-TR (APA, 2000) lists "an inability to recall an important aspect of the trauma" (p. 468) as a symptom of PTSD. Even though the meaning of this text is ambiguous, some clinicians have adduced that the described "symptom" is relevant to traumatic amnesia. The astute clinician will notice, however, that if someone does not remember a certain aspect of the trauma, it cannot be inferred whether that individual is unable to recall something that was encoded into memory, or if the detail was never encoded in the first place. After all, not all sensory inputs arising from an experience become encoded into memory. Therefore, failing to remember an event that was never encoded in the first place does not count as amnesia. Amnesia refers to material that is encoded, but not able to be retrieved.

Occasionally, traumatic amnesia is confused with everyday forgetfulness. That is, after having experienced a traumatic event, some people report difficulty concentrating and remembering things in everyday life. This kind of memory impairment, however, refers to everyday forgetfulness that develops following the trauma; it does not refer to a difficulty remembering the trauma itself.

Another misunderstanding regarding traumatic amnesia involves confusing it with childhood amnesia. That is, most people can remember very little of their lives before age four or five. Brain maturation and cognitive changes make it difficult for older children—let alone adults—to recall events encoded during their preschool years. Accordingly, a failure to recall an episode of childhood abuse from the preschool years may reflect childhood amnesia rather than traumatic amnesia.

Additionally, several studies have shown that adults with documented childhood abuse histories may not disclose these events. This failure to disclose abuse does not necessarily imply that one is unable to remember it. In a classic demonstration of this point, Femina, Yeager, and Lewis (1990) recontacted respondents who had described their abuse during a first interview, but had denied it during a second interview. When queried about the discrepancy in a follow-up interview, each respondent affirmed having recalled it during the second interview. Participants gave several reasons why they had been unwilling to disclose the abuse during the second interview (e.g., not wanting to talk about an upsetting experience). Whatever the reason, one cannot equate a failure to disclose with traumatic amnesia. Although it may imply forgetting, alternative explanations should be considered by practitioners.

## Traumatic versus Psychogenic Amnesia

The term traumatic amnesia has also been used when people refer to psychogenic amnesia, even though they are separate phenomena. Typical cases of psychogenic amnesia are characterized by an abrupt, massive retrograde memory loss, including loss of personal identity that cannot be attributed to a physical insult to the brain. The syndrome is sometimes preceded by exposure to a stressful event. The term *psychogenic* implies the absence of an obvious organic cause rather than an identified psychological one. Most cases of psychogenic amnesia remit within hours, days, or weeks, and often without any therapeutic intervention. With alleged traumatic amnesia, a person is unable to recall a specific traumatic event rather than being entirely unable to recall his or her past. Apart from psychogenic amnesia, traumatic amnesia has also been confused with organic amnesia, which results from direct damage to the brain.

# FALSE MEMORIES

Apart from research on traumatic amnesia, scholars have looked into how people can create memories of events that have *not* happened. In some cases these false memories pertain to traumatic events, such as childhood abuse.

At first sight, the idea that someone would recall a traumatic experience that has never occurred seems rather implausible. Yet, people have remembered all sorts of unlikely events. For instance, people have reported recovering memories of previous lives (Meyersburg, Bogdan, Gallo, & McNally, 2009), satanic ritual abuse (Scott, 2001), and even abduction by space aliens (Clancy, 2005). Most of these memories have surfaced with the help of mental health professionals and the use of techniques such as guided imagery and hypnosis. The earliest demonstration of an implanted trauma memory may have been described by Bernheim (1884/1889), who suggested to a hypnotized woman that she had witnessed a murder. The woman accepted Bernheim's suggestion and later reported the false event to someone in the role of a magistrate (Rosen, Sageman, & Loftus, 2003).

As human memory is fallible, people may engage in reconstructing an experienced event, thereby adding things to memory that may not have taken place. Moreover, people sometimes confuse the sources of their memories, frequently failing to distinguish things that they for example have imagined or seen in a movie, with things that truly happened to them. The dangers of such confusion grow when people participate in certain forms of therapy aimed at recovering memories. The use of such techniques as hypnosis, guided imagery, dream interpretation, and other highly suggestive treatments may create a situation in which it may be difficult for a person to discriminate fact from fiction (Loftus & Davis, 2006).

The controversy regarding false memories has produced great interest among cognitive psychologists on the topic of memory distortion. Some scholars have examined whether it is possible to implant false autobiographical memories. By suggesting critical but false information attributed to well-informed family members, researchers have succeeded in getting people to incorrectly believe in childhood events that never happened. Examples include being lost in a shopping mall for an extended period of time, being hospitalized overnight, and spilling a punch bowl at a family wedding (Hyman, Husband, & Billings, 1995; Loftus & Pickrell, 1995). In each of these studies, a significant minority of subjects came to accept all or part of the suggestion and claimed it as their own experience.

Might people fall sway to suggestion even when the falsely suggested event is highly emotional? The answer appears to be, yes. In one study, fully one third of subjects were persuaded that they had almost drowned as children, having been rescued by a lifeguard (Heaps & Nash, 2001). Another research group succeeded in getting about half of their subjects to believe they had experienced awful events as children, such as being a victim of a vicious animal attack (Porter, Yuille, & Lehman, 1999). Taken together, these studies demonstrate the power of suggestion, with on average, about 30% of subjects forming either partial or completely false memories (Lindsay, Hagen, Read, Wade, & Garry, 2004).

Another technique for planting false memories involves the use of fake photographs. Wade, Garry, Read, and Lindsay (2002) showed subjects a doctored photograph in which the subject and a relative were pasted into a prototype photograph of a hot-air balloon. Family members confirmed that the event never occurred. Subjects were instructed to tell everything they could remember about their experience in the balloon.

By the end of the experiment, which entailed three interviews, about half of the subjects had recalled, partially or clearly, the false hot-air balloon ride.

These studies and many more like them clearly show that people can develop false beliefs and memories for events that did not happen. But might such false beliefs and memories have repercussions on attitudes and behavior? Studies from Bernstein and colleagues (Bernstein, Laney, Morris, & Loftus, 2005) provide some clues: They falsely suggested to subjects that they had become ill after eating a certain food (e.g., strawberry ice cream, hard-boiled eggs,) when they were children. Subjects who accepted this false belief also reported decreased preference for the target food, accompanied by an increase in anticipated behavioral avoidance of the target food. A recent study conducted in our laboratory demonstrated that actual changes in *behavior* and avoidance of targeted foods does occur as a function of false beliefs (Geraerts et al., 2008).

Clearly, a large collection of studies on the creation of false memories has conclusively shown that suggestions can lead people to incorrectly believe in a childhood event that never occurred. To what extent are these conclusions relevant to the question of whether people develop false memories of traumatic events? Some have argued that experimental methods do not equate with real-life trauma, thereby limiting the import of research findings. Such objections have less force nowadays because researchers have demonstrated how it is possible to implant false memories for a diverse range of experiences. Moreover, and somewhat ironically, the most impressive demonstrations for the creation of false memories have arisen in clinical settings, not in the laboratory. These effects have occurred in the context of suggestive therapies in which therapist and patient join forces to uncover memories of abuse. Over many sessions, and with the aid of techniques such as guided imagination and hypnosis, false memories of childhood sexual abuse have arisen (Lynn, Knox, Fassler, Lilienfeld, & Loftus, 2004).

## RECOVERED MEMORIES

If we assume, as many theorists and clinicians do, that traumatic memories can be fragmented and totally forgotten, then a primary goal of therapy might be to "recover" and "make whole" the repressed material. This theoretical framework, and treatments that follow from its underlying assumptions, have been a source of heated debate. Unlike most controversies in psychology, this one has spread far beyond the clinic and laboratory. The topic of recovered memories has influenced legislation and outcomes in both civil suits and criminal trials. Famous cases of recovered memory have received intense media attention because of their legal implications. Interest in the topic has led to fictionalized cases that appear in films or books, and include a recovered memory as a main plot device.

In spite of intense interest, one very surprising aspect of the recovered memory debate has been the absence of research on the cognitive functioning of people who report experiencing the phenomenon. Until recently, scholars have argued their case by relying on evidence from either clinical experience, surveys of abuse survivors, or studies with college students (see review by McNally, 2003). Laboratory studies on the cognitive functioning of people reporting recovered memories have been entirely lacking. Recently, investigators from both the United States and The Netherlands have tried to examine the issues.

## Creating False Memories

Might it be that scholars are correct in arguing that at least some recovered memories are false, often instigated by suggestive therapeutic techniques? Are people who report recovered memories more prone to developing false memories, and can we observe this in the laboratory? To address this possibility, McNally's laboratory at Harvard University, and ours at Maastricht University and now at Erasmus University Rotterdam, used a paradigm to elicit false memories. In doing so, we tested the idea that people reporting recovered memories of childhood sexual abuse (CSA) would be more prone to falsely remember and recognize non-presented words. That is, they would have more difficulty differentiating between what they really saw and what they imagined. As hypothesized, we found that as a group, people with recovered CSA memories more often falsely recalled and recognized non-presented critical lures, relative to people with continuous CSA memories, and people with no history of abuse. Importantly, this was true for both neutral and trauma-related material (Clancy, Schacter, McNally, & Pitman, 2000; Geraerts, Smeets, Jelicic, van Heerden, & Merckelbach, 2005).

What do these findings tell us about the authenticity of reports of recovered abuse memories? Several researchers have suggested that deficits in source monitoring may lead to false memories. People with such deficits are prone to make incorrect judgments about the origins or sources of information. Our findings suggest that at least some individuals with recovered memories may have a source monitoring deficit for all types of material, whether the content is neutral or trauma-related. In other words, these individuals are more likely to conflate an internally generated thought with a real memory. In this way, individuals may develop false memories of abuse via a subtle interaction between pre-existing source monitoring difficulties and suggestive therapeutic techniques.

## Forgetting Prior Remembering

Research indicates that at least some recovered memories may be fictitious. At the same time, work outside the laboratory has shown the opposite, by demonstrating that some recovered memories may reflect genuine abuse events. Jonathan Schooler and co-workers (Schooler, Bendiksen, & Ambadar, 1997) published several case descriptions of individuals who experienced the discovery of apparently long-forgotten memories of abuse. All these memories were recovered outside the context of therapy. Importantly, corroborative information was found in each case. In several of these cases something else of interest was found: The partners of women who reported a recovered memory said their spouses had talked about the abuse, *prior* to the supposed recovery experience. Schooler et al. proposed that such cases demonstrate a forgot-it-all-along (FIA) mechanism, which leads to a false sense of recalling an event for the first time. Such a recollection is often paired with surprise and shock, particularly if the traumatic event is recalled in a qualitatively different way from past occasions of remembering. In such instances, an individual might reason, "If I am this shocked and surprised now, then I must have completely forgotten about the experience" (p. 283). Schooler's case studies put forward the possibility that at least some recovered memories reflect authentic abuse episodes that people may not have thought about for a long time.

In our laboratory we wanted to examine whether some people with recovered memories are not truly recalling an abuse event for the first time, but are forgetting prior cases of thinking about it. To explore this possibility, we (Geraerts et al., 2006) investigated whether people reporting recovered memories might be more likely to underestimate prior remembering. The experimental design used a task that tapped into the FIA effect (for a detailed description, see Geraerts, Smeets, Jelicic, Merckelbach, & van Heerden, 2006). Interestingly, a tendency to underestimate prior remembering (i.e., FIA phenomenon) was significantly greater for people who reported recovered memories as compared with people who reported continuously available memories, and people without any history of abuse. These findings support the hypothesis that people who have a recovered memory experience may simply have forgotten prior instances of remembering. The phenomenon is the same as observed in the case studies reported by Schooler et al., 1997.

## Two Types of Recovered Memory Experiences

We have seen that laboratory studies have produced conflicting findings. On the one hand, people with recovered memories show an increased susceptibility to false memory formation. In contrast, they also show pronounced underestimation of prior remembering. How can we integrate these phenomena? Careful examination of different recovered memory experiences may provide an answer. As we interviewed many people with recovered memories, we were able to identify two qualitatively different types of experiences. In one type, people came to realize they were abuse survivors, generally attributing current life difficulties to forgotten abuse memories. In this type of recovered memory experience, abuse events are often recalled slowly over time, and often induced by suggestive therapeutic techniques such as guided imagery, dream interpretation, and hypnosis. In the second type, people are suddenly reminded of events they had not thought about for many years. Typically, these individuals recollect the abuse when encountering salient retrieval cues (e.g., a book or movie in which CSA is clearly depicted, being in the same context in which the abuse happened, or participating in events involving the individual's children). This kind of recollection is clearly different from the one in which the person gradually recalls abuse. Further, one might expect that corroborative evidence would be easier to find for spontaneously recovered memories, as compared to previously unsubstantiated memories recovered through suggestive therapy.

To explore this issue, we studied individuals who fell into one of three groups: those who had always remembered their abuse; those who had a recovered abuse memory that arose during suggestive therapy; and, those who had a recovered memory arise spontaneously and outside a therapy context (Geraerts, Schooler, Merckelbach, Jelicic, Hauer, & Ambadar, 2007). All participants were queried systematically about sources of corroboration. Independent raters who were blind to group placement then made efforts to seek objective evidence, by interviewing other people who could possibly corroborate the event. A memory was considered corroborated if either (a) another individual reported learning about the abuse within a week after it happened, (b) another individual reported having been abused by the same perpetrator, or (c) the perpetrator admitted to committing the abuse. Memories that were recovered spontaneously, outside of therapy, were corroborated at a rate of 37%. This rate was quite comparable to that observed for people with continuously accessible memories of abuse (45%). In contrast, memories that had been recovered through suggestive therapy techniques were not corroborated in a single case. Although this lack of corroboration does not prove the recovered memories false, it does send out a warning to clinicians: first, to avoid suggestive recovery techniques in their own work; second, to be cautious when dealing with patients who have recovered memories with previous therapists.

In a subsequent study (Geraerts et al, 2009), we tested the same three types of participants with an experimental task that tapped the FIA effect. Strikingly, only those subjects who had recovered their memories spontaneously showed exaggerated forgetting of prior remembering; subjects who recovered their memories in suggestive therapy or subjects with continuous memories showed no such pattern. In contrast, when tested on a simple false memory task, only those individuals who recovered their memories in suggestive therapy showed increased false memory formation; neither the spontaneously recovered group nor people with continuous access to memories showed such a pattern. These findings strongly support the idea that individuals whose memories are recovered in suggestive therapy differ fundamentally from those for whom memories are spontaneously recovered. As a group, people who report having recovered a memory in suggestive therapy generally show a pronounced tendency to incorrectly claim experiences that have not occurred, as measured on a simple false memory test. Once again, research suggests that such reports of recovered memories should be viewed with a cautious eye, as they may reflect an interaction of suggestive therapy with pre-existing source monitoring deficits. When a therapist is convinced of the existence of repressed abuse memories, and a client starts to remember certain events, it may become difficult to appreciate that the memory may not be real, particularly when it provides a convenient explanation for current symptomatology. In contrast, people who believe they have spontaneously recovered a memory of abuse show no evidence of heightened susceptibility to the creation of false memories. These findings suggest that the latter group of individuals may be most likely to have simply failed to remember prior thoughts about early abuse experiences.

## CLINICAL IMPLICATIONS

Perspectives on trauma and memory have historically been polarized, leading one commentator to speak of the "memory wars" (Crews, 1995). Despite all the rancour, several points clearly emerge from decades of systematic research. First, accumulating evidence suggests that trauma memories are not processed and stored in a unique way. Further, memories of traumatic experiences (overwhelmingly terrifying, often life-threatening events) are nearly always remembered very well. Hence, PTSD is unlikely to represent a disorder resulting from fragmented memories and dissociative processes. Instead, processes such as normal forgetting, psychogenic amnesia, childhood amnesia, and encoding failures may explain why people sometimes report fragmented traumatic memories or no memory at all.

The implications of current research findings for clinical practice are clear. Efforts to help patients recall and then integrate trauma memories are largely misguided and based on unfounded theories. In this context, recovered memory therapies represent the clearest example of how treatment approaches based on fragmentation and dissociation theories can do significant harm. Clinicians are encouraged to take a different approach when treating PTSD and other posttraumatic disorders, one that is based on the latest scientific data. This data directs clinicians to focus their efforts on helping patients counter dysfunctional cognitions, alter maladaptive behaviors, and promote fear reduction.

## REFERENCES

American Psychiatric Association. (2000). *Diagnostic and statistical manual of mental disorders* (4th ed. – text revision). Author: Washington, DC.

Bernheim, H. (1884). De la suggestion dans l'etat hypnotique et dans l'etat de veille [On suggestion in the hypnotic state and the waking state]. *Revue Medicale de l'Est, 11e annee, Tome XVI*, No. 1 (1/1/84), 7–20.

Bernheim, H. (1889). *Suggestive therapeutics: A treatise on the nature and uses of hypnotism*. New York: Putnam.

Bernstein, D. M., Laney, C., Morris, E. K., & Loftus, E. F. (2005). False beliefs about fattening foods can have healthy consequences. *Proceedings of the National Academy of Sciences, 102*, 13724–13731.

Berntsen, D. (2001). Involuntary memories of emotional events: Do memories of traumas and extremely happy events differ? *Applied Cognitive Psychology, 15*, S135–S158.

Berntsen, D., & Rubin, D. C. (2007). When a trauma becomes a key to identity: Enhanced integration of trauma memories predicts posttraumatic stress disorder symptoms. *Applied Cognitive Psychology, 21*, 417–431.

Berntsen, D., Willert, M., & Rubin, D. C. (2003). Splintered memories or vivid landmarks? Qualities and organization of traumatic memories with and without PTSD. *Applied Cognitive Psychology, 17*, 675–693.

Brewin, C. R., Dalgleish, T., & Joseph, S. (1996). A dual representation theory of posttraumatic stress disorder. *Psychological Review, 103*, 670–686.

Bryant, R. A. (2007). Does dissociation further our understanding of PTSD? *Journal of Anxiety Disorders, 21*, 183–191.

Clancy, S. A. (2005). *Abducted: How people come to believe they were kidnapped by aliens*. Cambridge, MA: Harvard University Press.

Clancy, S. A., Schacter, D. L., McNally, R. J., & Pitman, R. K. (2000). False recognition in women reporting recovered memories of sexual abuse. *Psychological Science, 11*, 26–31.

Crews, F. (1995). *The memory wars: Freud's legacy in dispute*. New York: New York Review of Books.

Ehlers, A., & Clark, D. M. (2000). A cognitive model of posttraumatic stress disorder. *Behaviour Research and Therapy, 38*, 319–345.

Femina, D. D., Yeager, C. A., & Lewis, D. O. (1990). Child abuse: Adolescent records vs. adult recall. *Child Abuse and Neglect, 14*, 227–231.

Geraerts, E., Arnold, M. M., Lindsay, D. S., Merckelbach, H., Jelicic, M., & Hauer, B. (2006). Forgetting of prior remembering in persons reporting recovered memories of childhood sexual abuse. *Psychological Science, 17*, 1002–1008.

Geraerts, E., Bernstein, D. M., Merckelbach, H., Linders, C., Raymaekers, L., & Loftus, E. F. (2008). Lasting false beliefs and their behavioral consequences. *Psychological Science, 19*, 749–753.

Geraerts, E., Kozaric-Kovacic, D., Merckelbach, H., Peraica, T., Jelicic, M., & Candel, I. (2007). Traumatic memories of war veterans: Not so special after all. *Consciousness and Cognition, 16*, 170–177.

Geraerts, E., Lindsay, D. S., Merckelbach, H., Jelicic, M., Raymaekers, L., Arnold, M. M., & Schooler, J. S. (2009). Cognitive mechanisms underlying recovered memory experiences of childhood sexual abuse. *Psychological Science, 20*, 92–98.

Geraerts, E., & McNally, R. J. (2009). Trauma, recollective accuracy, and posttraumatic stress disorder. In C. Edwards (Ed.), *The behavioral science of forensic responsibility*. In A. Jamieson & A. Moenssens (Editors-in-Chief), *Encyclopedia of forensic sciences*). Hoboken, NJ: John Wiley and Sons.

Geraerts, E., Schooler, J. W., Merckelbach, H., Jelicic, M., Hauer, B. J. A., & Ambadar, Z. (2007). The reality of recovered memories: Corroborating continuous and discontinuous memories of childhood sexual abuse. *Psychological Science, 18*, 564–567.

Geraerts, E., Smeets, E., Jelicic, M., Merckelbach, H., & van Heerden, J. (2006). Retrieval inhibition of trauma-related words in women reporting repressed or recovered memories of childhood sexual abuse. *Behaviour Research and Therapy, 44*, 1129–1136.

Geraerts, E., Smeets, E., Jelicic, M., van Heerden, J., & Merckelbach, H. (2005). Fantasy proneness, but not self-reported trauma is related to DRM performance of women reporting recovered memories of childhood sexual abuse. *Consciousness and Cognition, 14*, 602–612.

Gray, M. J., & Lombardo, T. W. (2001). Complexity of trauma narratives as an index of fragmented memory in PTSD: A critical analysis. *Applied Cognitive Psychology, 15*, S171–S186.

Heaps, C. M., & Nash, M. (2001). Comparing recollective experience in true and false autobiographical memories. *Journal of Experimental Psychology: Learning, Memory and Cognition, 27*, 920–930.

Hyman, I. E., Husband, T. H., & Billings, F. J. (1995). False memories of child-hood experiences. *Applied Cognitive Psychology, 9*, 181–195.

Jones, E., Vermaas, R.H., McCartney, H., Beech, C., Palmer, I., Hymans, K., et al. (2003). Flashbacks and post-traumatic stress disorder: The genesis of a 20th-century diagnosis. *British Journal of Psychiatry, 182*, 158–163.

LaBar, K. S., & Cabeza, R. (2006). Cognitive neuroscience of emotional mem-ory. *Nature Reviews Neuroscience, 7*, 54–64.

Lindsay, D. S., Hagen, L., Read, J. D., Wade, K. A., & Garry, M. (2004). True photographs and false memories. *Psychological Science, 15*, 149–154.

Loftus, E. F., & Davis, D. (2006). Recovered memories. *Annual Review of Clinical Psychology. 2*, 469–498.

Loftus, E. F., & Pickrell, J. E. (1995). The formation of false memories. *Psychiatric Annals, 25*, 720–725.

Lynn, S. J., Knox, J. A., Fassler, O., Lilienfeld, S. O., & Loftus, E. F. (2004). Memory, trauma, and dissociation. In G.M. Rosen (Ed.), *Posttraumatic stress disorder: Issues and controversies* (pp. 163–186). Chichester, England: John Wiley & Sons.

McNally, R. J. (2003) *Remembering trauma*. Cambridge, MA: Belknap Press/ Harvard University Press.

Merckelbach, H., Dekkers, T., Wessel, I., & Roefs, A. (2003). Amnesia, flash-backs, nightmares, and dissociation in aging concentration camp survivors. *Behaviour Research and Therapy, 41*, 351–360.

Meyersburg, C. A., Bogdan, R., Gallo, D. A., & McNally, R. J. (2009). False memory propensity in people reporting recovered memories of past lives. *Journal of Abnormal Psychology, 118*, 399–404.

Parker, E. S., Cahill, L., & McGaugh, J. L. (2006). A case of unusual autobio-graphical remembering. *Neurocase, 12*, 35–49.

Porter, S., Yuille, J. C., & Lehman, D. R. (1999). The nature of real, implanted, and fabricated memories or emotional childhood events. Implications for the recovered memory debate. *Law and Human Behavior, 23*, 517–537.

Rosen, G. M., Sageman, M., & Loftus, E. (2003). A historical note on false traumatic memories. *Journal of Clinical Psychology, 60*, 137–139.

Rubin, D. C., Berntsen, D., & Bohni, M. K. (2008). A memory based model of posttraumatic stress disorder. *Psychological Review, 115*, 985–1011.

Schacter, D. L. (2001). *How the mind forgets and remembers. The seven sins of memory*. Boston: Houghton Mifflin.

Schooler, J. W., Bendiksen, M. A., & Ambadar, Z. (1997). Taking the middle line: Can we accommodate both fabricated and recovered memories of sexual abuse? In M. Conway (Ed.), *False and recovered memories* (pp. 251–292). Oxford: Oxford University Press.

Scott, S. (2001). *The politics and experience of ritual abuse: Beyond disbelief.* Buckingham, UK: Open University Press.

van der Kolk, B.A. (1994). The body keeps the score: Memory and the evolving psychobiology of posttraumatic stress. *Harvard Review of Psychiatry, 1,* 253–265.

Vasterling, J. J., Brailey, K., Constans, J. I., Borges, A., & Sutker, P. B. (1997). Assessment of intellectual resources in Gulf War veterans: Relationship to PTSD. *Assessment, 1,* 51–59.

Wade, K., Garry, M., Read, J. D., & Lindsay, D. S. (2002). A picture is worth a thousand lies. Using false photographs to create false childhood memories. *Psychonomic Bulletin and Review, 9,* 597–603.

Young, A. (2004). When traumatic memory was a problem: On the historical antecedents of PTSD. In G.M. Rosen (Ed.), *Posttraumatic stress disorder: Issues and controversies* (pp. 127–146). Chichester, England: John Wiley & Sons.

Zoellner, L. A., & Bittenger, J. N. (2004). On the uniqueness of trauma memories in PTSD. In G.M. Rosen (Ed.), *Posttraumatic stress disorder: Issues and controversies* (pp. 147–162). New York: John Wiley & Sons.

CHAPTER

# 5

# Searching for PTSD's Biological Signature

GERALD M. ROSEN
SCOTT O. LILIENFELD
SCOTT P. ORR


$N$*osology* is that branch of medical science whose goal is to "carve nature at its joints," in Plato's famous terms—in other words, to accurately identify and classify disorders as they occur in nature. Inevitably, any listing of conditions [nomenclature] is an evolving effort: New conditions may be added; an existing diagnosis may be "split" into two or more separate categories; or previously distinct diagnoses may be "lumped" when varied presentations come to be understood as manifestations of the same disorder. In every instance the goal is the same: to achieve a classification system that best reflects the true state of affairs in nature. The ultimate benefit of an accurate classification system is to further the development and implementation of effective treatments.

As is the intent of all diagnostic constructs, posttraumatic stress disorder (PTSD) was defined in the third edition of the American Psychiatric Association's diagnostic manual (DSM-III; American Psychiatric Association (APA), 1980) in an effort to more accurately carve nature at its joints and to further our understanding and treatment of posttraumatic morbidity. Prior to the diagnosis of PTSD, it had generally been held that stressful events could increase risk of illness, and that this held true across a wide range of events and disorders (e.g., Selye, 1946). At various points in time, several "event specific" disorders had been introduced by those concerned with psychiatric nosology (e.g., "soldier's heart," "shell shock," "war neurosis"). PTSD built on this model and postulated that a distinct class of stressors (Criterion A) created risk for a specific clinical syndrome (Criteria B through D).

Since the introduction of PTSD in DSM-III (APA, 1980), numerous challenges have been raised to its conceptual foundations. For example, Breslau and Davis (1987) questioned the assumption that a distinct class of stressors contributed to the condition's signs and symptoms. Others raised concerns about whether PTSD is a distinct disorder or merely an amalgam of such extant conditions as depression, generalized anxiety disorder, panic disorder, and specific phobia (March, 1990; Rosen, Spitzer & McHugh, 2008). Put another way, when PTSD was carved out of the general field of stress studies, was it simply an old wine in a new bottle? It was in the context of these concerns that researchers spoke of the critical task of distinguishing PTSD from other diagnostic constructs, to assure the "long-term survival of the construct" (King & King, 1991, p. 117).

Clinicians may find themselves taken aback to hear that academicians and researchers have questioned the widespread assumptions that underlie PTSD and the criteria that define this syndrome. Most clinicians have found that the PTSD diagnosis is of considerable utility in guiding their understanding and treatment of patients who have survived extremely adverse and life-threatening events, as well as helping patients to identify and better understand the nature of their emotional distress. For many of these clinicians, there is little doubt PTSD has successfully carved nature at its joints. Even so, the issues raised and addressed by researchers are of direct relevance to those who work with patients. If the features of PTSD that are truly distinctive can be clearly identified, we are more likely to accurately diagnose and effectively treat our patients.

## VALIDATING PSYCHIATRIC DIAGNOSES: PTSD AS A CASE EXAMPLE

In nosology, the strongest situation for establishing the validity of a diagnosis is when a specific pathology can be linked to a disorder's etiology.

Meehl (1977) referred to this situation as the "ideal type." In the field of medicine, a number of disease entities meet this condition. For example, tuberculosis is known to arise from exposure to a specific mycobacterium; the signs and symptoms of coronary artery disease result from plaque build-up; and so on. Few, if any, psychiatric disorders, boast this type of "hard" biological basis to establish their place in nature.

Short of Meehl's ideal type, various experts have considered what conditions should be met to demonstrate that a diagnostic entity is valid. Robins and Guze (1970) provided the classic exposition of this matter. These authors observed that merely labeling a set of signs and symptoms with a diagnosis does not demonstrate validity. Instead, a valid diagnosis must provide *surplus* information that is not contained in the signs and symptoms themselves. That is, to be valid, a diagnosis must afford us novel information that we did not have previously. In particular, Robins and Guze emphasized that valid diagnoses should (a) describe the core clinical features of the disorder; (b) distinguish the diagnosis from other, similar diagnoses; (c) predict family history of the diagnosis; (d) predict performance on laboratory measures, including biological indicators and personality test results; and (e) predict the natural history (course and outcome) of the diagnosis. Although not emphasized by Robins and Guze, other authors have argued that a valid diagnosis should ideally, although not necessarily, (f) predict treatment response (Waldman, Lilienfeld, & Lahey, 1995).

Later authors extended Robins and Guze's (1970) criteria by fleshing out their nomological network (Cronbach & Meehl, 1955) of external validating indicators (Kendall & Jablensky, 2003). For example, Kendler (1980) usefully distinguished among: (a) antecedent validators, such as premorbid personality traits and psychosocial stressors; (b) concurrent validators, such as performance on laboratory measures; and (c) predictive validators, such as natural history and response to treatment. Andreasen (1995) argued that particular emphasis be placed on potential "endophenotypic" markers (those that presumably lie in between the circuitous path between genes and observable phenotypes), such as levels of neurotransmitter metabolites and brain imaging findings, in the validation of diagnostic entities. Other extensions and clarifications regarding Robins and Guze's five criteria have been offered by experts in the field, but for our purposes, these criteria can serve as a minimal framework for considering the validity of a diagnosis.

Ideally, following Robins and Guze (1970), Andreasen (1995), and others, the construct validity of a diagnosis would be strengthened by the existence of diagnostic "markers," viz., laboratory (e.g., biological, personality trait) test results that indicate with strong certainty either the presence (an inclusion test), absence (an exclusion test), or both, of a diagnosis. Researchers refer to a marker that serves as either a perfect inclusion or exclusion test as one-way pathognomonic, and as both a perfect inclusion and exclusion test as two-way pathognomonic.

Traditionally, psychologists and psychiatrists have evaluated the validity of diagnostic markers using conditional probability indicators, especially sensitivity, specificity, positive predictive power (PPP), and negative predictor power (NPP) (Widiger, Hurt, Frances, Clarkin, & Gilmore, 1984). Sensitivity is the probability of a marker being positive (present) given the presence of a diagnosis; specificity, in contrast, is the probability of a marker being negative (absent) given the absence of a diagnosis. PPP is the probability of a diagnosis being present given the presence of a marker; NPP is the probability of a diagnosis being absent given the absence of a marker. Examples may help to illustrate these concepts. Let's say there is a sample of 1,000 individuals, among whom 100 have PTSD and 100 have Major Depression. A test with 100% sensitivity would identify all 100 of the PTSD cases, while a test with 100% specificity would not identify any of the 900 non-PTSD cases. Put another way, when a test's specificity and sensitivity are 100%, there are no false positives or false negatives, respectively. PPP and NPP are somewhat more complicated measures because they are affected by base rates (the prevalence of the condition in question), whereas sensitivity and specificity are not. Hence, PPP and NPP tend to be more sample-specific and more relevant to diagnostic decision-making than sensitivity and specificity. However, for our purposes, we will focus on the simpler indices.

With these introductory points clarified, we can now consider various attempts to identify biological markers or "signatures" for PTSD. As previously observed, success in such endeavors would not only serve to establish PTSD as a disorder in nature, but could also further our understanding and treatment of patients in need.

# THE "CORTISOL HYPOTHESIS"

One of the pioneers in stress studies was Hans Selye. Selye began his research in the 1930s, and later proposed a General Adaptation Syndrome (Selye, 1946). Within this model, stressors were etiologically nonspecific such that any event of sufficient intensity (the stressor) could produce a physiological adaptation response (stress syndrome) whose features were consistent regardless of the event. Integral to this model was the stress hormone *cortisol*. Produced by the adrenal glands, cortisol is associated with increased production when the organism is under stress. Researchers came to understand that elevated levels of cortisol among stressed subjects are related to activation of the hypothalamic-pituitary-adrenal (HPA) axis in the face of adverse or aversive events. Consistent with this model, prolonged states of stress and disorders associated with such stress (e.g., major depression) are typically associated with chronically elevated levels of cortisol. On the opposite end of the stress spectrum, massage therapy has been associated with low cortisol levels (Field, Hernandez-Reif, Diego, Schanberg, & Kuhn, 2005).

In the context of decades of research on stress and elevated cortisol, the finding that patients with chronic PTSD possess lower than normal urinary cortisol levels understandably aroused considerable interest (e.g., Yehuda, Southwick, Nussbaum, Giller, & Mason, 1990). Such findings of "hypocortisolimia" among PTSD-diagnosed patients led to the view that a specific HPA axis dysfunction could provide an underlying physiopathology for the disorder. These findings also appeared to provide support for the discriminant validity of PTSD from co-occurring disorders, such as depression, which are typically marked by hypercortisolimia.

Researchers were enthusiastic about these early biological findings, and some suggested that they provided "an essential first step in allowing the permanent validation of human suffering" (Yehuda & McFarlane, 1995, p. xv). Of course, as pointed out by McNally (2004), one might ask why it is necessary to have a biological marker to establish human suffering. All of us can appreciate that if we are mourning the death of a loved one, we don't need to measure stress hormones to validate the depths of our grief. Bioethicist Eric Racine has similarly referred to this line of reasoning as "neurorealism"—the logically flawed assumption that a subjective experience is not "real" until it has been validated by physiological findings (Racine, Bar-Ilan, & Illes, 2005). Accordingly, Yehuda and McFarlane might have better stated their enthusiasm by observing that biological findings might help to establish the diagnostic construct of PTSD as a valid entity in nature. Indeed, this was the goal that Yehuda and others believed they had accomplished with the counterintuitive finding of low cortisol levels among PTSD patients.

Despite early enthusiasm with the "cortisol hypothesis" of PTSD, multiple considerations have required a re-evaluation. For example, not all researchers have found lower cortisol levels among groups of PTSD patients (e.g., Metzger et al., 2008), and some studies have even reported the opposite, viz, high cortisol levels (e.g., Liberzon, Abelson, Flagel, Raz, & Young, 1999; Pitman & Orr, 1990). Epidemiologic studies have similarly not consistently revealed lower cortisol levels among individuals who report exposure to trauma and who meet the symptom criteria for PTSD (e.g., Young & Breslau, 2004; Young, Tolman, Witkowski, & Kaplan, 2004).

Further weakening the import of cortisol findings is the marked variability of cortisol levels within and among patients. Even when mean cortisol levels for PTSD-diagnosed groups differ statistically from those of controls, the findings can reflect group mean scores and fictive patients (i.e., prototypical patients who rarely exist in nature) rather than the majority of actual individuals. Young (2004) provided an example of this concern by analyzing data reported by Yehuda et al. (1990). In that study, Yehuda et al. found significantly lower urinary cortisol levels in 16 non-medicated male combat veterans diagnosed with PTSD compared with 16 age-comparable nonpsychiatric male control subjects ($p < .001$; Cohen's $d = 1.22$). Young observed that only 2 of the 16 PTSD patients in Yehuda and colleagues' study had cortisol levels that fell below the lowest score obtained in the comparison group. Put another way, although group means differed, the independent variable had little diagnostic utility.

Further concerns regarding the implications of cortisol findings with PTSD patients are raised by studies that report low cortisol levels among adults with fibromyalgia (Fries, Hesse, Hellhammer, & Hellhammer, 2005; Griep et al., 1998) and chronic fatigue syndrome (Demitrack et al., 1991; Roberts, Wessely, Chalder, Papadopoulos, & Cleare, 2004), and among children with conduct disorders (Oosterlaan, Geurts, Knowl, &

Sergeant, 2005; Shoal, Giancola, & Kirillova, 2003). These findings raise questions concerning the specificity of low cortisol for PTSD.

In the context of such findings, enthusiasm over the cortisol hypothesis has waned. It is now widely agreed that cortisol as a biological marker for PTSD lacks sufficient sensitivity and specificity to be clinically useful. Nevertheless, research over the past two decades has increased our appreciation for the complexity of stress reactions, with some patients demonstrating heightened levels of cortisol, and others lower levels. This is an area in which continued research may still yield new insights.

## NEUROANATOMY

Since the mid-1990s, several studies have found reduced hippocampal volumes among combat veterans, victims of childhood abuse, and other traumatized individuals (e.g., Bremner et al., 1995; Gurvits et al., 1996). Bremner (1999) related these findings to animal studies that had revealed a relationship between stress and reduced volumes of the hippocampus. The findings were thought to be particularly relevant to PTSD because the hippocampus is associated with learning and memory, and the intensity and durability of trauma memories have always been central to patient problems. Based on his review of this literature, Bremner (1999) concluded that stress can damage the brain.

Certainly, findings on brain structures and changes that may result from stress are of considerable interest to clinicians and researchers concerned with posttraumatic morbidity. At the same time, Bremner's (1999) conclusion that stress-induced brain damage underlies PTSD seems to have been premature. First, Bremner's analysis did not adequately consider alternative hypotheses that could account for reduced hippocampal volumes. For example, pre-existing reductions in hippocampal volume could predispose individuals to develop morbidity after trauma (Stein, Koverola, Hanna, Torchia, & McClarty, 1997). Support for this hypothesis comes from a study by Gilbertson et al. (2002), who examined male monozygotic (identical) twin pairs discordant for Vietnam combat exposure. In some twin pairs, the combat-exposed brother was diagnosed with PTSD, thereby providing a built-in control for genetic effects. As in earlier studies, Gilbertson et al. found reduced hippocampal volumes in the veterans with PTSD, compared with non-PTSD trauma-exposed veterans. Importantly, they also found similarly reduced volumes in the monozygotic twin brothers of the veterans with PTSD. These findings suggest that reduced hippocampal volumes among PTSD patients are a pre-trauma vulnerability factor rather than a consequence of trauma.

Further tempering the claim that stress damages the brain are studies that have failed to replicate the finding of smaller hippocampal volumes among PTSD diagnosed patients (e.g., Bonne et al., 2001; Fennema-Notestine, Stein, Kennedy, Archibald, & Jernigan, 2002). The interpretation of research on neuroanatomy and PTSD also is complicated by studies that report reduced hippocampal volumes among patients diagnosed with depression (e.g., Bremner et al., 2000; Mervaala et al., 2000), a condition that co-occurs substantially with PTSD and therefore represents an important confound. Other issues that weaken the empirical basis for claiming that stress damages the brain have been reviewed by Rosen and Lilienfeld (2008).

Finally, if hippocampal atrophy is a gradual process (absent direct physical trauma), then stress-induced brain damage is unlikely to account for posttraumatic symptoms that develop very soon after a traumatic event. This point is particularly relevant in light of research that finds that "delayed onset" PTSD is exceedingly rare (Frueh, Grubaugh, Yeager & Magruder, 2009), with most individuals exhibiting significant reactions in the immediate aftermath of a traumatic event. For example, North (2001) assessed individuals after the Oklahoma City bombing and found that 34% of the sample met criteria for PTSD. Although PTSD cannot be formally diagnosed until 1 month after the traumatic event, among PTSD diagnosed individuals, onset of symptoms was rapid, with 76% of individuals reporting that symptoms arose the first day, and another 18% reporting that symptoms arose within the first week. It remains a possibility that reduced hippocampal volumes occur over time and that this change contributes to development of chronic PTSD (i.e., PTSD that persists for years). However, a study by Bonne et al. (2001) using a longitudinal design with brain scans conducted within a week of a traumatic event and again six months later observed no change within this time frame for either right or left hippocampal volumes among ten participants who met PTSD criteria. Although this study is limited by its small sample and relatively brief follow-up period, it suggests that PTSD morbidity over a 6-month period is not associated with reductions in hippocampal volume.

As with the cortisol hypothesis, research on brain structures has yet to identify a biological marker or "signature" that distinguishes PTSD from other disorders. The possibility that premorbid variations in brain structure may be associated with emotional regulation difficulties, intellectual functioning, and an increased risk for developing PTSD is intriguing. But as observed by Pitman (2001), we shouldn't jump to conclusions regarding the possibility of stress-induced hippocampal damage in PTSD patients.

## PSYCHOPHYSIOLOGICAL REACTIVITY

When criteria for PTSD were revised in the DSM-III-R (APA, 1987) "physiologic reactivity" was added as one of the hyperarousal symptoms (Cluster D). This modification to PTSD's symptom criteria was based on studies showing that PTSD-diagnosed individuals demonstrated heightened reactivity (e.g., heart rate, skin conductance) to trauma relevant stimuli (e.g., Blanchard, Kolb, Pallmeyer, & Gerardi, 1982). An example of this type of research is provided by studies that have used the "script-driven imagery" procedure. This imagery-based approach involves the presentation of trauma-relevant narratives, as well as positive and "neutral" scripts, with measurement of skin conductance, heart rate, and facial electromyogram responses compared across conditions (e.g., Orr, Pitman, Lasko, & Herz, 1993). A sizable literature that documents increased reactivity of PTSD diagnosed patients to trauma-related imagery was reviewed by Orr, Metzger, Miller, and Kaloupek (2004). With the advent of DSM-IV (APA, 1994), the symptom of physiologic reactivity was moved to the re-experiencing symptoms listed as Cluster B. Orr et al. (2004) have discussed the conceptual significance of this change. Originally viewed as indicative of generally heightened arousal, physiologic reactivity was now seen as an index of emotional re-experiencing. This view places emphasis on PTSD as a disorder marked by emotional reactivity (fear) to traumatic memories and associated stimuli.

A second psychophysiological assessment that has shown promise as a test of PTSD is the loud-tones procedure. This assessment measures heart, skin conductance, and eye blink (electromyogram) responses to 15 presentations of a brief (1/2 second), loud (95 dB) pure tone (1000 Hz). One of the most replicable psychophysiologic findings in the PTSD literature is that of a larger averaged HR response to loud tones in individuals with, compared with individuals without, PTSD (see Orr, Metzger, et al., 2004, for review). Recent findings clearly suggest that this is an acquired feature of PTSD (Orr et al., 2003; Shalev et al., 2000). For example, in their study of monozygotic twins discordant for combat exposure, Orr et al. found that combat-exposed veterans with PTSD showed heightened HR responses to loud tones, whereas their twin brothers without PTSD did not. These results indicate that the larger HR responses to loud tones were associated with the development of PTSD and did not represent a pre-trauma (e.g., genetic) vulnerability. If heightened HR reactivity to loud tones is an acquired feature of PTSD, then it may be possible to use this measure as an index of PTSD symptom reduction and treatment outcome. In fact, a treatment study of rape-related PTSD using cognitive-behavioral therapy observed a significant reduction in HR responses to loud sounds from pre- to post-treatment in treatment responders, whereas treatment non-responders did not show a reduction (Griffin & Resick, 2004).

Could physiologic reactivity to trauma-relevant stimuli and/or loud tones provide a biological signature that helps to validate PTSD? The answer to this question appears to be a qualified "yes." First and foremost among the limiting qualifiers is that upwards of 40% of patients diagnosed with PTSD do not demonstrate heightened reactivity to trauma-relevant cues. This finding, that a sizable minority of PTSD diagnosed individuals do not demonstrate psychophysiologic reactivity, is consistent with early reports of "desynchrony" among various response modalities (e.g., behavior avoidance, cognitive threat statements, physiologic responses) among phobic subjects (Lang, 1968, 1979). Such findings limit the sensitivity of physiological measures for identifying PTSD-caseness.

The sensitivity of any potential biological marker is influenced by the reliability and validity of the diagnostic criterion used (e.g., the Clinician Administered PTSD Scale [CAPS]). If the best criterion available results in some diagnostic error, then even a theoretically perfect biological marker will produce less than 100% sensitivity. Therefore, when evaluating the performance of a potential biological marker, it is important to keep in mind whatever limitations exist for the diagnostic standard against which the biological marker is compared. This issue has been addressed in more detail with regard to PTSD and psychophysiological reactivity to script-driven imagery by Orr, McNally, Rosen, and Shalev (2004). In the context of these considerations, it is not entirely surprising to find that psychophysiologic reactivity has limited sensitivity as an index of PTSD.

Even when psychophysiologic reactivity occurs, the finding needs to be understood within a broad context of human emotion and arousal. For example, psychophysiologic reactivity to fear-related stimuli was long ago observed among individuals with specific phobia (e.g., Lang, 1968; Weerts, & Lang, 1978). In fact, it was this early work from Peter Lang's group that stimulated application of the script-driven imagery methodology to PTSD. At the same time, studies on other anxiety disorders, such as agoraphobia and panic disorder (e.g., Cook, Melamed, Cuthbert, McNeil, & Lang, 1988; Zander & McNally, 1988), and on borderline personality disorder (Kuo & Linehan, 2009), have not demonstrated heightened physiological reactivity to disorder-relevant stimuli. In addition, a small study that compared a group of veterans with combat-related PTSD with combat veterans having other anxiety disorders found that only veterans with PTSD showed heightened physiological reactivity during recall of their combat experiences (Pitman, Orr, Forgue, Altman, deJong & Herz, 1990). Thus, heightened physiologic reactivity to anxiety-related stimuli shows good specificity for PTSD, with the exception of conditions for which fear (rather than anxiety) is a central component (e.g., specific phobia). With regard to measures of reactivity to loud tones, a recent study of patients with obsessive-compulsive disorder (OCD) found that patients with OCD also showed a heightened average HR response to loud tones (e.g., Buhlmann, et al., 2007). This raises the possibility that heightened HR reactivity to loud tones also is not specific to PTSD, but may be a characteristic of anxiety disorders in general. With these limiting conditions in mind, it can be said that increased psychophysiological reactivity to trauma cues is a viable marker of PTSD. As such, psychophysiological reactivity is probably the closest approximation we have to a biological signature for the disorder, although it is far from serving as a one-way pathognonomic indicator.

Future research will want to investigate whether combining various measures from multiple assessment methods provides a biologically based method of triangulating on the PTSD diagnosis. For example, individuals with PTSD or specific phobia both show heightened psychophysiological reactivity to fear-relevant imagery. If it were shown that individuals with specific phobia do not show heightened HR reactivity to loud tones, this would serve to differentiate the two groups of patients. Clearly, more research is needed to refine assessment strategies and the nature of biological markers for PTSD.

## IMPLICATIONS FOR THE CLINICIAN

Recently, Zhang, Li, Benedek, Li, and Ursano (2009) issued an investigative call for identifying biological markers for PTSD with high sensitivity and specificity, stating that "a simple blood test or biomarker that could detect PTSD in its earliest and potentially most treatable stages would be beneficial for physicians and patients" (p. 404). Among the promising candidates mentioned by Zhang et al. were platelet MAO-B activity, platelet serotonin activity, rapid eye movement latency, heart rate responsivity to loud noises, and urinary dopamine levels. Nevertheless, they acknowledge that no diagnostic marker with adequate sensitivity and specificity for PTSD has yet been identified, a conclusion also drawn by Rosen and Lilienfeld (2008) in their comprehensive review of the PTSD literature. As they noted, efforts to identify highly sensitive and specific laboratory tests or biological markers, including hormonal (cortisol levels), neuroanatomical (e.g., hippocampal volume), and brain activity (e.g., amygdala reactivity) findings, have all fallen short of being useful diagnostic tests or markers. This also holds true for research on genetic influences, where it appears that any heritability for PTSD per se may result largely from a genetic predisposition toward negative emotionality in general (e.g., Koenen et al., 2008).

In agreement with Zhang et al.'s appraisal of the current state of affairs, a report issued by the Institute of Medicine (IOM, 2006) on the construct validity of PTSD concluded: "No biomarkers are clinically useful or specific in diagnosing PTSD, assessing the risk of developing it, or charting its progression" (p. 46). At first glance, this conclusion may surprise and disappoint some readers, at least in part because it appears to neglect the promise held by some of the psychophysiological measures, as previously discussed. However, on reflection there is nothing unexpected in observing that a highly sensitive and specific biological marker has not been found for PTSD. After all, considering the full range of psychiatric diagnoses, is there any disorder that is characterized by a clinically useful biological marker, viz., one with high sensitivity and specificity? With the potential exception of certain organic brain disorders, no DSM conditions can be characterized by even one-way pathognomonic indicators (Lilienfeld & Landfield, 2008). Certainly, we should be even less sanguine that a two-way pathognomonic marker for PTSD will ever be identified. In retrospect, the goal of finding a single biological marker that would somehow validate PTSD is probably unrealistic.

Also upon reflection, there is no reason to experience disappointment in the state of current findings. In actuality, we have made substantial progress in understanding the psychobiology of posttraumatic morbidity since the introduction of PTSD in 1980. There is now a better appreciation for the complexity of stress hormone reactions after trauma. Research findings point to the possibility that structural variations in neuroanatomy may be associated with risk and reduced ability to modulate emotional reactions. And a number of psychophysiological findings have converged to facilitate diagnoses in a large number of PTSD-suspected cases.

Findings from various research efforts that have searched for PTSD's biological signature hold several important implications for the practicing clinician. First, clinicians are well served if they appreciate the limits of our knowledge and adjust their vocabularies accordingly. Like most psychiatric diagnoses, PTSD has not been established as a disorder that carves nature at its joints. Unlike some clearly definable medical diseases with known pathologies, PTSD, like virtually all DSM categories and many medical disorders, remains a hypothetical construct. This means that PTSD defines a clinical syndrome in the hope of guiding research, advancing the development of effective treatments, and eventually furthering our identification and differentiation of disorders in nature. One implication of this state of affairs concerns the frequently used phrase,

"My patient has PTSD." In point of fact, it is at best questionable to assert that someone with nightmares, intrusive thoughts, emotional numbing, and hypervigilance "has" PTSD. Rather, clinicians should recognize that their patient has received the diagnosis of PTSD, at least in part, because they are experiencing nightmares, intrusive thoughts, or other reactions that are defined criteria of PTSD. This distinction in phrasing affects how we conceptualize causality. When we say that a patient "has" PTSD, we are implicitly suggesting that trauma nightmares, flashbacks, exaggerated startle and other symptoms are caused by the "disorder" (i.e., PTSD). To the contrary, nightmares and other symptoms are largely a consequence of being exposed to a traumatic event and the associated risk factors that influence one's response to the traumatic event (see Boorsboom, 2008, for a distinction between "common cause" and "causal chain" models). Until more is learned about the pathogenesis of posttraumatic morbidity, PTSD will remain a way to categorize, but not explain, its defining symptoms.

Second, clinicians ought to be wary of using popularized phrases that have made their way into the media, such as "stress damages the brain," or the biological functioning of PTSD patients has been "permanently changed." Instead, clinicians are advised to discuss the complex transactions between stress and physical functioning, the increased risks that stress *can* place on the individual, and how such considerations *may* apply to a specific individual.

In the midst of these several cautionary points, it can be said that there is promising, albeit preliminary evidence for a pattern of psychophysiological "signatures," such as increased psychophysiological reactivity to trauma-related cues, which may help to provide validation for the PTSD diagnosis. Increased HR response to loud tones may prove to be one of the most useful measures, as it is a valid and consistently replicated marker that appears to be acquired with the disorder. Although this measure's sensitivity and specificity are far from perfect (e.g., the response is not present in all individuals receiving a PTSD diagnosis, and the response is shared by some other anxiety disorders), it may nonetheless be a useful marker of pathological anxiety. Just as important, this measure may be a useful outcome index of treatment success, as the HR response should "normalize" with clinical improvement.

Findings on psychophysiologic reactivity also raise important questions regarding how we conceptualize PTSD and how we might conceptualize that disorder's distinctive or "hallmark" features. Might re-experiencing symptoms and associated anxiety reactions be central to our understanding of significant posttraumatic morbidity? Should greater emphasis be placed on an assessment of these reactions before making a PTSD diagnosis? Will continuing research efforts eventually find patterns of psychophysiologic reactions that differentiate PTSD from other anxiety disorders? Clearly, the search for PTSD's biological signature, should one exist, remains an ongoing endeavor.

## REFERENCES

American Psychiatric Association. (1980). *Diagnostic and statistical manual of mental disorder* (3rd ed). Washington, DC: Author.

American Psychiatric Association. (1987). *Diagnostic and statistical manual of mental disorders* (3rd ed, revised). Washington, DC: Author.

American Psychiatric Association. (1994). *Diagnostic and statistical manual of mental disorders* (4th ed). Washington, DC: Author.

Andreasen, N. C. (1995). The validation of psychiatric diagnosis: New models and approaches. *American Journal of Psychiatry, 152,* 161–162.

Blanchard, E. B., Kolb, L. C., Pallmeyer, T. P., & Gerardi, R. J. (1982). A psychophysiological post-traumatic stress disorder in Vietnam veterans. *Psychiatric Quarterly, 54,* 220–229.

Bonne, O., Brandes, D., Gilboa, A., Gomori, J. M., Shenton, M. E., Pitman, R. K., et al. (2001). Longitudinal MRI study of hippocampal volume in trauma survivors with PTSD. *American Journal of Psychiatry, 158,* 1248–1251.

Borsboom, D. (2008). Psychometric perspectives on diagnostic systems. *Journal of Clinical Psychology, 64,* 1089–1108.

Bremner, J. D. (1999). Does stress damage the brain? *Biological Psychiatry, 45,* 797–805.

Bremner, J. D., Narayan, M., Anderson, E. R., Staib, L. H., Miller, H. L., & Charney, D. S. (2000). Hippocampal volume reduction in major depression. *American Journal of Psychiatry, 157,* 115–118.

Bremner, J. D., Randall, P., Scott, T. M., Bronen, R. A., Seibyl, J. P., Southwick, S. M., et al. (1995). MRI-based measurement of hippocampal volume in patients with combat-related posttraumatic stress disorder. *American Journal of Psychiatry, 152,* 973–980.

Breslau, N., & Davis, G. C. (1987). Posttraumatic stress disorder: The stressor criterion. *The Journal of Nervous and Mental Disease, 175,* 255–264.

Buhlmann, U., Wilhelm, S., Dockersbach, T., Rauch, S. L., Pitman, R. K., & Orr, S. P. (2007). Physiologic responses to loud tones in individuals with obsessive-compulsive disorder, *Psychosomatic Medicine, 69,* 166–172.

Cook, E. W., Melamed, B. G., Cuthbert, B. N., McNeil, D. W., & Lang, P. J. (1988). Emotional imagery and the differential diagnosis of anxiety. *Journal of Consulting and Clinical Psychology, 56,* 734–740.

Cronbach, L. J., & Meehl, P. E. (1955). Construct validity in psychological tests. *Psychological Bulletin, 52,* 281–302

Demitrack, M., Dale, J., Straus, S., Laue, L., Listwak, S. J., Kruesi, M. J. P., et al. (1991). Evidence of impaired activation of the hypothalamic-pituitary-adrenal axis in patients with chronic fatigue syndrome. *Journal of Clinical Endocrinology and Metabolism, 73,* 1224–1234.

Fennema-Notestine, C., Stein, M. B., Kennedy, C. M., Archibald, S. L., & Jernigan, T. L. (2002). Brain morphometry in female victims of intimate partner violence with and without posttraumatic stress disorder. *Biological Psychiatry, 51,* 1089–1101.

Field, T., Hernandez-Reif, M., Diego, M., Schanberg, S., & Kuhn, C. (2005). Cortisol decreases and serotonin and dopamine increase following massage therapy. *International Journal of Neuroscience, 115,* 1397–1413.

Fries, E., Hesse, J., Hellhammer, J., & Hellhammer, D. H. (2005). A new view of hypocortisolism. *Psychoneuroendocrinology, 30,* 1010–1016.

Frueh, B. C., Grubaugh, A. L., Yeager, D. E., & Magruder, K. M. (2009). Delayed-onset post-traumatic stress disorder among war veterans in primary care clinics. *British Journal of Psychiatry, 194,* 515–520.

Gilbertson, M. W., Shenton, M. E., Ciszewski, A., Kasai, K., Lasko, N. B., Orr, S. P., et al. (2002). Smaller hippocampal volume predicts pathologic vulnerability to psychological trauma. *Nature Neuroscience, 5,* 1242–1247.

Griep, E. N., Boersman, J. W., Lentjes, E. G., Prins, A. P., van der Korst, J. K., & de Kloet, E. R. (1998). Function of the hypothalamic-pituitary-adrenal axis in patients with fibromyalgia and low back pain. *Journal of Rheumatology, 25,* 1374–1381.

Griffin, M. G., & Resick, P. A. (2004). Auditory startle modification following treatment for posttraumatic stress disorder. *Psychophysiology,* (Suppl. 1), S8.

Gurvits, T. V., Shenton, M. E., Hokama, H., Ohta, H., Lasko, N. B., Gilbertson, M. W., et al. (1996). Magnetic resonance imaging study of hippocampal volume in chronic, combat-related posttraumatic stress disorder. *Biological Psychiatry, 40,* 1091–1099.

Institute of Medicine. (2006). *Posttraumatic stress disorder: Diagnosis and assessment.* Washington, DC: National Academies Press.

Kendell, R., & Jablensky, A. (2003). Distinguishing between the validity and utility of psychiatric diagnoses. *American Journal of Psychiatry, 160,* 4–12.

Kendler, K. S. (1980). The nosologic validity of paranoia (simple delusional disorder): A review. *Archives of General Psychiatry, 37,* 699–706.

King, D. W., & King, L. A. (1991). Validity issues in research on Vietnam veteran adjustment. *Psychological Bulletin, 109,* 107–124.

Koenen, K. C., Fu, Q. J., Ertel, K., Lyons, M. J., Elsen, S. A., True, W. R., et al. (2008). Common genetic liability to major depression and posttraumatic stress disorder in men. *Journal of Affective Disorders, 105,* 109–115.

Kuo, J. R., & Linehan, M. M. (2009). Disentangling emotion processes in borderline personality disorder: Physiological and self-reported assessment of biological vulnerability, borderline intensity, and reactivity to emotionally evocative stimuli. *Journal of Abnormal Psychology, 118,* 531–544.

Lang, P. J. (1968). Fear reduction and fear behavior: Problems in treating a construct. *Research in Psychotherapy, 3,* 90–102.

Lang, P. J. (1979). A bio-information theory of emotional imagery. *Psychophysiology, 16,* 495–512.

Liberzon, I., Abelson, J. L., Flagel, S. B., Raz, J., & Young, E. A. (1999). Neuroendocrine and psychophysiologic responses in PTSD: A symptom provocation study. *Neuropsychopharmacology, 21,* 40–50.

Lilienfeld, S. O., & Landfield, K. (2008). Issues in diagnosis: Categorical vs. dimensional. In W. E. Craighead, D. J. Miklowitz, & L. W. Craighead (Eds.), *Psychopathology: History, diagnosis, and empirical foundations* (pp. 1–33). Hoboken, N.J.: John Wiley & Sons.

March, J. S. (1990). The nosology of posttraumatic stress disorder. *Journal of Anxiety Disorders, 4,* 61–82.

McNally, R. J. (2004). Conceptual problems with the DSM-IV criteria for posttraumatic stress disorder. In G. M. Rosen (Ed.), *Posttraumatic stress disorder: Issues and controversies* (pp. 1–14). Chichester: John Wiley & Sons.

Meehl, P. E. (1977). Specific etiology and other forms of strong influence: Some quantitative meanings. *The Journal of Medicine and Philosophy, 2,* 33–53.

Mervaala, E., Fohr, J., Kononen, M., Valkonen-Korhonen, M., Vainio, P., Partanen, K., et al. (2000). Quantitative MRI of the hippocampus and amygdala in severe depression. *Psychological Medicine, 30,* 117–125.

Metzger, L. J., Carson, M. A., Lasko, N. B., Paulus, L. A., Orr, S. P., Pitman, R. K., & Yehuda, R. (2008). Basal and suppressed salivary cortisol in female Vietnam nurse veterans with and without PTSD. *Psychiatry Research, 161*, 330–335.

North, C. S. (2001). The course of post-traumatic stress disorder after the Oklahoma City bombing. *Military Medicine, 166* (Suppl. 2), 51–52.

Oosterlaan, J., Geurts, H. M., Knowl, D. L., & Sergeant, J. A. (2005). Low basal salivary cortisol is associated with teacher-reported symptoms of conduct disorder. *Psychiatry Research, 134*, 1–10.

Orr, S. P., McNally, R. J., Rosen, G. M., & Shalev, A. (2004). Psychophysiologic reactivity: Implications for conceptualizing PTSD. In G.M. Rosen (Ed.), *Posttraumatic stress disorder: Issues and controversies* (pp. 39–61). Chichester: John Wiley & Sons.

Orr, S. P., Metzger, L. J., Lasko, N. B., Macklin, M. L., Shalev, A. Y., Hu, F., et al. (2003). Psychophysiologic responses to sudden, loud tones in monozygotic twins discordant for combat exposure: Relationship to posttraumatic stress disorder. *Archives of General Psychiatry, 60*, 283–288.

Orr, S. P., Metzger, L. J., Miller, M. W., & Kaloupek, D. G. (2004). Psychophysiological assessment of PTSD. In J. P. Wilson & T. M. Keane (Eds.), *Assessing psychological trauma and PTSD: A handbook for practitioners* (2nd ed.; pp. 289–343). New York: Guilford.

Orr, S. P., Pitman, R. K., Lasko, N. B., & Herz, L. R. (1993). Psychophysiologic assessment of posttraumatic stress disorder imagery in World War II and Korean combat veterans. *Journal of Abnormal Psychology, 102*, 152–159.

Pitman, R. K. (2001). Hippocampal dimunition in PTSD: More (or less?) than meets the eye. *Hippocampus, 11*, 73–74.

Pitman, R. K., & Orr, S. P. (1990). Twenty-four hour urinary cortisol and catecholamine excretion in combat-related posttraumatic stress disorder. *Biological Psychiatry, 27*, 245–247.

Pitman, R. K., Orr, S. P., Forgue, D. F., Altman, B., deJong, J. B., & Herz, L. R. (1990). Psychophysiologic responses to combat imagery of Vietnam veterans with post-traumatic stress disorder vs. other anxiety disorders. *Journal of Abnormal Psychology, 99*, 49–54.

Racine, E., Bar-Ilan, O., & Illes, J. (2005). fMRI in the public eye. *Nature Reviews Neuroscience, 6*, 159–164.

Roberts, A. D., Wessely, S., Chalder, T., Papadopoulos, A., & Cleare, A. J. (2004). Salivary cortisol response to awakening in chronic fatigue syndrome. *British Journal of Psychiatry, 184*, 136–141.

Robins, E., & Guze, S. B. (1970). Establishment of diagnostic validity in psychiatric illness: Its application to schizophrenia. *American Journal of Psychiatry*, *126*, 983–987.

Rosen, G. M., & Lilienfeld, S. O. (2008). Posttraumatic stress disorder: An empirical analysis of core assumptions. *Clinical Psychology Review*, *28*, 837–868.

Rosen, G. M., Spitzer, R. L., & McHugh, P. R. (2008). Problems with the PTSD diagnosis and its future in DSM-V. *British Journal of Psychiatry*, *192*, 394.

Selye, H. (1946). The general adaptation syndrome and the diseases of adaptation. *Journal of Clinical Endocrinology*, *6*, 117–230.

Shalev, A. Y., Peri, T., Brandes, D., Freedman, S., Orr, S. P., & Pitman, R. K. (2000). Auditory startle responses in trauma survivors with PTSD: A prospective study. *American Journal of Psychiatry*, *157*, 255–261.

Shoal, G. D., Giancola, P. R., & Kirillova, G. P. (2003). Salivary cortisol, personality, and aggressive behavior in adolescent boys: A 5-year longitudinal study. *Journal of the American Academy for Child and Adolescent Psychiatry*, *42*, 1101–1107.

Stein, M. B., Koverola, C., Hanna, C., Torchia, M. G., & McClarty, B. (1997). Hippocampal volume in women victimized by childhood sexual abuse. *Psychological Medicine*, *27*, 951–959.

Waldman, I. D., Lilienfeld, S. O., & Lahey, B. B. (1995). Toward construct validity in the childhood disruptive behavior disorders: Classification and diagnosis in DSM-IV and beyond. In T.H. Ollendick & R.J. Prinz (Eds.), *Advances in clinical child psychology* (Vol. 17). New York: Plenum.

Weerts, T. C., & Lang, P. J. (1978). Psychophysiology of fear imagery: Differences between focal phobia and social performance anxiety. *Journal of Consulting and Clinical Psychology*, *46*, 1157–1159.

Widiger, T. A., Hurt, S. W., Frances, A, Clarkin, J. F., & Gilmore, M. (1984). Diagnostic efficiency and DSM-III. *Archives of General Psychiatry*, *41*, 1005–1012.

Yehuda, R., & McFarlane, A. C. (1995). Conflict between current knowledge about posttraumatic stress disorder and its original conceptual basis. *American Journal of Psychiatry*, *152*, 1705–1713.

Yehuda, R., Southwick, S. M., Nussbaum, G., Giller, E. L., & Mason, J. W. (1990). Low urinary cortisol excretion in PTSD. *Journal of Nervous and Mental Disease*, *178*, 366–369.

Young, A. (2004). How narratives work in psychiatric science: An example from the biological psychiatry of PTSD. In B. Hurwitz, T. Greenhalgh, &

V. Skultans (Eds.), *Narrative research in health and illness* (pp. 382–396). Oxford: Blackwell.

Young, E. A., & Breslau, N. (2004). Cortisol and catecholamines in posttraumatic stress disorder: An epidemiologic community study. *Archives of General Psychiatry, 61*, 394–401.

Young, E. A., Tolman, R., Witkowski, K., & Kaplan, G. (2004). Salivary cortisol and posttraumatic stress disorder in a low-income community sample of women. *Biological Psychiatry, 55*, 621–626.

Zander, J. R., & McNally, R. J. (1988). Bio-informational processing in agoraphobia. *Behaviour Research and Therapy, 26*, 421–429.

Zhang, L., Li, H., Benedek, D., Li, X., & Ursano, R. (2009). A strategy for the development of biomarker tests for PTSD. *Medical Hypotheses, 73*, 404–409.

# Clinical Practice

# 6

# Assessing Trauma Exposure and Posttraumatic Morbidity

Jon D. Elhai
Julian D. Ford
James A. Naifeh

This chapter is intended as a resource for the mental health clinician who assesses clients for a history of psychological trauma exposure, posttraumatic stress disorder (PTSD), and associated psychopathology. We have aimed this chapter toward both clinicians and clinical trainees who are relatively unfamiliar with the technical aspects of trauma/PTSD assessment (regardless of level of general clinical experience), or who are experienced but interested in an update on key assessment issues and resources. We will cover three topics in this chapter: (a) assessing trauma exposure history, (b) assessing PTSD symptoms to establish a PTSD diagnosis, and (c) assessing other mental health problems associated with trauma exposure. For each area, we will consider important issues and controversies in assessment, discuss general assessment and diagnostic strategies, and sample available instruments. At the end of the chapter, we include a checklist to assist in assessing each of these areas.

## CASE STUDY INTRODUCTION

Mr. Gavin is a 45-year-old, Caucasian man who presented for treatment to an independent group mental health practice in his community of Bloomington, Indiana. He married his high school sweetheart after they graduated college in Illinois, and has been happily married since. Mr. Gavin reported some history of familial mental health problems; his biological sister and mother had been treated on an outpatient basis for depression. The client's only contact with mental health providers was as a college student, when he was treated during his freshman year by a campus counselor for adjustment problems related to his move to college. He denied any history of serious medical problems or previous head injuries.

Mr. Gavin had worked as a bank manager for 10 years. Two months prior to his psychological assessment, the bank was robbed while Mr. Gavin was on duty. Specifically, a noticeably agitated man walked into the bank with a gun, and instructed the teller to quickly hand over $50,000. Mr. Gavin, in attempting to manage the situation, inadvertently caused the man to discharge his gun. A customer was accidentally shot and later died from her wounds. Upon shooting the customer, the armed man quickly fled the scene and was never apprehended. Mr. Gavin immediately spent two weeks on paid administrative leave, instructed to do so by the bank's corporate headquarters. He subsequently returned to work after four weeks. At the time of the assessment, Mr. Gavin reported being depressed, having serious difficulty sleeping and concentrating, and drinking 10–12 beers daily to cope. Because his symptoms were not getting better, Mr. Gavin considered filing for worker's compensation. He also set up an appointment with a clinical psychologist, known locally to have expertise in treating posttraumatic problems.

In evaluating Mr. Gavin during the initial appointment, several questions had to be considered by the mental health professional. How should Mr. Gavin be assessed for trauma exposure? Given the sensitivity of this issue and referral question, how should a mental health professional broach the subject of assessment with him? Which instrument(s) should be administered to assess for PTSD? What other mental health problems should be assessed? Because of possible litigation from a worker's compensation case, should the case be treated differently than in standard clinical practice?

Later in this chapter, we will return to our case study as a means of demonstrating the methods and procedures in assessing and diagnosing Mr. Gavin.

# ASSESSING HISTORY OF EXPOSURE TO TRAUMATIC STRESSORS

Several issues related to the assessment of trauma history deserve consideration. These include the ethics of inquiring about traumatic experiences, the wording of trauma exposure questions, assessing the characteristics of traumatic events that have particular clinical implications, the nature of memory of traumatic events, and under- and over-reporting trauma exposure.

It is highly likely in clinical practice that a significant proportion of one's caseload will include individuals who have been exposed to psychological trauma and struggle with associated mental health problems. In fact, between 50 to 60% of the general adult population has reported at least one incident of psychological trauma exposure (Kessler, Sonnega, Bromet, Hughes, & Nelson, 1995), with similar estimates in children and adolescents (Copeland, Keeler, Angold, & Costello, 2007). Furthermore, exposure to traumatic events in childhood (e.g., Felitti et al., 1998) or in adulthood (e.g., Leverich et al., 2002) is associated with an increased risk of a range of serious mental and physical health problems, including but not limited to PTSD. In the seriously mentally ill, rates of trauma exposure are even higher. Yet, trauma histories are often not routinely assessed in practice (Cusack, Frueh, & Brady, 2004).

Clinicians will want to keep in mind that most trauma-exposed individuals do not develop PTSD, and among those who do, about half remit over time (e.g., Dohrenwend et al., 2006). In fact, many children and adults who experience traumatic stressors do not develop any clinically significant emotional problems. This has led some professionals to question whether it is appropriate to routinely screen for trauma exposure, since spontaneously asking about such experiences might cause clients significant distress. While this concern has intuitive appeal, research demonstrates that asking about potentially traumatic experiences is not distressing for most respondents. Even those who feel distressed do not regret responding to such questions. In fact, many respondents report that they benefited from an opportunity to disclose traumatic experiences to a concerned professional (Newman & Kaloupek, 2004).

Despite the above findings, it is important to be cautious when asking clients to disclose traumatic experiences. Laypersons (and many professionals) often incorrectly assume that trauma history assessment involves a detailed "dredging up" of memories of potentially traumatic experiences. So it is important to clearly state that the client should only disclose what she or he feels ready and able to disclose. One possible exception to this guideline is when months elapse in treatment while avoiding discussion of trauma exposure, with the proverbial "elephant in the room." In such cases, the clinician sometimes must nudge the patient to discuss difficult memories.

Questions should be as free from colloquial and academic terms as possible, particularly terms that may be both anxiety-provoking and subject to many different interpretations. Asking if a client has ever been "abused" or witnessed "domestic violence" may be problematic for a couple of reasons: (a) it does not assist the client in describing *their actual experience*, and (b) the emotionally charged nature of these terms may lead to under- or over-reporting. In fact, one author (JDE) treated a client who believed that when her dating partner forced her into sexual intercourse, this would not be considered "rape"; she mistakenly believed that the term "rape" only applied when the perpetrator was a stranger. This example is just one of many myths people have about traumatic events. In order to avoid some of these pitfalls, it is recommended that the clinician use standardized, behaviorally specific questions that briefly and matter-of-factly describe features of stressful experiences that research suggests are likely to elicit traumatic stress reactions. For example, rather than asking "Were you physically abused as a child," it is better to ask a question such as "When you were less than 18 years old, did anyone who was in charge of you (e.g., babysitter, relative, etc.) ever hit, slap, shove, kick, burn, or punch you in a way that left a mark/bruise or led you to miss school or go to the doctor?" Instruments that provide these types of trauma history questions will be described later in this chapter.

It also is important to therapeutically guide clients when they disclose potentially traumatic experiences so that they do not come away from the assessment feeling emotionally overwhelmed or stigmatized by their disclosure. The first step in this process is to clearly explain to each client why trauma history is being assessed. This explanation should communicate the importance of obtaining a complete psycho-social history, and normalize the various intra- and interpersonal dif-ficulties the client may be experiencing as a consequence of trauma exposure. If these difficulties are explained as "normal reactions to severe threats to your or someone else's life or safety," it helps clients recognize that even problematic symptoms are an understandable (and in many ways resilient) adaptation to severe threat. The other criti-cal step is to inform the client that it is best to approach disclosure of highly stressful experiences gradually, and only as the client feels ready. Specifically, the client should feel free to "pass" on disclosing any event(s) or aspects of events that she or he prefers not to think about or describe at the time of assessment. This provides the client with a mechanism for feeling in control of what is remembered and dis-closed (Harvey, 1996), rather than feeling in any way coerced or pres-sured. After all, perceived loss of control is a cardinal negative feature of traumatic stressors and should always be minimized during clinical encounters. In some cases, clients may reflexively describe traumatic experiences in great detail, even when cautioned to disclose selectively and gradually. It usually is helpful in such cases to empathically reflect the seriousness and distressing nature of the client's experience(s), while simultaneously reassuring the client that all of the specifics can and will be dealt with in treatment.

Often the purpose of inquiring about trauma exposure is to estab-lish or rule out a diagnosis of PTSD. PTSD's Criterion A1 in *DSM-IV* (American Psychiatric Association, 2000) requires that the trauma involved actual or threatened death or serious injury, or the threat to one's bodily integrity. Criterion A2 requires that the individual ini-tially responded to the trauma with intense fear, helplessness, or horror. Without a careful review of experiences that may meet these criteria, a diagnosis of PTSD may either be incorrectly given (if no specific trau-matic experiences can be documented) or inaccurately assumed to not be present. Because trauma exposure has been linked to the risk or severity of a range of mental disorders other than PTSD, even if PTSD is appro-priately ruled out, knowledge of a client's trauma history may inform the treatment of other diagnostic conditions.

In addition to the formal criteria for establishing whether an event meets DSM-IV PTSD criteria for a traumatic stressor, follow-up questions about traumatic event-related characteristics are important to query. Trauma characteristics may include variables such as: (a) severity and frequency with which traumatic stressors occurred, (b) client's initial emotional, cognitive, and biological reactions, (c) age and developmental period in which the stressor occurred, (d) other person(s) directly or indirectly involved during and after the event(s), and (e) social support and/or social pressures placed upon the client during and after the event(s). Many of these risk and protective factors are addressed in several of the trauma history instruments discussed below.

When assessing these issues it is important to realize that memory is quite fallible. Research has demonstrated that people have difficulty accurately reporting the details of their trauma history (Frueh, Elhai, & Kaloupek, 2004), and they often are inconsistent across different occasions when queried (e.g., Wessely et al., 2003).

An area of particular concern with regard to fallible memory is the matter of repressed memories of child sexual abuse when these are raised by adult patients. We acknowledge that this issue is controversial. It is difficult to determine clinically if any memory, including a memory of traumatic events, was "repressed" as opposed to having not been encoded in long-term memory or not recalled due to ordinary forgetting. It also is difficult to determine if a memory has been "recovered," as opposed to being constructed to fulfill a conscious or non-conscious psychological motivation (McNally, 2003). Clinicians are advised to not encourage patients to search for "repressed" memories, and to not directly or indirectly validate a "newly recovered" memory as definitely true or false; they should also not invalidate claims of "recovered" memories outright. Therefore, especially in a high-stakes clinical situation, such as when legal involvement is ongoing or imminent, corroboration of trauma exposure using medical, educational, military, police department, or other records is necessary.

On a related note, an important issue for the clinician to consider is whether there are any factors that may motivate a client to under- or over-report trauma exposure. Reasons to under-report trauma include wanting to preserve one's family (when the alleged perpetrator lives with, and even financially supports, the victim), fear of retribution by the perpetrator, fear of being stigmatized or blamed as a trauma victim, lack of encouragement to disclose and past negative experiences from disclosing trauma, and fear of emotional consequences (Acierno, Kilpatrick, & Resnick, 1999). Reasons to over-report trauma include attempts at financial compensation from litigation or disability application (Guriel & Fremouw, 2003), seeking of attention, or other motivations for taking on the patient role (Lacoursiere, 1993; Rosen & Taylor, 2007). In Veterans Affairs Medical Centers, disability compensation for PTSD can be associated with large monetary incentives when prior combat exposure is linked to current PTSD (Frueh, Grubaugh, Elhai, & Buckley, 2007).

In private practice contexts, assuming the patient is not involved in trauma-related litigation, a clinician can usually take the patient's self-report of trauma at face value. On the other hand, in cases where the patient has a large incentive to report being involved in a trauma (e.g., a veteran who claims combat-related PTSD, mitigation in a criminal case, personal injury litigation), the clinician should remain skeptical (but not necessarily suspicious) of the patient's report and seek to review objective documentation. In noting these concerns we must provide the caveat that over-reporting trauma exposure does not necessarily mean the client did not experience a trauma. Instead, an individual may be exaggerating or over-reporting a bona fide experience as an expression of severe distress.

## Strategies for Trauma History Assessment

We recommend the following major steps when inquiring about a client's history of exposure to potentially traumatic events. First, since asking about trauma exposure involves sensitive questions, it is wise to begin the query with a preface statement. This statement can orient the respondent to the trauma query and convey the clinician's knowledge that most people have experienced traumatic stressors at some point. It also is important to communicate that stress reactions following such exposure are not uncommon, may occur immediately or after a delay, and reflect a healthy self-protective attempt to survive and be prepared for future threats. Clients also benefit from reassurance that it is only when stress reactions interfere with a person's well-being or functioning that treatment is needed. Lastly, it can be explained that effective treatments require that the clinician knows enough about the client's past traumatic experiences to teach the client ways to cope with specific stress reactions that have become problematic. This overview demonstrates that the clinician is empathetic, while also communicating how an understanding of trauma history can benefit the patient (Acierno, Kilpatrick, & Resnick, 1999).

Second, the clinician should ideally use a psychometrically sound, standardized interview or self-report instrument that contains a list of behaviorally specific questions regarding types of trauma, querying whether the respondent has experienced these events. Follow-up probe questions should ideally be used judiciously after each trauma question to gain a comprehensive picture of relevant trauma characteristics. These follow-up probes will help to rule in/out a PTSD diagnosis (i.e., DSM-IV Criterion A1 and A2), as well as identify trauma-related reactions and adaptations that should be addressed in treatment. Similar to other components in a structured mental health assessment (e.g., family, health care, or educational history), probing should not be open-ended, but instead should be done with the fewest questions necessary to efficiently target specific risk or protective factors. In high-stakes clinical or forensic contexts, objective documentation of trauma exposure should be sought.

Third, if the client endorses more than one type of traumatic stressor, which in clinical mental health samples is more common than not, she or he should be asked to nominate a particular "index" event (e.g., the event that currently causes the most distress) in relation to which PTSD symptoms will subsequently be assessed. We will discuss this issue in greater detail later in this chapter.

## Instruments

Several instruments are available to assess trauma history. Each measure has its own advantages and disadvantages. We will not review all of these measures, but will focus on measures that appear to be relatively widely used and are psychometrically sound. When mentioning interviews, we provide information on administration time, since longer times can burden a clinician's resources. The interested reader should refer to several other sources for more specific details on measures for adults (Briere, 2004; Frueh, Elhai, & Kaloupek, 2004) and children (Nader, 2008; Ohan, Myers, & Collett, 2002). Table 6.2, provided at the end of this chapter, lists contact information for obtaining these measures.

*Adults:* For a brief, simple self-report checklist of traumatic events, the 17-item Life Events Checklist (LEC, Gray, Litz, Wang, & Lombardo, 2004) can serve well, although its items have very little behavioral specificity and contain no follow-up probes. Two slightly longer self-report measures with better behavioral specificity for assessing traumatic event characteristics include the Stressful Life Events Screening Questionnaire (SLESQ, Goodman, Corcoran, Turner, Yuan, & Green, 1998), which queries 12 specific traumatic events, and the Trauma History Questionnaire (THQ, e.g., Mueser et al., 2001), which inquires about 24 traumatic events.

Several more comprehensive self-report instruments of trauma exposure are available, each assessing trauma-related characteristics using follow-up probes. Adapted from the Traumatic Event Screening Instrument for children (TESI), the Traumatic Events Screening Inventory for Adults (TESI-A, Ford & Fournier, 2007) inquires about 18 discrete types of traumatic events (Ford & Fournier, 2007). The Traumatic Life Events Questionnaire (TLEQ, Kubany et al., 2000) queries exposure to 23 traumatic events, and the Trauma Assessment for Adults (TAA; with an interview version available as well) has excellent behavioral specificity and newly published psychometric analyses (Gray, Elhai, Owen, & Monroe, 2009). Finally, the Childhood Trauma Questionnaire (e.g., Scher, Stein, Asmundson, McCreary, & Forde, 2001) is a 28-item self-report scale that is especially useful for assessing neglect and abuse histories reported by adults.

*Children:* Fewer child measures that query trauma exposure are available (though some child PTSD interviews also query trauma exposure, as discussed below). The TESI can be administered directly to a child via interview (TESI-C) or self-report (TESI-C/SR), or to the child's parent via interview (TESI-PRR) (e.g., Ford, Hartman, Hawke, & Chapman, 2008). Additionally, the Dimensions of Stressful Events Rating Scale is a 50-item interview measure of trauma exposure that includes follow-up questions and takes about 15 to 30 minutes to administer (Fletcher, 1996). Finally, in addition to being used with adults, the Childhood Trauma Questionnaire can be used with adolescents who are older than age 12.

## Discussion

We prefer comprehensive trauma exposure instruments such as the TLEQ, TESI, and TAA because of their behavioral specificity, broad coverage of traumatic events, and the detail they gather via follow-up questions. Among these instruments, the TLEQ stands out because it has been subjected to the most careful psychometric scrutiny. Nonetheless, we have used shorter measures such as the SLESQ in mental health clinics and primary care settings where longer measures were not logistically feasible. While some of these measures do not inquire about PTSD's criterion A2, they can be supplemented with appropriate questions. Finally, it should be emphasized that results from trauma history measures always should be taken with a grain of salt in the absence of objective documentation that trauma exposure occurred.

## ASSESSING PTSD'S SYMPTOM CRITERIA

Several issues deserve discussion regarding the assessment of the 17 symptom criteria that define PTSD (See Chapter 1, Table 1.2.). These include linking PTSD symptoms to a particular traumatic event, ensuring that a sufficient amount of time has elapsed before assigning a PTSD diagnosis, selecting PTSD symptom queries or questions, identifying a PTSD symptom as clinically significant, considering PTSD's symptom structure, considering special populations, and assessing the client's response style.

### Linking Symptoms to a Traumatic Event

Theoretically, PTSD symptoms can be assessed by referencing a specific traumatic event. However, since most trauma survivors report experiencing more than one type of trauma (Kessler et al., 1995), PTSD symptoms can alternatively be assessed in relation to one's trauma history in general, without reference to a specific event. Additionally, symptoms can be assessed more globally by inquiring about symptoms in relation to a particular time in one's life (during which trauma had occurred intermittently). Finally, some investigators have queried PTSD symptoms without referencing any particular trauma or time-frame.

Let us consider just one symptom example—PTSD's symptom Criterion C5: feeling detached from other people. In this instance, a clinician could ask if the respondent felt detached from people: (a) as a direct result of a specific traumatic event, (b) as a consequence of one's traumatic events in general (when more than one trauma is reported), (c) as a consequence of a period in life (e.g., military experience), or (d) in general (without referencing any traumatic or lifetime experience).

There are two important reasons to take the first approach and link PTSD symptom queries to a single, index trauma (Long & Elhai, 2009). First, when global/unreferenced symptom queries are conducted, a respondent may endorse a PTSD symptom that arose from causes other than trauma. For example, PTSD's symptom C3 (difficulty remembering aspects of the trauma) can be caused by normal forgetting or by age-related cognitive impairment; symptom D1 (sleep difficulty) can be caused by a host of alternative issues (e.g., medical problems, change in work schedule, other stressors); symptom D3 (difficulty concentrating) can be attributed to other disorders (e.g., depression, insomnia), and so on. In fact, evidence suggests that when asking individuals to rate PTSD symptoms from events that do not satisfy PTSD's Criterion A1, relatively high levels of PTSD severity can result (Long et al., 2008)—suggesting that PTSD symptoms can indeed be attributed to other causes than trauma. Second, some of PTSD's symptoms overlap with other mood and anxiety disorders (Elhai, Grubaugh, Kashdan, & Frueh, 2008; Rosen, Spitzer, & McHugh, 2008). Consequently, the primary means of distinguishing PTSD from other disorders is based on whether the symptoms are linked to a specific trauma. By definition, for a diagnosis of PTSD to be made, all symptoms must be satisfied in reference to at least one single trauma; it is not permissible to satisfy one symptom criterion from one trauma, and another criterion from another trauma (American Psychiatric Association, 2000).

Trying to link PTSD symptoms to an index trauma does not come without costs. In many cases, trauma survivors may not adequately sequester their PTSD symptom ratings as resulting from one trauma versus another. Clearly, a nightmare about a rape can be sequestered from a nightmare about a natural disaster; but some of PTSD's symptoms are less clear. For example, can we expect an individual who has been in two motor vehicle accidents to accurately state which one is responsible for their difficulty concentrating or their irritability? In this type of case, the most distressing instance might be nominated for PTSD symptom query, but this would not necessarily resolve the matter.

## Time Since the Trauma

It is important to be mindful of the time that has elapsed between the occurrence of an index trauma and the PTSD evaluation. A DSM-IV PTSD diagnosis requires that symptoms last for more than one month. Therefore, the clinician is advised not to diagnose a client with PTSD if the evaluation happens to take place less than one month between the trauma's occurrence and the evaluation date. In such a case (e.g., a recent traumatic loss; ongoing domestic, community, or military violence), acute stress disorder (ASD) rather than PTSD can be considered. Per the DSM-IV, ASD involves similar symptoms to PTSD, with the addition of a set of dissociative symptoms (Bryant & Harvey, 2000).

A related issue involves PTSD symptoms that are reported with delayed onset. The concept of delayed onset is provided as a DSM-IV PTSD diagnostic specifier to indicate that symptoms did not develop until months or years after a traumatic event. Research has found that presentations of delayed PTSD are uncommon, if not nonexistent, unless the person previously experienced acute stress or posttraumatic stress symptoms (Andrews, Brewin, Philpott, & Stewart, 2007; Frueh, Grubaugh, Yeager, & Magruder, 2009). Thus when meeting with a patient who presents with delayed onset PTSD, the possibility that some of his or her PTSD symptoms actually appeared earlier needs to be ruled out.

## Assessing Symptoms

The clinician is cautioned to take DSM-IV's structure of PTSD symptoms (i.e., re-experiencing, avoidance/numbing, and arousal) with a grain of salt. Studies examining how well PTSD symptoms are intercorrelated (or hang together) demonstrate that this three-factor model does not adequately represent PTSD's latent structure. Instead, two competing models have emerged as best fitting PTSD's structure: (a) a four-factor model similar to the DSM-IV PTSD model, but separating PTSD's effortful avoidance and emotional numbing symptoms; and (b) a four-factor model of re-experiencing, avoidance, dysphoria and hyperarousal. These models are reviewed by Asmundson, Stapleton, and Taylor (2004). What this means clinically is that effortful avoidance and emotional numbing symptoms should not be considered one and the same. Further, some symptoms like difficulties concentrating and sleeping may be considered as general symptoms of distress rather than specific posttraumatic sequelae.

An assessment of PTSD's symptom clusters can be reliably and validly conducted by using a standardized list of queries. Several of these instruments are discussed later in this chapter. It is important to emphasize that only an interviewer-administered instrument should be used in firmly deciding whether a client has PTSD, since interviews allow for clinical judgment. Therefore, a self-report instrument (e.g., symptom checklist) should not be the sole basis for determining a PTSD diagnosis. Checklists often do not assess functional impairment, and consequently, they can result in false positives and overestimations of PTSD's prevalence (Ruggiero, Del Ben, Scotti, & Rabalais, 2003). Despite their limitations, self-report measures can be used to track a patient's symptom course during treatment.

Clinicians should consider not only whether PTSD symptoms are present, but also the severity of reported problems. Using a "yes"/"no" rating format makes it impossible to track gradations of symptom improvement over the course of treatment. Additionally, without information on the severity of a symptom, it cannot be determined if a reaction should be considered "clinically significant." There is no universal agreement on which various levels of symptom severity meet criteria for being a "significant symptom," and DSM-IV provides no assistance in arriving at such a determination. Thus clinical judgment often is required.

Gauging PTSD symptom severity can be done primarily in two ways. Symptoms can be assessed for how frequently (e.g., nightmares occurring once per month vs. once per week) and/or how intensely they occur (e.g., nightmares keeping the client awake for one hour vs. three hours after). The majority of PTSD assessment measures query symptoms either based on frequency *or* intensity, although a few measures assess both dimensions. As it turns out, emerging research suggests the two severity dimensions are so highly intercorrelated that they are essentially redundant (Elhai et al., 2006). On the other hand, from a clinical standpoint, the impact on a client's well-being and functioning can be altered by different combinations of frequency and intensity. Compare, for example, a flashback that occurs once every few months, but is so intense the client requires acute psychiatric hospitalization, with a series of moderately disabling flashbacks that occur several times a week. The experienced clinician will appreciate that treatment for these two "comparably severe" PTSD symptoms is likely be quite different (e.g., crisis prevention and emotion regulation as a focus in the first case, versus stress inoculation and exposure therapy in the latter case). Therefore, it is important to carefully define symptom "severity" in each PTSD case with specific reference to frequency and intensity, rather than simply labeling symptoms as more or less severe.

## Special Populations

Clinicians should always be sensitive to cultural differences when assessing PTSD, as symptoms can have differing expression in non-Western cultures. At the same time, differences should not be created when they do not exist. For example, with regard to racial differences between Caucasian and African Americans, we have found little support for racial differences in the expression of PTSD, both among civilian (Davis et al., 2006) and military trauma samples (Frueh, Elhai, Monnier, Hamner, & Knapp, 2004; Grubaugh et al., 2006).

Working with the seriously mentally ill who report trauma exposure and subsequent PTSD deserves special consideration as well. PTSD is often given short shrift among patients identified as suffering from serious mental illness such as psychosis or bipolar disorder (Cusack et al., 2004). However, the presence of serious mental illness does not necessarily mean that the patient's posttraumatic emotional difficulties pale in comparison to their psychosis or mania; PTSD may be just as or more burdensome than other serious mental disorders. And in fact interventions can be used and are efficacious for treating such patients' PTSD (Frueh, Grubaugh, Cusack, Kimble, Elhai, & Knapp, 2009).

## Assessing Response Style

PTSD symptoms can be minimized or under-reported for reasons similar to why any psychopathology may be minimized (e.g., fear of losing child custody, application for a job, military rank demotion). However, over-reporting PTSD is probably more likely in a clinical or forensic setting. Possible reasons for over-reporting PTSD include seeking mental health treatment, financial compensation for a work-related traumatic injury or disability application, acquittal or mitigation from a criminal trial, or discharge from the military (Guriel & Fremouw, 2003; Rosen & Taylor, 2007). Thus, the setting in which the PTSD evaluation is conducted should be taken into context. In settings such as jails, prisons, and VA medical centers where there is a clear incentive to appear symptomatic with PTSD, the clinician should be skeptical of PTSD reports and use proper methods to rule out malingering (Guriel & Fremouw, 2003; Resnick, West, & Payne, 2008; Rosen, 2004).

## Strategies

We have two recommendations to make for the clinician who assesses PTSD symptoms. First, assuming that the clinician elicited the client's most currently distressing past traumatic experience (or the presenting trauma for specific forensic or clinical purposes), the client should be instructed to rate all PTSD symptoms with reference to that traumatic stressor. When approaching this phase of the assessment, it is not uncommon for clients to select a technically sub-traumatic stressor (e.g., a difficult divorce; work or financial crises; or other incident not meeting Criterion A) as their most distressing past experience. While non-Criterion A experiences may be extremely stressful and relevant to the overall clinical management of a patient, it is necessary for purposes of a PTSD diagnosis that reference is made to an event or experience that fulfills the DSM's objective and subjective stressor criteria (A1 and A2). A different consideration is when a client has experienced multiple or prolonged traumatic stressors that all cause significant levels of distress. In such cases, it is best to encourage the client to prioritize one event or series of events (e.g., a series of incest or physical abuse events over a period of months or years) as the most currently distressing. Some clients will have difficulty making this determination because different symptoms may be endorsed in reference to different traumatic stressors (e.g., triggered reminders of a severe accident along with nightmares of being physically assaulted and avoidance of reminders of a sexual assault).

Our second recommendation is that the clinician should use a psychometrically sound PTSD self-report or interviewer-administered instrument. Ideally, this measure should be a continuously scaled or dimensional instrument (rather than including binary items that simply inquire whether the symptom is or is not present) that assesses the frequency and/or intensity of symptoms. When conducting diagnostic evaluations, an interviewer-administered instrument is always preferred over written self-report formats. When the clinician has reason to suspect an altered response set (i.e., under- or over-reporting), additional measures should be administered to rule out malingering or defensiveness.

## Instruments

Numerous instruments are available to assess PTSD symptoms in adults and children/adolescents, each with unique advantages and disadvantages. As with our coverage of trauma exposure instruments, we will focus on measures that appear to be relatively widely used and psychometrically sound. The interested reader should refer to several other sources for more specific details on adult (Briere, 2004; Frueh, Elhai, & Kaloupek, 2004; Norris & Hamblen, 2004) and child (Nader, 2008; Ohan et al., 2002) measures. Table 6.2 at the end of our chapter provides contact information.

*Adults:* With regard to adults, several self-report PTSD instruments are available that mirror DSM-IV's PTSD symptoms. With only 17 symptoms to assess, these measures probably do not overly burden the respondent. Among these measures is the PTSD Checklist (PCL, e.g., Ruggiero et al., 2003), a widely used measure of PTSD symptom intensity in military and civilian trauma samples (Elhai, Gray, Kashdan, & Franklin, 2005). A similar instrument is the PTSD Symptom Scale (PSS), which measures symptom frequency, examined primarily in civilian trauma samples (Foa & Tolin, 2000). The PSS was subsequently modified to create two alternative instruments: (a) a brief screen of trauma exposure and assessment of PTSD's duration and functional impairment criteria were added to create the Posttraumatic Diagnostic Scale (PDS, e.g., Griffin, Uhlmansiek, Resick, & Mechanic, 2005); and (b) queries of symptom intensity were added to create the Modified PTSD Symptom Scale (e.g., Falsetti, Resnick, Resick, & Kilpatrick, 1993, June). Additionally, there are self-report measures that do not map onto DSM-IV's PTSD symptom criteria, but rather were developed empirically or before DSM-IV's publication. Some widely used examples include the Impact of Event Scale-Revised, and the 100-item Trauma Symptom Inventory (Briere, 2004; Frueh, Elhai, & Kaloupek, 2004; Norris & Hamblen, 2004).

When the goal of assessment is to screen for potential PTSD, self-report measures such as the PCL and PSS may be useful, but even briefer instruments have been developed and validated. Measures such as the four-item Startle, Physiological Arousal, Anger, and Numbness (SPAN) and 10-item Trauma Screening Questionnaire are discussed in Brewin (2005). Additionally, four- to six-item PTSD screens for use in primary care clinics have proven useful (Kimerling, Trafton, & Ngyuen, 2006; Lang & Stein, 2005).

Finally, several interview-based PTSD measures are available. The PSS, already discussed, can be used as an interviewer-administered measure. It takes approximately 20 to 30 minutes to administer and assess PTSD symptoms, without taking into account duration or functional impairment as required for a diagnosis. The Structured Interview for PTSD allows assessment of either item frequency or intensity, and uses fairly precise behavioral anchors for rating symptoms, resulting in improved reliability across raters, and about 20 to 30 minutes of administration time (Davidson, Kudler, & Smith, 1997). The Clinician-Administered PTSD Scale (CAPS) is the most comprehensive and widely used PTSD interview (Elhai et al., 2005). It is packaged with the Life Events Checklist to assess trauma exposure, and it is the only PTSD interview that assesses both item frequency *and* intensity. It has precise behavioral anchors for unambiguous rating and has been scrutinized across various trauma-exposed samples (Weathers, Keane, & Davidson, 2001). Unfortunately, the CAPS is lengthy to administer, taking 40 to

60 minutes. Other PTSD interviews only assess the presence or absence of symptoms, not symptom severity (e.g., PTSD modules of the Structured Clinical Interview for DSM-IV Axis I Disorders, Composite International Diagnostic Interview).

*Children:* Several PTSD self-report measures are available, generally for children aged 6 or 7 and older. The Child PTSD Symptom Scale is a child version of the PDS, and maps well onto DSM-IV's PTSD criteria (Foa, Johnson, Feeny, & Treadwell, 2001). Other child PTSD self-report measures do not really follow DSM's criteria. These measures inquire about only some symptoms, or they query all PTSD symptoms along with others that are only tangentially related to PTSD. Two notable measures fairly widely used are the Trauma Symptom Checklist for Children (TSCC) and the Trauma Symptom Checklist for Young Children (TSCYC). The TSCC is a 54-item scale developed for 8- to 16-year-olds (e.g., Sadowski & Friedrich, 2000). The TSCYC is a 90-item scale developed for 3- to 12-year-olds (Briere, 2005).

Standardized or "structured" interviews also are available for child PTSD assessment, again generally for ages 6 or 7 and older. The Clinician-Administered PTSD Scale for Children and Adolescents (CAPS-CA) is patterned after the adult CAPS. It is packaged with the Life Events Checklist to assess trauma exposure and assess PTSD item frequency and intensity, offering the same unique features as the adult version of the CAPS, and taking between 30 to 120 minutes to administer. The Children's PTSD Inventory takes 15 to 20 minutes of administration time. It includes a preface about typical traumatic events, and assesses PTSD symptoms, albeit using binary items (e.g., Saigh et al., 2000). Other notable possibilities include PTSD modules of the Diagnostic Interview for Children and Adolescents-Revised (DICA-R), Diagnostic Interview Schedule for Children (DISC) and others (Ohan et al., 2002).

## Discussion

To minimize time constraints in busy clinical practices, we are generally supportive of the following options: (a) use of a broad-based diagnostic interview to assess for a range of psychopathology, with inclusion of a PTSD module, followed by an assessment of PTSD severity using a shorter measure such as the PCL or PSS if a client screens positive for PTSD, or (b) in a setting that likely has a large proportion of PTSD-diagnosed individuals (e.g., rape shelter, VA combat PTSD clinic), routinely administering a relatively short PTSD interview such as the PSS. In other settings where it is not permissible or feasible to administer a measure longer than a few items (e.g., a medical clinic, mass disaster shelter), use of a four-to-six item PTSD assessment instrument is still better than none at all. Finally, we should note that many PTSD measures that include validity scales (e.g., TSI) should be viewed with caution, in that these validity scales are not adequately validated and do not appear to robustly discriminate between malingered and genuine PTSD (e.g., Elhai et al., 2005; Rosen et al., 2006).

## ASSESSING COMORBIDITY

PTSD is highly comorbid with other mental disorders. This fact was demonstrated by Kessler and colleagues (1995) who used data from the National Comorbidity Survey, a nationally representative sample of U.S. respondents, to estimate PTSD's lifetime comorbidity rates. They found that 44% of women and 59% of men diagnosed with PTSD also met criteria for at least three additional mental disorders, with the highest comorbidity rates found for major depression and dysthymic disorder; specific and social phobia; agoraphobia; and substance use. Based on these findings, it is probably wise to assess trauma survivors for mental disorders other than PTSD.

A potentially problematic issue in assessing issues of comorbidity is that several of PTSD's symptom criteria are also found in criteria for other anxiety and mood disorders (Rosen et al., 2008). The following scenario demonstrates the issue's complexity. A client with a history of trauma exposure meets full diagnostic criteria for major depressive disorder (MDD; with all symptoms met), and she meets the six required PTSD symptoms for a PTSD diagnosis. However, one of these PTSD symptoms is anhedonia, a symptom of major depressive disorder. That is, by virtue of having an MDD diagnosis, the client naturally has to meet some criteria for PTSD because of the symptom overlap. Should the client be diagnosed with PTSD, MDD, both disorders, or neither disorder? An objection to diagnosing the client with both disorders could be that we would essentially be "double-dipping"—diagnosing two conditions unnecessarily and therefore overpathologizing a client's presentation. We investigated this issue empirically and examined the effect on PTSD's comorbidity rates by removing overlapping symptoms from the diagnoses. What we found was that comorbidity rates were identical whether using or removing these overlapping symptoms (Elhai et al., 2008). Thus, it may be appropriate to diagnose a client with all disorders for which criteria are met, even if symptoms overlap.

We recommend the following two major steps when inquiring about mental disorders other than PTSD among trauma survivors. First, a broadband structured or semi-structured diagnostic interview should be used that assesses the full range of clinical disorders—one that has been found reliable and valid from psychometric studies. Second, based on which disorders the client appears to meet criteria for (e.g., generalized anxiety disorder), these disorders should be subsequently probed further with specific self-report measures to inquire about the frequency or intensity of symptoms (e.g., a measure specifically tapping generalized anxiety disorder severity).

We have found that some clinicians are opposed to structured interviews because they believe this approach takes too much time to administer; interferes with rapport during the initial session and therefore is not favored by clients; does not allow for nuanced questions or clinical judgment; and, proves too financially costly. All of these concerns can be addressed. Thus, some structured interviews take only 15 to 20 minutes to complete; clients can appreciate the rationale for this approach when informed that diagnostic accuracy is maximized; adjunct questions and clinical judgment can still be used; and some are available at no financial charge. We therefore advise the clinician who is unfamiliar with structured diagnostic interviews to locate one, try it with a couple of clients, solicit their feedback, and then make an informed decision about whether to continue their use.

In the United States, the most widely used structured diagnostic interview for adult clinical disorders is the SCID-I (First, Spitzer, Gibbon, & Williams, 1996). It is semi-structured, in that it provides flexible probes, and a version for clinical practice is available, as well as a slightly expanded version for research purposes. Administration time can range from 45 to 90 minutes. Because of concerns about administration time for clinicians in practice, a good but shorter diagnostic interview alternative is the Mini International Neuropsychiatric Interview (Sheehan et al., 1998). The MINI only requires about 15 to 20 minutes of administration, and has yielded comparable psychometric properties when compared against the longer SCID and CIDI. The MINI is modeled after the aforementioned structured interviews, but it is streamlined with skip-out rules to substantially reduce administration time and required paper quantity. Other adult structured diagnostic interviews are discussed elsewhere (Segal & Coolidge, 2003; Summerfeldt & Antony, 2004).

Several structured diagnostic interviews are available for children and adolescents. The DICA-R (e.g., Reich, 2000) is a semi-structured interview and takes about 2 to 3 hours to administer. Next, the Diagnostic Interview Schedule for Children (DISC, e.g., Shaffer, Fisher, Lucas, Dulcan, & Schwab-Stone, 2000) is highly structured and takes about 70 to 120 minutes to administer. For a less time-consuming alternative, a version of the MINI is available for children, and we have found this instrument useful. Other similar measures are discussed elsewhere (Hughes & Melson, 2008).

Many clinicians, especially those working in VA settings, use the Minnesota Multiphasic Personality Inventory-2 (MMPI-2) to assess personality and psychopathology. This broad-based assessment measure may be helpful when assessing issues of comorbidity. At the same time, special considerations are needed when interpreting MMPI-2 profiles for victims of severe trauma exposure. First, research examining profiles of civilian (e.g., Elhai, Klotz Flitter, Gold, & Sellers, 2001) and military trauma (e.g., Elhai, Frueh, Davis, Jacobs, & Hamner, 2003) demonstrate that a relatively large proportion of trauma victims evidence significant, extreme elevations on the MMPI-2's Infrequency Scale (F) and Scale 8 (Schizophrenia). Although high elevations on the F scale can indicate symptom overreporting, previous research has found that common trauma-related mental health problems largely accounted for variation in F scale scores, especially dissociation (Klotz Flitter, Elhai, & Gold, 2003). Therefore, other MMPI-2 validity scales have been developed that are less confounded with genuine trauma-related distress (e.g., Elhai et al., 2004; Elhai et al., 2002). Additionally, depression and dissociation among trauma survivors largely accounted for variation in Scale 8 scores, suggesting that psychosis should not be over-interpreted in MMPI-2 profiles among this population (Elhai, Frueh, Gold, Hamner, & Gold, 2003; Elhai, Gold, Mateus, & Astaphan, 2001).

## CASE STUDY: METHODS AND RESULTS

Presented below is a checklist that identifies the key issues and assessment strategies that we have presented thus far.

### Table 6.1 Checklist for Issues and Strategies in Assessing Trauma Survivors

**Assessing History of Exposure to Traumatic Stressors**

1 Feel confident about the ethics in making such queries.
2 Provide a rationale for such inquiry, and an empathic preface statement.
3 Use items with standardized, behaviorally specific language, from a psychometrically sound instrument.
4 Probe trauma-related event characteristics.
5 Ask the respondent to nominate an index traumatic event.
6 Consider memory recall problems.
7 Consider the possibility of under- or over-reporting, and, in some settings, attempt to obtain objective documentation of trauma exposure.

**Assessing Posttraumatic Stress Disorder**

1 Link symptom queries to an index traumatic event incident.
2 Ensure that symptoms have lasted the appropriate duration of time.
3 Use a validated symptom instrument, with frequency and/or intensity ratings.
4 Consider cultural issues.
5 Consider under-or over-reporting of symptoms, and in some settings, attempt to rule out malingering and defensiveness.

**Assessing Other Mental Health Problems**

1 Assess additional disorders than PTSD using a broadband measure of personality or diagnosis.
2 Further probe other mental health problems using specific symptom measures.

With this checklist in mind, we can now return our attention to the case study introduced at the beginning of this chapter. Armed with knowledge on methods, procedures and instruments for assessing trauma, PTSD and other mental health problems, this case represents a practical illustration, albeit with a fictional patient. We should emphasize that the selection of instruments discussed below represents merely one example of the many possibilities previously covered.

In the case of Mr. Gavin, the clinician was especially careful to conduct a thorough evaluation because of the likely possibility of legal involvement. Legal concerns clearly applied because the client reported that his bank was being sued by customers, and Mr. Gavin possibly had a worker's compensation claim. The clinician gathered a detailed demographic, educational, employment, social, legal, family, mental health, and medical history.

After gathering historical information discussed above, the clinician assessed trauma history using the TLEQ. He began administering the TLEQ by first providing a preface indicating empathy and understanding. Results of the TLEQ revealed two other specific traumatic events reported by Mr. Gavin who had witnessed as a child his father occasionally hitting his mother, and who on occasion had himself been hit by his father with sufficient force to cause injury (thus meeting PTSD's Criterion A1). The clinician asked Mr. Gavin to nominate the trauma that currently caused him the most distress, and the attempted robbery was chosen (though in our clinical experience, the most distressing trauma chosen is not necessarily the one that the clinician would predict is the most distressing). Mr. Gavin additionally stated that when the customer was shot, he felt horrified (thus meeting PTSD's Criterion A2). The clinician did not need to obtain additional proof of the recent traumatic stressor, since its occurrence had been covered on the local news.

After a general clinical interview asking Mr. Gavin about the problems he was having, the clinician administered the PSS-Interview version, instructing Mr. Gavin to rate PTSD symptoms based on his experience with the attempted robbery. The client endorsed three re-experiencing symptoms (intrusive thoughts, nightmares, and emotional reactivity when first returning to the bank; Criterion B), four avoidance and numbing symptoms (persistent avoidance of thoughts and activities related to the incident, anhedonia, and social detachment; Criterion C), and three hyperarousal symptoms (difficulty sleeping and concentrating, and hypervigilance; Criterion D). Most symptoms were endorsed as occurring at least several times per week. Mr. Gavin reported that the symptoms had lasted for nearly two months (Criterion E) and had disrupted work functioning (Criterion F). Based on these results, the clinician provided a diagnosis of PTSD, Acute. Note that because the traumatic event, although recent, happened more than four weeks beforehand, a diagnosis of Acute Stress Disorder was not appropriate.

The clinician administered the MINI to explore comorbid psychopathology. Based on this interview, Mr. Gavin additionally met diagnostic criteria for major depressive disorder, single episode, moderate; and alcohol dependence, without physiological dependence. He therefore was administered short self-report measures of depression and alcohol use to probe symptom severity.

Finally, because of the forensic implications of this case, the clinician assessed Mr. Gavin's response style by administering the MMPI-2. Test results demonstrated a clinical profile that was consistent with the client's self-report. Validity scale scores, while somewhat elevated, were not invalid and suggested instead the presence of significant distress.

## CONCLUSION

In this chapter, we have reviewed methods for assessing trauma history, PTSD, and other mental health problems among individuals presenting with trauma-related issues. We discussed important issues to consider in assessing these domains and strategies for conducting such assessments. A brief overview of available instruments for assessment was presented, along with a case study to demonstrate assessment with a trauma survivor. We hope clinicians find these strategies and resources of assistance as they carefully and sensitively assess their clients. The proper assessment of trauma history and PTSD symptoms will allow the clinician to accurately diagnose or rule out this diagnosis, while developing treatment plans for trauma-related and comorbid psychopathology.

## Table 6.2  Assessment Instruments

| Instrument | Contact Information for Obtaining the Instrument |
| --- | --- |
| Childhood Trauma Questionnaire | Available for purchase from Pearson Assessments: www.pearsonassessments.com |
| Children's Posttraumatic Stress Disorder Inventory | Available for purchase from the Psychological Corporation: www.PsychCorp.com |
| Clinician Administered Posttraumatic Stress Disorder Scale for Children and Adolescents | Available for order at no charge from the National Center for PTSD: www.ncptsd.va.gov/ncmain/ assessment |
| Composite International Diagnostic Interview | Available for purchase from Washington University's Epidemiology Web site: www.epi.wustl.edu/epi/assess .htm |
| Diagnostic Interview for Children and Adolescents-Revised | Available for purchase from Multi-Health Systems, Inc.: www.mhs.com |
| Diagnostic Interview Schedule for Children | Available for purchase from the Columbia DISC Development Group, Division of Child and Adolescent Psychiatry, 1051 Riverside Drive, New York, NY 10032, (888) 814-DISC, disc@worldnet.att.net |
| Dimensions of Stressful Events Rating Scale | Available at no charge from Kenneth Fletcher, Ph.D., Psychiatry Department, 55 Lake Avenue North, Worcester, MA 01655-0001, (508) 856-3329, Kenneth.Fletcher@umassmed.edu |
| Impact of Event Scale-Revised | Available at no charge from Daniel Weiss, Ph.D., Department of Psychiatry, University of California - San Francisco, Box F-0984, San Francisco, CA 94143-0984, daniel.weiss@ucsf.edu |
| Life Events Checklist | Available for order as part of the CAPS at no charge from the National Center for PTSD: www.ncptsd .va.gov/ncmain/assessment  Available as part of the CAPS for purchase from Western Psychological Services: www.wpspublish.com |
| Mini International Neuropsychiatric Interview | Available at no charge by download from Medical Outcomes: www.medical-outcomes.com |
| Modified Posttraumatic Stress Disorder Symptom Scale | Available at no charge from Sherry Falsetti, Ph.D., Dept. of Family and Community Medicine, College of Medicine at Rockford, University of Illinois at Chicago, 1221 East State Street, Rockford, IL 61104, falsetti@uic.edu |

*(continued)*

**Table 6.2** *(continued)*

| Instrument | Contact Information for Obtaining the Instrument |
| --- | --- |
| Posttraumatic Diagnostic Scale | Available for purchase from Pearson Assessments: www.pearsonassessments.com |
| Posttraumatic Stress Disorder Checklist (Civilian version, Military version, and Specific Stressor version | Available for order at no charge from the National Center for PTSD: www.ncptsd.va.gov/ncmain/assessment |
| Posttraumatic Stress Disorder Symptom Scale (Child version and Adult version) | Available at no charge from Edna Foa, Ph.D., Department of Psychiatry, University of Pennsylvania, 3535 Market Street, 6th Floor, Philadelphia, PA 19104, (215) 746-3327, foa@mail.med.upenn.edu |
| Startle, Physiological Arousal, Anger, and Numbness scale (SPAN) | Available for purchase from Multi-Health Systems, Inc.: www.mhs.com |
| Stressful Life Events Screening Questionnaire | Available at no charge from Bonnie L. Green, Ph.D., Department of Psychiatry, Georgetown University Medical School, 310 Kober Cogan Hall, Washington, DC 20007, (202) 687-6529, bgreen01@georgetown.edu |
| Structured Clinical Interview for DSM-IV Axis I Disorders | Available for purchase from Columbia University's Biometrics Research Department: www.scid4.org |
| Structured Interview for Posttraumatic Stress Disorder | Available for download at no charge from Duke University's Anxiety and Traumatic Stress Program: http://psychiatry.mc.duke.edu/Research/Research.html |
| Trauma Assessment for Adults (Interview version and Self-Report version) | Available at no charge from Heidi Resnick, Ph.D., National Crime Victims Research and Treatment Center, Department of Psychiatry and Behavioral Sciences, 171 Ashley Avenue, Charleston, SC 29425-0742, resnickh@musc.edu |
| Trauma History Questionnaire | Available at no charge from Bonnie L. Green, Ph.D., Department of Psychiatry, Georgetown University Medical School, 310 Kober Cogan Hall, Washington, DC 20007, (202) 687-6529, bgreen01@georgetown.edu |
| Trauma Screening Questionnaire | Available at no charge from Chris Brewin, Ph.D., Sub-Department of Clinical Health Psychology, University College London, Gower Street, London WC1E 6BT, UK, c.brewin@ucl.ac.uk. Also included in its entirety in Brewin, C. R., Rose, S., Andrews, B., Green, J., Tata, P., McEvedy, C., et al. (2002). Brief screening instrument for post-traumatic stress disorder. *British Journal of Psychiatry, 181*, 158–162. |

| Instrument | Contact Information for Obtaining the Instrument |
| --- | --- |
| Trauma Symptom Checklist for Children | Available for purchase from Psychological Assessment Resources: www.parinc.com |
| Trauma Symptom Checklist for Young Children | Available for purchase from Psychological Assessment Resources: www.parinc.com |
| Trauma Symptom Inventory | Available for purchase from Psychological Assessment Resources: www.parinc.com |
| Traumatic Event Screening Instrument (Child Interview version, Child Self-Report version, Child's Parent version, Adult version) | The original Child Interview version is available for download at no charge from the National Center for PTSD: www.ncptsd.va.gov/ncmain/assessment. Other versions are available at no charge from Julian D. Ford, Ph.D., University of Connecticut Health Center, Psychiatry Department, 263 Farmington Avenue, MC 1410, Farmington, CT 06030, ford@ psychiatry.uchc.edu |
| Traumatic Life Events Questionnaire | Available for purchase from Western Psychological Services: www.wpspublish.com |
| When Bad Things Happen Scale | Available at no charge from Kenneth Fletcher, Ph.D., Psychiatry Department, 55 Lake Avenue North, Worcester, MA 01655-0001, (508) 856-3329, Kenneth.Fletcher@umassmed.edu |

# REFERENCES

Acierno, R., Kilpatrick, D. G., & Resnick, H. S. (1999). Posttraumatic stress disorder in adults relative to criminal victimization: Prevalence, risk factors, and comorbidity. In P. A. Saigh & J. G. Bremner (Eds.), *Posttraumatic stress disorder: A comprehensive text* (pp. 44–68). Boston: Allyn and Bacon.

American Psychiatric Association. (2000). *Diagnostic and statistical manual of mental disorders* (4th ed. – text revision). Washington, DC: Author.

Andrews, B., Brewin, C. R., Philpott, R., & Stewart, L. (2007). Delayed-onset posttraumatic stress disorder: A systematic review of the evidence. *American Journal of Psychiatry, 164*, 1319–1326.

Asmundson, G. J. G., Stapleton, J. A., & Taylor, S. (2004). Are avoidance and numbing distinct PTSD symptom clusters? *Journal of Traumatic Stress, 17*, 467–475.

Brewin, C. R. (2005). Systematic review of screening instruments for adults at risk of PTSD. *Journal of Traumatic Stress, 18*, 53–62.

Briere, J. (2004). *Psychological assessment of adult posttraumatic states: Phenomenology, diagnosis, and measurement.* Washington, DC: American Psychological Association.

Briere, J. (2005). *Trauma symptom checklist for young children: Professional manual.* Odessa, FL: Psychological Assessment Resources Inc.

Bryant, R. A., & Harvey, A. G. (2000). *Acute stress disorder: A handbook of theory, assessment, and treatment.* Washington, DC: American Psychological Association.

Copeland, W., Keeler, G., Angold, A., & Costello, E. J. (2007). Traumatic events and posttraumatic stress in childhood. *Archives of General Psychiatry, 64,* 577–584.

Cusack, K. J., Frueh, B. C., & Brady, K. T. (2004). Trauma history screening in a community mental health center. *Psychiatric Services, 55,* 157–162.

Davidson, J. R. T., Kudler, H. S., & Smith, R. (1997). Structured interview for PTSD (SIP): Psychometric validation for DSM-IV criteria. *Depression and Anxiety, 5,* 127–129.

Davis, J. L., Borntrager, C. F., Combs-Lane, A. M., Wright, D. C., Elhai, J. D., Falsetti, S. A., et al. (2006). Comparison of racial groups on trauma and post-trauma functioning. *Journal of Trauma Practice, 5*(2), 21–36.

Dohrenwend, B. P., Turner, J. B., Turse, N. A., Adams, B. G., Koenen, K. C., & Marshall, R. (2006, August 18). The psychological risks of Vietnam for U.S. veterans: A revisit with new data and methods. *Science, 313,* 979–982.

Elhai, J. D., Frueh, B. C., Davis, J. L., Jacobs, G. A., & Hamner, M. B. (2003). Clinical presentations in combat veterans diagnosed with posttraumatic stress disorder. *Journal of Clinical Psychology, 59,* 385–397.

Elhai, J. D., Frueh, B. C., Gold, P. B., Hamner, M. B., & Gold, S. N. (2003). Posttraumatic stress, depression and dissociation as predictors of MMPI-2 scale 8 scores in combat veterans with PTSD. *Journal of Trauma and Dissociation, 4*(1), 51–64.

Elhai, J. D., Gold, S. N., Mateus, L. F., & Astaphan, T. A. (2001). Scale 8 elevations on the MMPI-2 among women survivors of childhood sexual abuse: Evaluating posttraumatic stress, depression, and dissociation as predictors. *Journal of Family Violence, 16,* 47–57.

Elhai, J. D., Gray, M. J., Kashdan, T. B., & Franklin, C. L. (2005). Which instruments are most commonly used to assess traumatic event exposure and posttraumatic effects?: A survey of traumatic stress professionals. *Journal of Traumatic Stress, 18,* 541–545.

Elhai, J. D., Gray, M. J., Naifeh, J. A., Butcher, J. J., Davis, J. L., Falsetti, S. A., et al. (2005). Utility of the Trauma Symptom Inventory's Atypical Response Scale in detecting malingered post-traumatic stress disorder. *Assessment, 12,* 210–219.

Elhai, J. D., Grubaugh, A. L., Kashdan, T. B., & Frueh, B. C. (2008). Empirical examination of a proposed refinement to DSM-IV posttraumatic stress disorder symptom criteria using the National Comorbidity Survey Replication data. *Journal of Clinical Psychiatry, 69*, 597–602.

Elhai, J. D., Klotz Flitter, J. M., Gold, S. N., & Sellers, A. H. (2001). Identifying subtypes of women survivors of childhood sexual abuse: An MMPI-2 cluster analysis. *Journal of Traumatic Stress, 14*, 157–175.

Elhai, J. D., Lindsay, B. M., Gray, M. J., Grubaugh, A. L., North, T. C., & Frueh, B. C. (2006). Examining the uniqueness of frequency and intensity symptom ratings in posttraumatic stress disorder assessment. *Journal of Nervous and Mental Disease, 194*, 940–944.

Elhai, J. D., Naifeh, J. A., Zucker, I. S., Gold, S. N., Deitsch, S. E., & Frueh, B. C. (2004). Discriminating malingered from genuine civilian posttraumatic stress disorder: A validation of three MMPI-2 infrequency scales (F, Fp, and Fptsd). *Assessment, 11*, 139–144.

Elhai, J. D., Ruggiero, K. J., Frueh, B. C., Beckham, J. C., Gold, P. B., & Feldman, M. E. (2002). The Infrequency-Posttraumatic Stress Disorder scale (Fptsd) for the MMPI-2: Development and initial validation with veterans presenting with combat-related PTSD. *Journal of Personality Assessment, 79*, 531–549.

Falsetti, S. A., Resnick, H. S., Resick, P. A., & Kilpatrick, D. G. (1993, June). The Modified PTSD Symptom Scale: A brief self-report measure of posttraumatic stress disorder. *Behavior Therapist, 16*, 161–162.

Felitti, V., Anda, R., Nordenberg, D., Williamson, D., Spitz, A., & Edwards, V., et al. (1998). Relationship of childhood abuse and household dysfunction to many of the leading causes of death in adults. *American Journal of Preventive Medicine, 14*, 245–258.

First, M. B., Spitzer, R. L., Gibbon, M., & Williams, J. B. (1996). *Structured Clinical Interview for DSM-IV Axis I Disorders, Clinician Version (SCID-CV)*. Washington, DC: American Psychiatric Press.

Fletcher, K. (1996). Psychometric Review of Dimensions of Stressful Events (DOSE) Ratings Scale. In B. H. Stamm (Ed.), *Measurement of stress, trauma, and adaptation* (pp. 144–151). Lutherville, MD: Sidran Press.

Foa, E. B., Johnson, K. M., Feeny, N. C., & Treadwell, K. R. H. (2001). The Child PTSD Symptom Scale: A preliminary examination of its psychometric properties. *Journal of Clinical Child Psychology, 30*, 376–384.

Foa, E. B., & Tolin, D. F. (2000). Comparison of the PTSD Symptom Scale-Interview version and the Clinician-Administered PTSD Scale. *Journal of Traumatic Stress, 13*, 181–191.

Ford, J. D., & Fournier, D. (2007). Psychological trauma, post-traumatic stress disorder, and health-related functioning of low-income urban women receiving community mental health services for severe mental illness. *Journal of Psychiatric Intensive Care, 3*, 27–34.

Ford, J. D., Hartman, J. K., Hawke, J., & Chapman, J. (2008). Traumatic victimization, posttraumatic stress disorder, suicidal ideation, and substance abuse risk among juvenile justice-involved youths. *Journal of Child and Adolescent Trauma, 1*, 75–92.

Frueh, B. C., Elhai, J. D., & Kaloupek, D. G. (2004). Unresolved issues in the assessment of trauma exposure and posttraumatic reactions. In G. M. Rosen (Ed.), *Posttraumatic stress disorder: Issues and controversies* (pp. 63–84). New York: John Wiley & Sons.

Frueh, B. C., Elhai, J. D., Monnier, J., Hamner, M. B., & Knapp, R. G. (2004). Symptom patterns and service use among African American and Caucasian veterans with combat-related PTSD. *Psychological Services, 1*, 22–30.

Frueh, B. C., Grubaugh, A. L., Cusack, K. J., Kimble, M. O., Elhai, J. D., & Knapp, R. G. (2009). Exposure-based cognitive behavioral treatment of PTSD in adults with schizophrenia or schizoaffective disorder: A pilot study. *Journal of Anxiety Disorders, 23*, 665–675.

Frueh, B. C., Grubaugh, A. L., Elhai, J. D., & Buckley, T. C. (2007). US Department of Veterans Affairs disability policies for posttraumatic stress disorder: Administrative trends and implications for treatment, rehabilitation, and research. *American Journal of Public Health, 97*, 2143–2145.

Frueh, B. C., Grubaugh, A. L., Yeager, D. E., & Magruder, K. M. (2009). Delayed-onset post-traumatic stress disorder among war veterans in primary care clinics. *British Journal of Psychiatry, 194*, 515–520.

Goodman, L., Corcoran, C., Turner, K., Yuan, N., & Green, B. L. (1998). Assessing traumatic event exposure: General issues and preliminary findings for the Stressful Life Events Screening Questionnaire. *Journal of Traumatic Stress, 11*, 521–542.

Gray, M. J., Elhai, J. D., Owen, J. R., & Monroe, J. R. (2009). Psychometric properties of the Trauma Assessment for Adults. *Depression and Anxiety, 26*, 190–195.

Gray, M. J., Litz, B. T., Wang, J., & Lombardo, T. W. (2004). Psychometric properties of the Life Events Checklist. *Assessment, 11*, 330–341.

Griffin, M. G., Uhlmansiek, M. H., Resick, P. A., & Mechanic, M. B. (2005). Comparison of the Posttraumatic Stress Disorder Scale versus the Clinician-Administered Posttraumatic Stress Disorder Scale in domestic violence survivors. *Journal of Traumatic Stress, 17*, 497–503.

Grubaugh, A. L., Frueh, B. C., Elhai, J. D., Monnier, J., Knapp, R. G., & Magruder, K. M. (2006). Racial differences in psychiatric symptom patterns and service use in VA primary care clinics. *Psychiatric Services, 57*, 410–413.

Guriel, J., & Fremouw, W. (2003). Assessing malingered posttraumatic stress disorder: A critical review. *Clinical Psychology Review, 23*, 881–904.

Harvey, M. (1996). An ecological view of psychological trauma and trauma recovery. *Journal of Traumatic Stress, 9*, 3–23.

Hughes, C. W., & Melson, A. G. (2008). Child and adolescent measures for diagnosis and screening. In A. J. Rush, M. B. First, & D. Blacker (Eds.), *Handbook of psychiatric measures* (2nd ed.; pp. 251–308). Arlington, Virginia: American Psychiatric Publishing.

Kessler, R. C., Sonnega, A., Bromet, E., Hughes, M., & Nelson, C. B. (1995). Posttraumatic stress disorder in the National Comorbidity Survey. *Archives of General Psychiatry, 52*, 1048–1060.

Kimerling, R., Trafton, J., & Ngyuen, B. (2006). Validation of a brief screen for post-traumatic stress disorder with substance use disorder patients. *Addictive Behaviors, 31*, 2074–2079.

Klotz Flitter, J. M., Elhai, J. D., & Gold, S. N. (2003). MMPI-2 F scale elevations in adult victims of child sexual abuse. *Journal of Traumatic Stress, 16*, 269–274.

Kubany, E. S., Haynes, S. N., Leisen, M. B., Owens, J. A., Kaplan, A. S., Watson, S. B., et al. (2000). Development and preliminary validation of a brief broad-spectrum measure of trauma exposure: The Traumatic Life Events Questionnaire. *Psychological Assessment, 12*, 210–224.

Lacoursiere, R. B. (1993). Diverse motives for fictitious post-traumatic stress disorder. *Journal of Traumatic Stress, 6*, 141–149.

Lang, A. J., & Stein, M. B. (2005). An abbreviated PTSD checklist for use as a screening instrument in primary care. *Behaviour Research and Therapy, 43*, 585–594.

Leverich, G., McElroy, S., Suppes, T., Keck, P., Denicoff, K., Nolen, W., et al. (2002). Early physical and sexual abuse associated with an adverse course of bipolar illness. *Biological Psychiatry, 51*, 288–297.

Long, M. E., & Elhai, J. D. (2009). Posttraumatic stress disorder's traumatic stressor criterion: History, controversy, clinical and legal implications. *Psychological Injury and Law, 2*, 167–178.

Long, M. E., Elhai, J. D., Schweinle, A., Gray, M. J., Grubaugh, A. L., & Frueh, B. C. (2008). Differences in posttraumatic stress disorder diagnostic rates and symptoms severity between Criterion A1 and non-Criterion A1 stressors. *Journal of Anxiety Disorders, 22*, 1255–1263.

McNally, R. J. (2003). Progress and controversy in the study of posttraumatic stress disorder. *Annual Review of Psychology, 54,* 229–252.

Mueser, T., Rosenberg, S. D., Fox, L., Salyers, M. P., Ford, J. D., & Carty, P. (2001). Psychometric evaluation of trauma and posttraumatic stress disorder assessments in persons with severe mental illness. *Psychological Assessment, 13,* 110–117.

Nader, K. (2008). *Understanding and assessing trauma in children and adolescents: Measures, methods and youth in context.* New York: Routledge.

Newman, E., & Kaloupek, D. G. (2004). The risks and benefits of participating in trauma-focused research studies. *Journal of Traumatic Stress, 17,* 383–394.

Norris, F. H., & Hamblen, J. L. (2004). Standardized self-report measures of civilian trauma and PTSD. In J. P. Wilson & T. M. Keane (Eds.), *Assessing psychological trauma and PTSD* (2nd ed.; pp. 63–102). New York: Guilford.

Ohan, J. L., Myers, K., & Collett, B. R. (2002). Ten-year review of rating scales. IV: Scales assessing trauma and its effects. *Journal of the Academy of Child and Adolescent Psychiatry, 41,* 1401–1422.

Reich, W. (2000). Diagnostic Interview for Children and Adolescents (DICA). *Journal of the Academy of Child and Adolescent Psychiatry, 39,* 59–66.

Resnick, P. J., West, S., & Payne, J. W. (2008). Malingering of posttraumatic disorders. In R. Rogers (Ed.), *Clinical assessment of malingering and deception* (3rd ed.; pp. 109–127). New York: Guilford.

Rosen, G. M. (2004). Malingering and the PTSD data base. In G. M. Rosen (Ed.), *Posttraumatic stress disorder: Issues and controversies* (pp. 85–99). Chichester, England: John Wiley & Sons.

Rosen, G. M., Sawchuk, C. N., Atkins, D. C., Brown, M., Price, J. R., & Lees-Haley, P. R. (2006). Risk of false positives when identifying malingered profiles using the Trauma Symptom Inventory. *Journal of Personality Assessment, 86,* 329–333.

Rosen, G. M., Spitzer, R. L., & McHugh, P. R. (2008). Problems with the posttraumatic stress disorder diagnosis and its future in DSM-V. *British Journal of Psychiatry, 192,* 3–4.

Rosen, G. M., & Taylor, S. (2007). Pseudo-PTSD. *Journal of Anxiety Disorders, 21,* 201–210.

Ruggiero, K. J., Del Ben, K., Scotti, J. R., & Rabalais, A. E. (2003). Psychometric properties of the PTSD Checklist-Civilian Version. *Journal of Traumatic Stress, 16,* 495–502.

Sadowski, C. M., & Friedrich, W. N. (2000). Psychometric properties of the Trauma Symptom Checklist for Children (TSCC) with psychiatrically hospitalized adolescents. *Child Maltreatment, 5*, 364–372.

Saigh, P., Yaski, A. E., Oberfield, R. A., Green, B. L., Halamandaris, P. V., Rubenstein, H., et al. (2000). The Children's PTSD Inventory: Development and reliability. *Journal of Traumatic Stress, 30*, 369–380.

Scher, C. D., Stein, M. B., Asmundson, G. J. G., McCreary, D. R., & Forde, D. R. (2001). The Childhood Trauma Questionnaire in a community sample: Psychometric properties and normative data. *Journal of Traumatic Stress, 14*, 843–857.

Segal, D. L., & Coolidge, F. L. (2003). Structured interviewing and *DSM* classification. In M. Hersen & S. M. Turner (Eds.), *Adult psychopathology and diagnosis* (4th ed.; pp. 72–103). New York: John Wiley & Sons.

Shaffer, D., Fisher, P., Lucas, C., Dulcan, M., & Schwab-Stone, M. (2000). NIMH Diagnostic Interview Schedule for Children version IV (NIMH DISC-IV): Description, differences from previous versions, and reliability of some common diagnoses. *Journal of the Academy of Child and Adolescent Psychiatry, 39*, 28–38.

Sheehan, D. V., Lecrubier, Y., Sheehan, K. H., Amorim, P., Janavs, J., & Weiller, E., et al. (1998). The Mini-International Neuropsychiatric Interview (MINI): The development and validation of a structured diagnostic psychiatric interview for DSM-IV and ICD-10. *Journal of Clinical Psychiatry, 59* (Suppl. 20), 22–33.

Summerfeldt, L. J., & Antony, M. M. (2004). Structured and semistructured diagnostic interviews. In M. M. Antony & D. H. Barlow (Eds.), *Handbook of assessment and treatment planning for psychological disorders* (pp. 3–37). New York: Guilford.

Weathers, F. W., Keane, T. M., & Davidson, J. R. (2001). Clinician-administered PTSD scale: A review of the first ten years of research. *Depression and Anxiety, 13*, 132–156.

Wessely, S., Unwin, C., Hotopf, M., Hull, L., Ismail, K., Nicolaou, V., et al. (2003). Stability of recall of military hazards over time: Evidence from the Persian Gulf War of 1991. *British Journal of Psychiatry, 183*, 314–322.

# 7

# Early Intervention in the Aftermath of Trauma

RICHARD GIST
GRANT J. DEVILLY

A commuter aircraft carrying two dozen passengers attempts an approach to a mid-sized community airport as a line of storms is clearing the area. It is late evening as they begin their final descent. About two miles short of landing, the plane experiences some type of massive disruption and crashes nose-first into a populated suburban neighborhood. Rescue workers from the city, supplemented by volunteer firefighters from outlying communities, are at first overwhelmed by fire from both the airplane and homes in the area of impact. They work through the night to contain the flames, while also organizing search and rescue activities. By morning, it is clear that all passengers and crew on the airplane have perished, along with several members of at least two households in the impact area. Others on the ground, ranging from children to older adults, are treated for injuries of various extents. Many people—perhaps more than a hundred—find themselves displaced from the neighborhood as rescue activities continue; many watch in horror before leaving the area. A Red Cross shelter is established but only a handful come and none elect to stay.

(continued)

(*continued*)

You, along with other mental health professionals in the area, have been asked by local community leaders to provide assistance to those living in the vicinity of the crash. Among the tasks identified are helping families who await identification of remains; assisting others in the neighborhood with a multitude of needs; working with career and volunteer firefighters who were controlling fires and recovering victims; and recommending other measures that might be needed to help the community recover. You will be playing a lead role in planning and directing whatever measures are taken and the mayor's office wants to know how you plan to begin.

The more we understand, sometimes, the less we seem to know. Years ago there was little guidance as to what clinicians should do in the aftermath of trauma. Now, despite a plethora of competing models, there still is confusion as to what constitutes best practice.

## THE DEBRIEFING MODEL

Decades ago, a schism in practice began to develop, with two very different approaches to early intervention. The best known approach, and subsequently most criticized model, to guide efforts in the aftermath of trauma was termed Critical Incident Stress Debriefing (CISD; Mitchell, 1983). Born from work with paramilitary/emergency organizations (e.g., ambulance, fire brigades, police) this protocol advocated a one-size-fits-all, seven-step approach for all who have been exposed to trauma. In the original debriefing model, there was to be a one-off intervention, of one to three hours, to be delivered within 72 hours of the trauma. Within this one prolonged meeting were the seven steps or phases: (1) the introductory phase (rules, process and goals outlined); (2) the "fact" phase (recitation of what participants saw, did, and heard); (3) the "thoughts" phase (recounting of participants' first thoughts as awareness of the event and its magnitude developed); (4) the "reaction" phase (emotional reactions to the experience, sometimes labeled the "feelings" phase); (5) the "symptoms" phase (global assessment of physical or psychological symptoms based on participant disclosures); (6) the "teaching" phase (educating the participants about common, likely, or possible stress responses); (7) the "re-entry" phase (referral information provided). In the example vignette that began this chapter, a mental health practitioner using the debriefing model would have become visible, prominent, and central to the unfolding events. A group debriefing based on the seven steps would have been made available (possibly in demountable or mobile therapy rooms) to the primary victims of a disaster and to the attending professionals (e.g., firefighters possibly mandated to attend the session).

Initially lauded as a current best practice or gold standard response to trauma, the scientific evidence slowly eroded claims of efficacy. By the late 1990s/early 2000s, this practice was repudiated by most practitioners, companies, and government bodies. To understand how CISD fell from grace, a brief review of the history is in order. First, however, it is important to appreciate that science, it has been said, progresses at one of two speeds: tectonic in most instances or, when accelerated due to extreme urgency, glacial. Science tends to be conservative, tedious, and understandably cautious. Clinical applications tend to be bolder and less averse to risky shifts—the urgency of relieving suffering and limiting morbidity often motivates practitioners to try new ideas and approaches before science has had the full opportunity to test their safety and efficacy. We do not advocate this hurried approach, but are aware of its existence in the community. Accordingly, it is not at all uncommon to find today's "drug du jour" the subject of tomorrow's recall when controlled clinical testing finds that unforeseen risks outweigh demonstrable impact.

So it has been with disaster mental health. Popularized approaches such as debriefing appeared, on the surface, to be quite compelling. Their premises were consistent with then-current thought and theory regarding psychological trauma and its sequelae (providing succor for those exposed is always right); the actions recommended were seemingly reasonable and informed (be systematic and be well trained). Given the basic "appeal" of the model, the deployment of psychological interventions at disaster scenes grew. In little more than a decade, the counselors clamoring to provide assistance began to outnumber the victims seeking help. One reporter who studied the response in Manhattan following the 9/11 attacks noted that 9,000 counselors reported being present in New York, outnumbering known victims by at least three-to-one (Kadet, 2002). It is surprising that out-of-town firefighters and personnel ancillary to the rescue effort found any hotel space considering the number of counselors and therapists who made themselves available for service in the New York area. An estimated 800 Scientology "therapists" descended upon the scene, along with a flood of other therapy purveyors (Devilly, 2005).

Despite CISD's popularity, controlled studies on individual debriefings demonstrated either (a) no effect, or (b) paradoxical inhibition of recovery. In other words, despite the appeal to "clinical intuition," and the seeming logic of its underlying assumptions, the actual provision of debriefings was without benefit at best, and actively harmful at worst. By 2006, the scientific literature had led most reviewers to discourage the continued use of debriefings in the aftermath of trauma (e.g., Devilly, Gist, & Cotton, 2006; McNally, Bryant, & Ehlers, 2003; Rose, Bisson, Churchill, & Wessely, 2002; van Emmerik, Kamphuis, Hulsbosch, & Emmelkamp, 2002).

One criticism of the empirical evidence has always been that debriefings in randomized controlled trials were given on a one-to-one basis and so they lacked ecological validity. This argument was made because most debriefings are typically administered to groups of people. More recently, we have conducted analog studies of group debriefing following viewing of a stressful video. This line of investigation looked at whether providing group debriefing had any discernable effects one way or the other. Participants (mainly from the community and from the university) were shown a very harrowing video of paramedics attending the scene of a real-life motor vehicle accident. In one study (Devilly & Annab, 2008), participants randomly received either classic CISD debriefing in groups (treatment), or tea and biscuits with instructions simply to chat (control). The results showed no beneficial effects of debriefing over an unstructured social interaction. Of greater concern, there appeared to be a worrying trend for the debriefed to access fewer social supports following the video. It was also noted that those who received the debriefing later said they were glad that someone had talked to them about the video content, yet those in the control reported more satisfaction with having not been spoken to about what they had seen. Such cognitive dissonance explanations add weight to a finding from community debriefing studies in which participants are "glad they had been debriefed," even though clinical outcome measures found no benefits, and sometimes negative effects.

In a follow-up study (Devilly, Varker, Hansen & Gist, 2007) using a similar protocol, we found that overheard misinformation during a group debriefing session was likely to be later recalled as an eyewitness account. It was also worrying to find that irrespective of condition, people were more confident in their incorrect answers than their correct ones. Such contagion of false information, which is then believed with increased conviction, is worrisome, particularly if someone receives a group debriefing before giving evidence in court about details that are open to debate (e.g., witness saw or heard only part of an affray). Further, and consistent with individual debriefing studies (Mayou, Ehlers & Hobbs, 2000), we found in a recent study that the more severe the stressor, the more likely it was that debriefing would have negative effects relative to controls (Devilly & Varker, 2008).

Despite the growing literature that calls into question the use of debriefings, many mental health professionals continue to remain attached to the model. This attachment has been maintained, in part, by the exaggerated claims of those who have an interest in promoting debriefing workshops and other related products. Just as importantly, if not more so, attachment to the debriefing model has been maintained because of our urgent compulsion to bring whatever skills and information we might hold to bear on the human aftermath of crisis, cataclysm, and catastrophe. We have historically rushed, usually with the very noblest of intentions, to piece together whatever we may have heard, deduced, or simply believed to be useful and effective in such circumstances and to mount aggressive efforts to deliver such ministrations *en masse* at the times and places of visible turmoil. We bring what we sincerely believe to be the best of our tools and the best of our intent to the worst of times and the most difficult of situations—not surprisingly, we also tend to believe that we deliver in the process the best of care. Once we have mounted such an effort, we typically seek to share what we believe we have learned with other practitioners. Despite such noble intentions, it is important that clinicians deliver *evidence-informed interventions*. In the case of critical incident stress debriefings, it is clear that good intentions are not enough. Thus, studies have repeatedly found that these widely prescribed prophylactic interventions are not only inert with respect to prevention of PTSD, but they can actually inhibit recovery in at least some recipients. These findings present a compelling case for reexamination—not simply of the techniques and their application, but, more pressingly, of the axioms, assumptions, and pragmatics on which the entire debriefing model was constructed (Gist, Woodall, & Magenheimer, 1999).

## Intervention by Analogy

*Trauma* is a medical term used to describe an injury inflicted on the body through an external physical force. Its metaphorical application in psychiatry has frequently conflated the injury with the incident, leading to a tendency to think of a trauma as an event rather than a consequent reaction to the experience of an event and to focus our attention on the nature of traumatic incidents. We often assume that because the event is deemed "traumatic," the outcome is *de facto* injurious. We have accordingly reached for interventions to match the nature of traumatic events rather than treatments to match observed and assessed injuries. This can often prove counterproductive.

Consider a parallel from emergency medicine. Torsion forces to the ankle can lead to traumatic injuries; these are among the most commonly seen traumas in accident and emergency care. Most such injuries, while painful, are relatively benign and resolve with only supportive care (typically captured by the mnemonic acronym RICE: rest, ice, elevation, compression). Some injuries, due to the magnitude of the force applied, the angle or torque involved, the relative strength or weakness of the patient's tendons and ligaments, or the remnant impact of prior injuries, may require more intensive and more personalized intervention. A certain number may involve fractures that must be orthopedically mended; a few may require surgical repair and some may result in life-altering damage.

The design of treatment and intervention cannot be determined from the nature of the event from which the injurious force arose. Treatment of a specific patient's injury must be predicated on thorough and specific assessment of the patient's condition, including history, tolerances, and response. Mechanism of injury indeed plays a role in understanding the context of the injury and guiding the practitioner toward a focused and informed assessment, but it is assessment and diagnosis of the injury (if any) incurred that determines the nature and timing of appropriate care.

Analogies regarding preventive prophylaxis in public health have also been advanced to support widespread immediate intervention efforts. Vaccination has been a specifically prevalent analogy. But vaccination is preventative of infection rather than injury, which strains the analogy from the outset. It is widely known that vaccines present a risk to some but offer protection from serious disease to many more; the balance is between risk and benefit. Early prophylactic interventions (particularly the ubiquitous debriefing exercise) have become increasingly suspect in this regard. Indeed, in the most comprehensive meta-analysis to date (van Emmerik et al., 2002) such interventions showed no clear benefit, yielded indications of paradoxical impacts with respect to natural recovery, and fared less well overall than essentially other strategies against which they had been systematically compared (Gist & Devilly, 2002).

## COMMUNITY RESPONSES

At the beginning of this section we mentioned a schism in suggested approaches. One was the road most frequently traveled: debriefing. The alternative approach focuses on community responses to trauma. Early efforts at a community focus (Gist & Lubin, 1989; Gist & Stolz, 1982) suggested that psychologists could, in times of catastrophe, step back from the interventionist mindset of the debriefing model, and apply instead their basic knowledge and consultative skills to help communities reclaim autonomy and self-efficacy in the face of social disruption. It seemed clear in our experience that the fundamental determinants of individual reactions arose at least as much from social context, social comparison, and social construction as from any particular configuration of individual impingements. We came away with a profound respect for the resilience of the human spirit rather than any fascination with its limits.

A recent report from a number of leading researchers regarding the impact of disasters on the community is noteworthy for the extent to which it reiterates most of the basic premises that drove our early efforts. Hobfoll et al. (2008) listed what they contend to be five essential elements of appropriate community assistance, informed by the now substantial empirical literature in disaster mental health:

1. Restoring a sense of safety;
2. Calming (reducing anxiety and agitation);
3. Establishing a sense of community and self-efficacy;
4. Building connectedness; and
5. Facilitating hope.

These are not, the astute practitioner will quickly note, typical clinical objectives to be carried out by counselors through psychological intervention. Most involve instead the sorts of factors that flow from the actions taken by those who represent a community's formal and informal leadership. Here practitioners are seen as typically doing their best work by quietly advising those whose duty places them at the forefront of public trust regarding the consequences of events and situations—mayors, state emergency service chiefs, and the like. An additional objective for clinicians is to focus on identifying and properly addressing cases that present demonstrable need for clinical intervention.

A recent approach to provide evidence informed intervention was outlined in a consensus project led by the National Fallen Firefighters Foundation (Gist, Taylor, & Neeley, 2009). The project focused on early intervention strategies derived from current best practices guidelines (e.g., Australian Centre for Posttraumatic Mental Health, 2007; National Institute for Clinical Excellence, 2005; Rose, Wessely, & Bisson, 2005), consensus recommendations (e.g., National Institute of Mental Health, 2002), and systematic reviews (e.g., Devilly, Gist, & Cotton, 2006; Gray & Litz, 2005; McNally, Bryant, & Ehlers, 2003). Core principles included the following:

## 1. Immediate Assistance Should Be Proximal, Nonintrusive, and Ecologically Intact

Contacts utilizing principles of *psychological first aid* (PFA; see Brymer et al., 2006) represent the current standard for evidence-informed best practice in providing immediate support to victims of trauma. PFA represents a very different set of notions and assumptions than those which underlie debriefing models. Debriefing approaches are very prescriptive, protocol driven, and relatively rigid; there were set rules for what would be said, by whom, and in what order—sometimes even for such minute details as how chairs would be arranged and who should sit where. The techniques were rhetorically tied to presumptions of relatively high risk for PTSD and coupled to suggestions that these approaches could prevent its development.

PFA, on the other hand, specifically avoids the now well-established pitfalls of one-size-fits-all interventions. It embraces a wide range of techniques and anticipates that methods will change as evidence develops. Its strength is in its flexibility. PFA principles assume, in keeping with a growing body of empirical evidence, that victims of disaster are typically resilient, their concerns are principally instrumental and adaptive, and their reactions are generally transient and situational in nature—in short, they will get better as their situation gets better. Accordingly, the best way to help a disaster victim deal with the stress of losing his or her home may well be to get a roof over the victim's head.

First aid was never envisioned as something to be delivered by doctors and nurses—it was designed to be the province of baseball coaches and babysitters, of those who are most likely to be in first contact with the ill or injured. To return to our earlier analogy, first aid was aimed at those carrying the footballer from the field, not the surgeon reattaching the tendons of the ankle. The intent in severe cases was to provide sufficient skills (the ABCs: airway, breathing, and circulation) to stabilize serious problems until definitive help could be secured. Just as important, first aid was to enable folks to safely, effectively, and confidently deal with minor injuries such as scrapes and bruises. For PFA in disaster settings, the persons most likely to make a difference are those who encounter victims as a part of response and relief duties. That's not to say that there are not times when the direct help of a counselor or social worker will prove needed and valuable. What it does suggest is that emotional support, especially in the beginning, may be better received from first responders, disaster relief volunteers, shelter workers, and others in the context of their primary roles. It also means that those who need more focused, specialized assistance must be properly identified and given access to forms of treatment that have been solidly demonstrated as effective for the problems they present.

PFA is a manualized approach that has been made easily available in the public domain (e.g., through the Web sites of the National Center for Post Traumatic Stress Disorder and the National Child Traumatic Stress Network). Its core elements are outlined in Table 7.1.

Although PFA has endeavored to choose its labels carefully, we caution providers to be vigilant for messages lurking in the terms it selects. Consider the term "potentially traumatic event" (PTE), utilized with the deliberate intent to clarify that the event itself is not traumatic and the reactions of those exposed may, for many or most, never reach a pathologic level of intensity or duration. Nonetheless, even indicating that exposure *might* prove traumatic may increase the risk of reactions conforming to that expectation. Consider, for example, how referring to the suspect in a robbery as "the thief" during statement gathering by police vastly increases the likelihood of the suspect being confirmed as guilty by witnesses. Telling other witnesses after a trauma that you saw two helicopters increases the likelihood of those same

**Table 7.1  Core Elements of Psychological First Aid**

- *Contact and engagement*: Making contact with those in need of assistance; providing practical, instrumental assistance with compassion and care.
- *Safety and comfort*: Take all needed steps to provide those affected with as safe an environment as situations permit; provide for comfort as circumstances allow.
- *Stabilization*: Attenuate anxiety, provide a calming presence, help ground and orient the distraught, refer for emergency care in cases where clearly indicated.
- *Information gathering (current needs and concerns)*: Determine the pressing needs *as seen by the person in need;* tailor assistance efforts to address current needs while anticipating emerging situations.
- *Practical assistance*: Provide practical, instrumental help with identified needs; assist with problem-solving strategies and access to helping resources.
- *Connection with social supports*: Help those affected make contact with sources of social support important to them (e.g., friends, family, community, and spiritual resources) and integrate their support into problem solving and recovery.
- *Information on coping*: Simple, practical, proven tips on managing stress and coping with demands of disaster recovery—timed to match the situations and challenges at hand at any given juncture—can be useful and well received, especially when delivered in the context of practical assistance and social support.
- *Links to collaborative services*: Most disaster victims are unfamiliar with resources available to help with their various needs; assistance in navigating the resource network in a given community is important to sustained recovery.

witnesses incorporating two helicopters into their eyewitness accounts at a later date (Devilly et al., 2007). In effect, people incorporate into their thinking that which they have been told. This will occur more when the memory trace is weak, information is delivered by a credible source, and the information is not obviously incorrect (Wells, Wright, & Bradfield, 1999). Likewise we are concerned that referring to the term Psychological First Aid during the planning or provision of services increases the expectancy of *needing* psychological help, which in turn may retrospectively increase the threat appraisal of the event.

Describing the event as potentially traumatic, without considering the victim's perceptions, may itself increase the probability of such attributions. As the saying holds, "I didn't realize I was sick until you called for the doctor."

## 2. Early, Reliable, and Nonintrusive Assessment

Appropriate assessment is essential to any effective protocol for early intervention. Most persons respond to even deeply unsettling experiences with resilience and do not require mental health services (Bonanno, 2004). While the majority of Americans report exposure to situations sufficient to classify as Criterion A stressors, fewer than 10% experience clinically diagnosable PTSD (Breslau, 2009). This does not mean that most people experience no discomfort, distress, or disequilibrium; it means that they work through these experiences, sometimes even demonstrating growth. Yet it has become commonplace to see normal disequilibrium described as "symptoms of trauma," or to see subsyndromic distress labeled "partial PTSD" (Breslau, Lucia, & Davis, 2004; Mylle & Maes, 2004).

*Symptom* is another term borrowed somewhat metaphorically from medical traditions. Unlike a *sign*, an objective indicator of a condition that often holds some specificity, a symptom is a subjective element of the patient's reported experience that may or may not be a specific manifestation of the illness or injury in question. Most of the indicators we recognize as symptoms of disorders, as with PTSD, may simply be indicators that a person is reacting to a demanding and disturbing set of challenges. They do not become symptoms indicative of any particular dysfunction unless and until they fail to abate as the situation matures and resolves.

It is only when distress is atypically broad, persistent, and intense that it reaches a diagnosable threshold. Following the 9/11 attacks, some mental health spokespersons initially projected that one in four New Yorkers, and perhaps many more, would experience diagnosable PTSD and require treatment. Systematic epidemiologic studies showed that at four weeks—the current diagnostic threshold for persistence—only about 7.5% showed probable "caseness" (Galea et al., 2003). More significantly, by the time six months had passed—the original threshold for symptom persistence under the DSM-III (APA, 1980)—only about 0.6% had continued to show probable PTSD.

Put another way, 92% of those who were likely to have been diagnosable under current standards had resolved their reactions to less than clinical levels by the original time threshold for symptom duration (six months), typically without professional help or intervention. Indeed, the perceived underutilization of mental health services offered to New Yorkers following 9/11 has been one of the more intriguing "non-stories" of the episode (Sommers & Satel, 2005). Similar underutilization has been reported among Hurricane Katrina evacuees (Wang et al., 2007).

Fortunately, there are PTSD screening instruments available now that are simple to use, straightforward to score, and decently selective. A good screening test must have good *sensitivity* (capacity to detect cases that are actually present) coupled with decent *specificity* (capacity to find those cases without generating an undue number of "false positives"). For broad screens, high *negative predictive validity* (NPV) is desirable, indicating that those who screen negative for the condition are highly unlikely to manifest the disorder or require treatment. While *positive predictive validity* (PPV) is also desirable, positive screens are typically seen as indicators for more complete diagnostic testing; where the "hit rate" is reasonably low and the NPV suitably high, a lower PPV can still prove acceptable.

The Trauma Screening Questionnaire (TSQ) is a simple, straightforward, and nonintrusive self-report instrument that has demonstrated efficacy at three to six weeks post-exposure in distinguishing for whom resolution is progressing well and suggesting who may require fuller assessment for clinical treatment of PTSD (Brewin et al., 2002). The scale consists of 10 dichotomized queries regarding whether an indicated symptom has been experienced more than twice in the preceding week. Scoring is by rote count of affirmative responses with six or more affirmative replies indicating a positive screen. It accordingly provides an efficient screen in primary care settings and lends itself to workplace and self-assessment applications. Initial trials showed sensitivity > .85 with specificity > .90; negative predictive power was reported as .93 with positive predictive power calculated at .86. Overall screening efficiency was computed to be 90%.

Combined with a short depression screen such as that suggested by Henkel et al. (2004), the TSQ can provide a simple but effective instrument for a primary screen. Its brevity, simplicity of scoring, and very good psychometric properties make it an effective tool for use in disaster application centers, primary care clinics, or even as a self-screening tool. Its creators have deliberately kept it in the public domain to facilitate its ready use without license or fees. The TSQ's content is reproduced in Table 7.2.

**Table 7.2  Trauma Screening Questionnaire**

|  | YES, AT LEAST TWICE IN THE PAST WEEK | NO |
|---|---|---|
| 1. Upsetting thoughts or memories about the event that have come into your mind against your will | | |
| 2. Upsetting dreams about the event | | |
| 3. Acting or feeling as though the event were happening again | | |
| 4. Feeling upset by reminders of the event | | |
| 5. Bodily reactions (such as fast heartbeat, stomach churning, sweatiness, dizziness) when reminded of the event | | |
| 6. Difficulty falling or staying asleep | | |
| 7. Irritability or outbursts of anger | | |
| 8. Difficulty concentrating | | |
| 9. Heightened awareness of potential dangers to yourself and others | | |
| 10. Being jumpy or being startled at something unexpected | | |

Source: Brewin et al, 2002.

## 3. Stepped Care

Providing treatment that is titrated to demonstrated clinical need is now recommended in place of preemptive prophylaxis. Studies of cardiac patients following major coronary events have found that a significant minority actually do better if not enrolled in seemingly benign interventions such as psycho-educational support and symptom education (Frasure-Smith et al., 2002; Ginzberg, Solomon, & Bleich, 2002). Studies of early interventions based on debriefing techniques have also shown these sorts of paradoxical impacts (Bisson, Jenkins, Alexander, & Bannister, 1997; Mayou et al., 2000). Cardiac patients who typically used repressive coping strategies fared as well or better than others if left to their own devices, but deteriorated when involved in ostensibly supportive interventions that challenged their normal patterns of coping. Given that those who appear to cope repressively have often been among those targeted for intervention, it is particularly imperative to avoid presumptive over-intervention. Transient but subsyndromic discomfort that proves recalcitrant or troublesome may be addressed by targeted symptom management using focused elements of cognitive behavior therapy (CBT; Ehlers & Clark, 2003). Early intervention using CBT techniques in patients at heightened risk for PTSD has demonstrated specific efficacy in preventing transition from Acute Stress Disorder to full PTSD (Bryant, 2007). Self-help programs with demonstrated efficacy in bolstering symptom management skills and addressing external stressors may also show utility, especially if made accessible to those reluctant to accept clinical referral (see Litz, Engel, Bryant, & Papa, 2007, for a pilot study of an online self-management program). Where symptom manifestation reaches clinical thresholds, referral to specialty providers for evidence-based treatment is warranted.

## 4. Evidence-Based Treatment

Empirically supported interventions offered by competent and credentialed specialty providers should be considered the standard of care for cases that reach diagnostic thresholds. Evidence-based treatments consistent with current authoritative guidelines should form the basis for clinical intervention. Current treatment guidelines (e.g., Australian Centre for Posttraumatic Mental Health, 2007; National Institute for

Clinical Excellence, 2005; National Institute of Mental Health, 2002) favor trauma-focused variants of cognitive behavior therapy (CBT) utilizing graded exposure (see also Institute of Medicine, 2006, 2007, for detailed overview of evidence regarding assessment and clinical treatment of PTSD). Therefore, documented training and supervised experience in CBT should be considered imperative when providing clinical services to this population.

## ACQUIRING FUNDAMENTAL SKILL SETS

The baseline skills needed to participate productively in planning, coordinating, and delivering early interventions for trauma are, for the most part, extensions of basic clinical capabilities. In most cases, the additional information and training needed to expand the clinician's existing skill base are readily available. For example:

### 1. Psychological First Aid (PFA)

As previously discussed, PFA is an evidence-informed best practices strategy for providing immediate support (Brymer et al., 2006). It was developed by a coalition of the National Child Traumatic Stress Network, the National Center for PTSD, and the Substance Abuse and Mental Health Services Administration. Adaptations have been commissioned for such constituencies as spiritual care providers and the Medical Reserve Corps. It is a recognized strategy of choice (e.g., Australian Centre for Posttraumatic Mental Health, 2007), providing a list and range of strategies/skills that may be selected as needed during a case-formulated approach, rather than any rigid prescription of interventions. Full manuals and supporting materials are accessible on the Internet.

### 2. Resources for Complete PTSD Assessment

Assessment is a critical part of professional training, and appropriately licensed practitioners should have substantial training in this general arena. Assessment for PTSD and related issues connected to exposure to critical events may not, however, be a frequently demanded aspect of practice for many practitioners and, hence, may not be a well-developed area of expertise.

There are resources in the public domain to help address this need. The Institute of Medicine (2006) has published a state-of-the-art review regarding diagnosis and assessment of PTSD. This document is available on their Web site for online review. The National Center for PTSD has dedicated a section of its Web site to assessment strategies and instruments. Instruments and strategies developed by the Center are directly available, and information regarding access to other instruments is provided.

The *Trauma Screening Questionnaire* (provided in Table 7.2) and the WHO-5 are screening instruments with established efficacy and utility in primary settings (Brewin et al., 2002; Henkel et al., 2003). The WHO-5 may provide useful and reliable screening for depression when adapted to include as few as two queries (Henkel et al., 2004). Both instruments are in the public domain. Scoring for each is exceedingly direct and requires no specialized training.

### 3. Training in Case Formulation

The ability to view a specific person's (or company's) presenting problem in light of their history, current circumstances, assets, and deficits is fundamental to providing help (or to be able to recognize the lack of help needed). Whether this is seen through the lens of the 7 "P's" (Predisposition, Precipitation, Pattern, Perpetuation, Presentation, Prognosis, Potentials) and a treatment plan instigated through a functional analysis or whether some other *system* is used, the ability and necessity to case formulate is central to evolving standards of care.

### 4. Training in Evidence Based Treatments

*Appropriate training* (specifically CBT) is essential for competent treatment of clinically diagnosable cases. This has been a substantial limiting factor in many areas and many practice settings. The National Crime Victims Research and Treatment Center at the Medical University of South Carolina, with support from the National Child Traumatic Stress Network and the Substance Abuse and Mental Health Services Administration, has developed and implemented a Web-based training program in Trauma Focused Cognitive Behavior Therapy (TF-CBT) directed toward journeyman clinicians dealing with child sexual abuse; it has generated wide subscription with an outstanding completion rate. It exists in the public domain. Practitioners who are not themselves competent to deliver CBT interventions should be prepared to identify appropriate sources of referral and be prepared to refer as indicated.

## SUGGESTED PROTOCOLS FOR COMMUNITY- AND PATIENT-LEVEL INTERVENTION

A basic timeline and schematic for community-level response is outlined in Figure 7.1. A flow chart model from the patient perspective, based on the National Fallen Firefighter Foundation consensus model (Gist, Taylor, & Neeley, 2009), is presented in Figure 7.2 on the following page. These approaches assume that immediate response will be guided by PFA principles applied *in situ* by the range of aid workers and community resources providing instrumental assistance to the victim community. Preexisting clinical disorders may be exacerbated by the impact of these stressors and must be dealt with in the context of their ongoing clinical care; outreach strategies within clinical populations deserve specific attention, especially in the immediate impact period. Screening as indicated using TSQ or a similar established instrument becomes effective after three to four weeks.

Those screening positively are likely to benefit from short-cycle CBT with a specific trauma focus. Early intervention using these methods for those displaying heightened risk has been shown to prevent progression to PTSD. Diagnosable PTSD should be treated using evidence-based techniques (most specifically, CBT). Contextual efforts directed at instrumental support should continue on both community and case levels to enhance resiliency and support recovery.

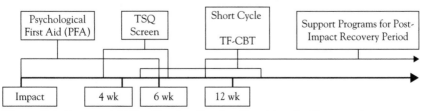

**Figure 7.1 Sequential Timeline for Service Provision in Community**

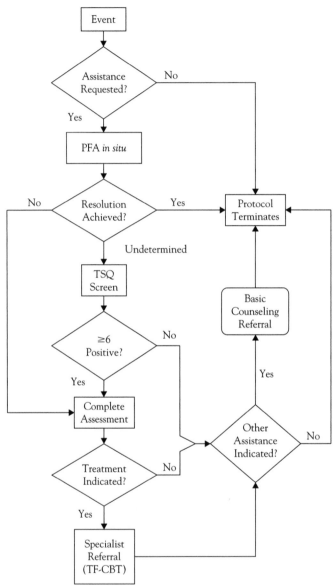

**Figure 7.2  Patient-level Protocol**

## APPLYING A COMMUNITY-BASED MODEL

Evidence informed best practices that can address the role demands presented in our opening vignette are increasingly available to guide the clinician in the provision of efficacious early interventions. These practices typically represent extensions and enhancement of basic clinical skills, although preparation before an event is always recommended for competent execution. Avenues for that preparation are easily accessible and can support not just disaster response, but daily clinical practice.

So, how might you, a well-informed practitioner, best approach the many and very pressing demands presented by the opening vignette? First, and most critically, it is important to resist the well-meaning compulsion toward immediate intervention. The most important issues in the immediate aftermath of trauma are rarely clinical in nature or implication. Most are best addressed by supporting actions already underway and within the domain of legitimate first responders. Your first effort should be to learn how those operations work so that you can offer appropriate support that may be needed. It is also critical to ensure that you do not unintentionally complicate, interfere with, duplicate, or obstruct the critical primary services.

The airline, for example, will be working with the National Transportation Safety Board (NTSB). They will coordinate with local authorities (e.g., law enforcement, emergency medical services, fire and rescue, emergency management, Red Cross) as they work to identify the passengers and crew, locate and notify next of kin, gather needed records and information, and the like. There will typically be a point of contact established for inquiries, and in most cases, a Family Assistance Center will be established. Here, families will have a safe place to come for information and assistance and there will be a central location for necessary interviews and interactions. Competent, trustworthy local resources are often utilized to provide consistent contacts for individual families. Mental health providers with good listening skills and strong boundaries can be helpful if they have an appropriately circumspect view of their role and a willingness to stay within its bounds.

Local families displaced by the event will need similar sources of contacts and support. These may be less quick to emerge since less structure and guidance exists regarding how this should be done. While a Red Cross shelter may be opened for those displaced, most will typically look for temporary shelter with family or friends. Still, they will have needs for information and assistance at all points, and especially as the focus shifts from the incident itself to rebuilding the neighborhood. Providers can similarly be helpful in staffing and assisting as various needs evolve.

Rescue workers will typically have organizational plans for dealing with the impact. The information provided in this chapter can be supplied to organizations to help them consider their options. Should there be survivors in the community, or rescuers for whom lasting difficulties become apparent, providers skilled in clinical assessment and evidence-based treatment will be needed as referees. If you have those skills to offer, making your availability known to the agencies will be helpful.

The issue is, again, not to saturate the incident and those involved with preordained interventions but to assure that there will be ready, informed, prepared, and appropriate resources to meet the needs of those impacted. There also may be a role for you after such an event in helping to identify lessons learned, so that your community can prepare for events that may come its way. Having a blueprint before disaster strikes and established relationships from which to work is the single most important determinant of effective and helpful response to disaster.

## REFERENCES

American Psychiatric Association. (1980). *Diagnostic and statistical manual of mental disorder*. (3rd ed.). Washington, DC: Author.

Australian Centre for Posttraumatic Mental Health. (2007). Australian guidelines for the treatment of adults with acute stress disorder and posttraumatic stress disorder. Melbourne, Australia: Author.

Bisson, J. I., Jenkins, P. L., Alexander, J., & Bannister, C. (1997). A randomised controlled trial of psychological debriefing for victims of acute harm. *British Journal of Psychiatry, 171*, 78–81.

Bonanno, G. A. (2004). Loss, trauma, and human resilience—Have we underestimated the human capacity to thrive after extremely aversive events? *American Psychologist, 59*, 20–28.

Breslau, N. (2009). The epidemiology of trauma, PTSD, and other posttrauma disorders. *Trauma, Violence, and Abuse, 10*, 198–210.

Breslau, N., Lucia, V. C., & Davis, G. C. (2004). Partial PTSD versus full PTSD: An empirical examination of associated impairment. *Psychological Medicine, 34*, 1205–1214.

Brewin, C. R., Rose, S., Andrews, B., Green, J., Tata, P., McEvedy, C., et al. (2002). Brief screening instrument for posttraumatic stress disorder. *British Journal of Psychiatry, 181*, 158–162.

Bryant, R. A. (2007). Early intervention in posttraumatic stress disorder. *Early Intervention in Psychiatry, 1,* 19–26.

Brymer, M., Jacobs, A., Layne, C., Pynoos, R., Ruzek, J., Steinberg, A., et al. (2006). *Psychological first aid: Field operations guide* (2nd ed.). National Center for PTSD. Accessed February 1, 2009 at: http://www.ncptsd.va.gov/ncmain/ncdocs/manuals/PFA_2ndEditionwithappendices.pdf.

Devilly, G. J. (2005). Power therapies and possible threats to the science of psychology and psychiatry. *Australian and New Zealand Journal of Psychiatry, 39,* 437–445.

Devilly, G. J., & Annab, R. (2008). A randomised controlled trial of group debriefing. *Behavior Therapy and Experimental Psychiatry, 39,* 42–56.

Devilly, G. J., Gist, R., & Cotton, P. (2006.) Ready! Fire! Aim! Psychological debriefing services and intervention in the workplace. *Review of General Psychology, 10,* 318–345.

Devilly, G. J., & Varker, T. (2008). The effect of stressor severity on outcome following group debriefing. *Behaviour Research and Therapy, 46,* 130–136.

Devilly, G. J., Varker, T., Hansen, K., & Gist, R. (2007). The effects of psychological debriefing on eyewitness memory. *Behaviour Research and Therapy, 45,* 1245–1254.

Ehlers, A., & Clark, D. (2003). Early psychological interventions for adult survivors of trauma: A review. *Biological Psychiatry, 9,* 817–826.

Frasure-Smith, N., Lespérance, F., Gravel, G., Masson, A., Juneau, M., & Bourassa, M. G. (2002). Long-term survival differences among low-anxious, high-anxious and repressive copers enrolled in the Montreal heart attack readjustment trial. *Psychosomatic Medicine, 64,* 571–579.

Galea, S., Vlahov, D., Resnick, H., Ahern, J., Susser, E., Gold, J., et al. (2003). Trends of probable post-traumatic stress disorder in New York City after the September 11 terrorist attacks. *American Journal of Epidemiology, 158,* 514–524.

Ginzburg, K., Solomon, Z., & Bleich, A. (2002). Repressive coping style and adjustment following myocardial infarction (MI). *Psychosomatic Medicine, 64,* 748–757.

Gist, R., & Devilly, G. J. (2002). Post-trauma debriefing: The road too often traveled? *The Lancet, 360,* 741–742.

Gist, R., & Lubin, B. (Eds.). (1989). *Psychosocial aspects of disaster.* New York: John Wiley & Sons.

Gist, R., & Stolz, S. B. (1982). Mental health promotion and the media: Community response to the Kansas City hotel disaster. *American Psychologist, 37,* 1136–1139.

Gist, R., Taylor, V. H., & Neeley, J. F. (2009). *Consensus meeting on Initiative 13: Occupational behavioral health in the fire service.* Emmitsburg, MD: National Fallen Firefighters Foundation.

Gist, R., Woodall, S. J., & Magenheimer, L. K. (1999). And then you do the Hokey-Pokey and you turn yourself about. In R. Gist & B. Lubin (Eds.), *Response to disaster: Psychosocial, community, and ecological approaches* (pp. 269–290). Philadelphia: Taylor & Francis.

Gray, M. J., & Litz, B. T. (2005). Behavioral interventions for recent trauma: Empirically informed practice guidelines. *Behavior Modification, 29,* 189–215.

Henkel, V., Mergl, R., Kohnen, R., Maier, W., Möller, H. J., & Hegerl, U. (2003). Identifying depression in primary care: a comparison of different methods in a prospective cohort study. *British Medical Journal, 326,* 200–201.

Henkel, V., Mergl, R., Coyne, J. C., Kohnen, R., Möller, H. J., & Hegerl, U. (2004). Screening for depression in primary care: Will one or two items suffice? *European Archives of Psychiatry & Clinical Neurosciences, 254,* 215–223.

Hobfoll, S. E., Watson, P. J., & Bell, C. C. et al. (2008). Five essential elements of immediate and mid-term mass trauma intervention: empirical evidence. *Psychiatry, 70,* 283–316.

Institute of Medicine. (2006). *Posttraumatic stress disorder: Diagnosis and assessment.* Washington, DC: National Academies Press.

Institute of Medicine. (2007). *Treatment of posttraumatic stress disorder: An assessment of the evidence.* Washington, DC: National Academies Press.

Kadet A. (2002, June). Good grief! *Smart Money, 11*(6), 108–114.

Litz, B. T., Engel, C. C., Bryant, R. A., & Papa, A. (2007). A randomized, controlled proof-of-concept trial of an internet-based, therapist-assisted self management treatment for posttraumatic stress disorder. *American Journal of Psychiatry, 164,* 1676–1683.

Mayou, R. A., Ehlers, A., & Hobbs, M. (2000). Psychological debriefing for road traffic accident victims: Three-year follow-up of a randomized controlled trial. *British Journal of Psychiatry, 176,* 589–593.

McNally, R. J., Bryant, R. A., & Ehlers, A. (2003). Does early psychological intervention promote recovery from posttraumatic stress? *Psychological Science in the Public Interest, 4*(2).

Mitchell, J. T. (1983). When disaster strikes . . . The critical incident stress debriefing process. *Journal of Emergency Services, 8,* 36–39.

Mylle, J., & Maes, M. (2004). Partial posttraumatic stress disorder revisited. *Journal of Affective Disorders, 78,* 37–48.

National Institute for Clinical Excellence. (2005). *Posttraumatic stress disorder: The management of PTSD in adults and children in primary and secondary care.* Trowbridge, Wiltshire, UK: Cromwell Press Ltd.

National Institute of Mental Health. (2002). *Mental health and mass violence: Evidence-based intervention for victims/survivors of mass violence* (NIH Publication No. 02-5138). Washington, DC: U.S. Government Printing Office.

Rose, S., Bisson, J., Churchill, R., & Wessely, S. (2002). *Psychological debriefing for preventing post traumatic stress disorder (PTSD).* Cochrane Database of Systematic Reviews, Issue 2. [DOI: 10.1002/14651858.CD000560]

Rose, S., Bisson, B., & Wessely, S. (2005). A systematic review of brief psychological interventions ("debriefing") for the treatment of immediate trauma related symptoms and the prevention of Post-traumatic Stress Disorder. *The Cochrane Collaboration* (database online). Updated issue 3. Hoboken, NJ: Wiley.

Sommers, C. H., & Satel, S. (2005). September 11, 2001: The mental health crisis that wasn't. In C. H. Sommers & S. Satel, *One nation under therapy* (pp. 177–214). New York: St. Martin's Press.

Van Emmerik, A. A. P., Kamphuis, J. H., Hulsbosch, A. M., & Emmelkamp, P. M. G. (2002). Single session debriefing following psychotrauma, help or harm: A meta-analysis. *The Lancet, 360,* 766–771.

Wang, P. S., Gruber, M. J., & Powers, R. E. et al. (2007). Mental health service utilization in Hurricane Katrina survivors in the eight months after the disaster. *Psychiatric Services, 58,* 1403–1411.

Wells, G. L., Wright, E. F., & Bradfield, A. L. (1999). Witnesses to crime: Social and cognitive factors governing the validity of people's reports. In R. Roesch, S. D. Hart, & J. R. P. Ogloff, (Eds.), Psychology and law: The state of the discipline. *Perspectives in Law and Psychology,* Volume 10.

# Cognitive Behavioral Treatments for PTSD

Elizabeth A. Hembree
Edna B. Foa

R esearch on cognitive behavioral treatments (CBT) for posttraumatic stress disorder (PTSD) has flourished over the past 20 years. In testament to this, the second edition of the PTSD treatment guidelines published in 2009 by the International Society of Traumatic Stress Studies (ISTSS; Foa, Keane, Friedman, & Cohen, 2009) lists nearly 100 studies of CBT for PTSD—65 randomized controlled trials and 31 additional non-randomized trials (Cahill, Rothbaum, Resick, & Follette, 2009). Evidence from these outcome studies is unequivocal: Cognitive behavioral therapies including exposure therapy, cognitive therapy, stress inoculation training, eye movement desensitization and reprocessing, and combinations of these treatments have repeatedly been shown to significantly reduce symptoms of PTSD, depression, anxiety, and other trauma-related problems.

In this chapter, we begin with a review of the theory underlying CBT treatment of PTSD, with emphasis on what maintains trauma-related symptoms long after the traumatic event has ended, and what therapy must provide in order to ameliorate PTSD severity. After presenting a theoretical framework, we focus more specifically on exposure treatment, and describe its core or essential elements. Following this background, we briefly summarize findings from outcome studies that have compared CBT treatments for PTSD, and have investigated whether combining interventions enhances outcomes (e.g., whether exposure combined with cognitive therapy or anxiety management training obtains better outcome than either treatment alone). We then illustrate the implementation of these techniques via a detailed case presentation of a woman treated with a specific exposure treatment that has amassed considerable empirical support: Prolonged Exposure (Foa, Hembree, & Rothbaum, 2007). We conclude with a discussion of implications for clinical practice.

## TRAUMA AND PTSD

Traumatic experiences are quite common. Fortunately, the majority of survivors recover from traumatic experiences via natural processes and without need for intervention. Trauma survivors commonly experience high levels of PTSD symptoms in the immediate aftermath of an event, and then show a decline in their symptoms over time, especially in the first three months. For example, Cahill, Street, Jayawickreme, and Foa (unpublished manuscript) found in a sample of 277 female survivors of rape and nonsexual assault that at an average of 10 days following the assault, 89% of rape survivors and 64% of non-sexual assault survivors met symptom criteria for PTSD. By the 4-week assessment (at which point the DSM duration criterion for acute PTSD would be met) the incidence of PTSD had dropped to 71% for sexual and 45% of non-sexual assault survivors, and by the 3-month assessment (the point at which duration criterion for chronic PTSD would be met), 50% of sexual and 22% of non-sexual assault survivors met the diagnosis for PTSD. By one year post-assault, the incidence of PTSD was 26% for rape survivors and 12% for non-sexual assault survivors.

Rates of PTSD for other types of trauma (e.g., motor vehicle accidents, natural disasters) tend to be less. Across the full spectrum of potential traumatic stressors, PTSD is estimated to effect 7 to 9% of the population (Breslau, Davis, Andreski, & Peterson, 1991; Kessler et al., 2005). Regardless of trauma type, the overall pattern of identifiable reactions in the immediate aftermath of trauma, followed by natural recovery for the majority of individuals, holds true. However, a sizable minority fails to recover and continues to suffer from PTSD symptoms for years.

## EMOTIONAL PROCESSING THEORY

The fact that many survivors are able to successfully process a traumatic experience has long interested researchers and clinicians. *Why* do some trauma survivors develop chronic PTSD or other trauma-related disturbances while some recover over the early post-trauma period? The answer to this question is important, because psychotherapeutic treatments must facilitate or kindle our natural recovery processes when for some reason they have been impeded. Within the theoretical framework of cognitive behavioral treatment approaches, the development of PTSD has been conceptualized as a failure to adequately process and gain a realistic perspective on the traumatic experience. This leads to a strong propensity to view the world as an extremely dangerous place and to view oneself as weak or incompetent (Foa, Steketee Rothbaum, 1989). Accordingly, the aim of CBT treatments has been to provide experiences that facilitate learning and reduce excessive fear and unrealistic expectations of harm. These concepts originate in emotional processing theory (Foa & Kozak, 1986; Foa & Cahill, 2001; Foa, Huppert, Cahill, & Riggs, 2006) and are also prominent in cognitive theories of trauma recovery and treatment (e.g., Ehlers & Clark, 2000; Resick & Schnicke, 1992).

Emotional processing theory, developed by Foa and Kozak (1985, 1986), provides an understanding of pathological fear and how it is modified via exposure therapy. The theory adopts Lang's view of fear as a cognitive structure in memory that includes information about the feared stimuli and fear responses for the purpose of escaping danger. Foa and Kozak emphasized the central role of the meaning associated with the stimuli and responses and made the distinction between normal and pathological fear structures. Normal fear structures are useful and necessary for survival, as they provide a template for effective action in response to realistic threat. For example, it is prudent and helpful to see a charging and menacing dog as a feared stimulus, to perceive it as dangerous, and to have one's body react energetically by running to safety.

When is a fear structure pathological? Foa and Kozak (1986) suggested that a fear structure is pathological and may interfere with functioning when certain characteristics are present: associations among stimulus elements are inaccurate or unrealistic; physiological and escape/avoidance responses are triggered by harmless stimuli; excessive and easily triggered response elements interfere with normal, adaptive behavior; and harmless stimulus and response elements are erroneously associated with threat meaning. For example, the fear structure of a person with social anxiety disorder includes representations of the feared stimuli (e.g., being on a stage giving a talk in front of 100 people), associated fear responses (e.g., muscle tension, heart pounding, trembling, urge to run away), and the meaning associated with the stimuli (e.g., rejection, criticism) and responses (e.g., I am afraid).

Foa and Kozak (1986) posited that treatment reduces anxiety symptoms by providing information that is incompatible with the pathological elements and thereby modifying the fear structure. Such modification is the essence of emotional processing. For treatment to successfully modify a pathological fear structure, it must first activate the fear structure, and then provide corrective information. These conditions can be met by engaging in repeated confrontation with stimuli (e.g. memories, situations, objects) that are feared, yet safe or with low likelihood of harm. Exposure to feared but harmless stimuli activates the fear structure and also provides realistic information about the probability and the cost of feared consequences. For example, a person phobic of bridges can be treated in exposure therapy by driving over a series of progressively higher and longer bridges. Driving over bridges initially activates the person's fear, yet over successive experiences (in which no harm befalls the person), the patient's fear of bridges is ameliorated.

Since Foa and Kozak's (1985, 1986) original work, emotional processing theory has been further developed and elaborated, accounting for the development and maintenance of PTSD. According to the theory, PTSD reflects a trauma memory that contains certain pathological elements. First, it has an especially large number of stimulus elements that are erroneously associated with the meaning of danger. For example, the trauma memory of a female rape survivor suffering PTSD may include representations of men who physically resemble her attacker, the smell of the ocean, and darkness. The excessively large number of stimuli that can activate the fear structure leads people with PTSD to perceive the world as highly dangerous. Second, fear structures associated with PTSD contain representations of physiological arousal and behavioral reactions. These elements of the fear structure (e.g., representations of the survivor's responses during the trauma such as screaming and freezing, flashbacks and intrusive thoughts about the trauma, and interpretation of the PTSD symptoms like "these symptoms mean that I am weak") are associated with the meaning of incompetence. Consequently, two prominent views, that "The world is entirely dangerous," and "I am completely incompetent," underlie the structure of PTSD (Foa & Riggs, 1993).

## Emotional Processing and Natural Recovery

Foa and Cahill's (2001) expansion of emotional processing theory offered an account of the mechanisms underlying natural recovery. They proposed that recovery involves emotional processing that occurs in the course of daily life by repeated activation of the trauma memory through engagement with trauma-related thoughts and feelings, talking about the trauma with others, and being confronted with situations, activities, or objects that serve as reminders of the trauma. *In the absence of additional trauma*, these naturally occurring experiences disconfirm the post-trauma perception that the world is entirely dangerous and that the survivor is incompetent. Natural exposures to trauma reminders enable the survivor to differentiate the trauma itself from memories about the trauma. Opportunities to share the story of the traumatic experience with other people, as well as to re-evaluate assumptions and emotional responses, all help the survivor organize the traumatic memory and achieve a realistic perspective.

## Failure to Emotionally Process Trauma

So what is occurring when this natural process doesn't proceed or is insufficient to prevent development of PTSD? According to emotional processing theory, extensive avoidance of trauma reminders prevents processing of the traumatic memory. Avoidance of trauma memories and related reminders is maintained through the process of negative reinforcement: avoidance leads to more avoidance, because it works well to reduce distress in the short term. For example, a man who fears swimming in deep water tries to swim the entire length of the pool, which includes swimming over to the deep end. Every time he approaches the deep water his anxiety rises. When he turns back towards the shallow water and avoids the deep end, his anxiety drops immediately. This decrease strongly reinforces his "turning back" behavior, and makes it more likely that the next time he approaches the deep end he will again turn away. But in the long run, such escape and avoidance maintain the fear that he may drown in deep water. Continuing to turn away from the deep end prevents our swimmer from learning he *can* safely swim in water that is over his head, and that his fear will subside as he reaches the other side of the pool.

## Exposure Therapy

Within emotional processing theory, it follows that treatment for PTSD must unleash or activate processes that occur naturally when recovery proceeds smoothly. Prolonged Exposure (PE) (Foa, Hembree, & Rothbaum 2007; Foa & Rothbaum, 1998) for PTSD works through activation of the fear structure by deliberate imaginal and in vivo exposure to trauma-related thoughts, images, and situations. These exposures contain information that correct clients' negative perceptions about themselves and the world. In exposure for PTSD, approaching or confronting the memories and reminders of the traumatic experience prevents negative reinforcement of cognitive and behavioral avoidance, reducing one of the primary factors that maintain PTSD.

Imaginal and in vivo exposure in the treatment of PTSD also helps clients to differentiate the traumatic event itself from situations, activities, or places that are similar or remind the person of the trauma, but unlike the trauma itself, are not dangerous or harmful. This allows them to see the trauma as a unique event occurring in space and time, which helps to counter the perception that the world is entirely dangerous and that they are weak and incompetent. Imagine that the swimmer in our example fears deep water because he once witnessed a friend drown in a deep pool. Swimming in deep water activates the memory of his friend's death and the associated fear of deep water. By repeatedly swimming over deep water himself, he differentiates the memory of his friend's death from other instances of being near deep water. He learns that he can swim in deep water as well as he swims in shallow water, decreasing his general fear and enhancing his sense of competence and confidence.

Repeated imaginal exposure to the trauma memory also promotes discrimination between the past and present by helping clients realize that, although remembering the trauma can be emotionally upsetting, *thinking about the trauma* is not the same as being *in* the trauma, nor is it dangerous. In addition, repeatedly revisiting the trauma memory in imaginal exposure provides the client with the opportunity to accurately evaluate aspects of the event about which he may have had some inaccurate perceptions. For example, if our swimmer also feels guilty about not having saved his friend, revisiting the memory may help him come to the realization that he was physically incapable of reaching his friend and there was nothing he could have done to prevent the death.

These experiences support another mechanism involved in emotional processing, which is habituation of anxiety. The anxiety and distress associated with the feared and avoided memories and situations decreases over time, which disconfirms erroneous beliefs that anxiety will last forever or will only reduce with escape from the situation. Importantly, clients also learn that they can tolerate their anxiety and associated symptoms and that confronting these trauma-related situations will not make them "go crazy" or "lose control," fears commonly held by individuals with PTSD. All of these changes reduce PTSD symptoms and bring about a greater sense of mastery and competence.

## Cognitive Therapy

As mentioned above, theoretical concepts central to emotional processing theory are also present in cognitive theories of trauma recovery and treatment (e.g., Ehlers & Clark, 2000; Resick & Schnicke, 1992). In cognitive theory, it is the interpretation of events that leads to specific emotional responses. Our interpretations may be realistic and accurate or may be unrealistic, as when safe or harmless events are viewed as threatening or dangerous. In the latter case, inaccurate interpretations can lead to unrealistic or excessive fear and anxiety. Conceptualizations that emphasize the role of appraisal naturally led to using and investigating the efficacy of cognitive therapy as a treatment for PTSD. As treatment for this disorder, the aim of cognitive therapy has been to provide experiences that reduce unrealistic expectations of harm and facilitate reduction of excessive fear.

Ehlers and Clark (2000) proposed a cognitive model of the development, maintenance, and treatment of PTSD. In their model, PTSD becomes persistent when individuals process the trauma in a way that leads to a sense of serious and current threat. For example, according to this theory, a core cognitive distortion underlying PTSD is the interpretation of the re-experiencing symptoms as threatening. Ehlers and Clark suggested that this perception of pervasive and persistent threat results from excessively negative appraisals, trauma memories characterized by poor elaboration and contextualization, strong associative connections, and strong perceptual priming. Ehlers and Clark's theory is similar to emotional processing theory in suggesting that change in negative perceptions and trauma memories are prevented by the use of avoidance strategies.

Like exposure therapy, cognitive therapy directly addresses the organization of the trauma memory and helps the trauma survivor to develop realistic perspectives toward the event. The primary difference between the two therapies is the tools they use and the degree to which exposure is implemented to address negative cognitions. An exposure therapist asks the PTSD client to approach trauma memories and reminders directly, and to experience the thoughts and feelings that are elicited, thereby creating opportunities for corrective information to be incorporated into the representation of the trauma in memory. In addition, in exposure therapy, the therapist helps the client articulate changes in their perception of themselves and the world. The cognitive therapist asks the PTSD client to identify and challenge the ways in which the trauma has colored thoughts, beliefs, and expectations about the world and self. Changing the way a client thinks and what the client believes will lead to changes in feelings and behavior. In addition, cognitive therapists sometimes make use of imaginal exposure to activate trauma-related cognitions, and they employ in vivo exposure as behavioral experiments that provide an opportunity to test out assumptions and expectancies.

# TREATMENT OUTCOME STUDIES

As stated in the opening to this chapter, close to 100 studies and case reports examining the efficacy of CBT interventions for PTSD have been conducted over the past several decades. For a current and extensive review of the literature, the reader is referred to the volume *Effective Treatments for PTSD, Second Edition: Practice Guidelines from the International Society for Traumatic Stress Studies* (Foa, Keane, Friedman, & Cohen, 2009), with particular attention to the chapter on CBT by Cahill, Rothbaum, Resick, and Follette.

Psychosocial treatment interventions whose efficacies have been studied in randomized trials include exposure therapy, anxiety management programs such as stress inoculation training, cognitive therapy, combinations of exposure with anxiety management and/or cognitive restructuring, and eye movement desensitization and reprocessing. All have been shown to be effective at ameliorating PTSD and other trauma-related psychopathology, although the number and quality of studies on different interventions varies widely.

Since the early days when the efficacy of cognitive behavioral treatment was demonstrated with male war veterans (Keane et al., 1989) and with female rape survivors (Foa et al., 1991, 1999), the populations that have been studied in CBT trials include female as well as male veterans, survivors of sexual and non-sexual assault and childhood abuse, motor vehicle accident victims, refugees, survivors of disasters such as earthquakes as well as those affected by terrorist attacks like the World Trade Center attack on September 11, 2001, and the 1998 terrorist bomb attack in Omagh, Northern Ireland. Thus, current knowledge regarding the efficacy of CBT treatment is based on a wide range of individuals of both genders, including adults and children, and a good representation of traumatic events.

## Exposure Therapy

Of the various treatment approaches subsumed under CBT, exposure therapy has amassed the greatest amount of empirical support thus far. Indeed, the committee charged with reviewing all available outcome data on psychotherapeutic and pharmacologic treatments for PTSD for the 2008 Institute of Medicine report on efficacy of treatments concluded that only exposure therapy had sufficient empirical support to be pronounced effective for treatment of PTSD (IOM, 2008).

Cahill and colleagues (2009) reported in their review of the CBT literature that individual exposure therapy has been studied in 24 randomized controlled trials (RCTs) and in nine non-randomized studies, and at least one more relatively large RCT has been published (Bryant et al., 2008) since their review. Nearly all of these studies reported statistically and clinically significant decreases in PTSD symptom severity and other trauma-related pathology (e.g., depression and anxiety) from pre- to post-treatment, with excellent maintenance of gains through follow-up periods of up to a year.

All 25 RCTs compared the outcome of participants treated with exposure therapy to those in control conditions and/or to those receiving other forms of CBT. In all comparisons with control conditions (e.g., supportive counseling, relaxation training, wait list or delayed treatment), exposure was found more effective at reducing trauma-related pathology. The vast majority of studies comparing participants randomized to exposure therapy with those randomized to another active CBT treatment have found no significant differences in reduction of PTSD or depression (e.g., Foa et al., 1999; Foa et al., 2005).

Perhaps of greatest interest to the practicing clinician, two recent investigations have demonstrated the effectiveness, or "real world" applicability, of prolonged exposure therapy. Foa et al. (2005) compared PE alone with PE combined with trauma-focused cognitive restructuring (CR) in a large sample of women with chronic PTSD resulting from rape, non-sexual assault, and/or childhood sexual abuse. Nearly half were treated by MA-level counselors and social workers in an inner-city, community-based rape treatment center with little specific training or prior experience with CBT. The participants they treated in the study were natural referrals to that clinic. The other half of the participants in this study were treated by Ph.D.-level, expert clinicians in the Center for the Treatment & Study of Anxiety, an academic research clinic specializing in the study and treatment of anxiety disorders. Both PE and PE combined with CR produced substantial reductions in PTSD and depression.

Importantly, results indicated *no differences* in outcome between the clients treated at the two sites. This extremely significant finding for clinicians indicates that PE can be successfully transported to a community setting and implemented effectively by non-CBT experts, thereby helping a wide group of clients.

The second recent study demonstrating the effectiveness and efficacy of PE is also notable for being one of the largest sized samples included in an RCT. Schnurr, Friedman, Engel, Foa, Shea, Resick, et al. (2007) compared PE with present-centered therapy (PCT) in a large sample of female veterans and active duty personnel (*N*=284) with chronic PTSD. PCT was an individual supportive counseling that focused on the here and now. Women who received PE experienced greater reduction in PTSD symptoms at post-treatment and at 3-month follow-up, and were less likely to meet diagnostic criteria for PTSD and more likely to achieve remission. However, by the 6-month follow-up evaluation differences in PTSD were no longer evident between the two treatment groups. It should be noted that PCT was a manualized intervention that also included education about PTSD and a focus on problem solving, including problems that may have developed from trauma or PTSD. The therapists implementing PCT received careful training and supervision throughout the study, and displayed a high degree of adherence and competence. Thus the PCT treatment implemented in this study may have been more rigorous and focused than counseling typically provided in community settings.

Studies like those of Foa et al. (2005) and Schnurr et al. (2007), which demonstrate the successful implementation of efficacious CBT treatments in the "real world" (e.g., in community-based clinical settings and in the hands of non-CBT clinicians), are crucial. After all, what good are treatments if they are only effective in the hands of highly trained, academically based CBT experts? It is important for clinicians to appreciate that dissemination of effective treatments to large populations of individuals in need (e.g., veterans returning from Iraq and Afghanistan, patients in community clinics) is an attainable goal. Indeed, prolonged exposure and cognitive processing therapy are being disseminated or "rolled-out" to clinicians working in Veteran's Affairs medical centers and Department of Defense settings across the United

States. PE has also been systemically disseminated in Israel and Japan, with numerous RCTs being conducted in these countries.

## Cognitive Therapy

The number of published studies evaluating cognitive therapy for PTSD has increased substantially over the past several years. However, studies investigating "pure" cognitive therapy are rare; the majority include some form of exposure to trauma-related memories or cues. For example, Resick and colleagues (2002) developed and studied the efficacy of Cognitive Processing Therapy (CPT). In its original form, CPT contained exposure in the form of having clients write a "trauma narrative" and repeatedly rereading that narrative during the early sessions. More recently, CPT has been shown effective when implemented without the written trauma narratives (Resick, Galovski, Uhlmansiek, Scher, Clum, & Young-Xu, 2008).

Cahill and colleagues (2009) identified 14 studies, 11 of them randomized trials, which have examined CT or CPT for trauma survivors with PTSD. To summarize overall findings, several different CT programs have been quite effective in reducing PTSD severity and depression compared to waitlist or control conditions (e.g., self-help booklets, relaxation training). Six studies (of them RCTs) of cognitive processing therapy, with female assault survivors, male and female veterans, and male and female refugees, have shown significant improvement in reduction of PTSD and other trauma-related pathology (e.g., Monson et al., 2006).

In summary, outcome studies examining cognitive behavioral interventions for chronic PTSD have clearly demonstrated the strong efficacy of several interventions in ameliorating PTSD symptoms, depression, and anxiety. Studies comparing exposure and cognitive therapy, and combinations of these interventions, have generally found strong and equivalent outcomes. All but one study comparing exposure alone to exposure combined with another active intervention (e.g., cognitive restructuring or stress management training) have failed to find enhanced outcomes from the added component. The exception was a recent study by Bryant et al. (2008) in which optimal treatment outcome was achieved by combining cognitive therapy with exposure therapy. However, in this study a critical component of exposure therapy (processing of imaginal exposure) was modified to ensure that no cognitive restructuring (CR) was done with clients in the non-CR conditions. The resulting restrictions imposed on therapists' discussions with their clients may have limited the benefit of exposure treatment, thereby tilting in favor of the combined intervention. On balance, the general literature on treatment components demonstrates the robustness of exposure therapy alone (e.g., Foa et al., 1999; Foa et al., 2005). At the same time, learning derived from exposure exercises is likely enhanced by helping the client process thoughts and feelings that arise from these powerful experiences.

## Eye Movement Desensitization and Reprocessing (EMDR)

Eye Movement Desensitization and Reprocessing (EMDR; Shapiro, 1989; 1995) is a form of exposure accompanied by a series of rapid eye movements or some other form of what has been called "bilateral stimulation." EMDR also has a strong cognitive component, with the aim of identifying and replacing negative cognitions with more desirable ways of perceiving or viewing the trauma and oneself. Briefly, the technique involves asking the client to think about or imagine a scene from the trauma, focusing on some salient aspect of the experience (e.g., the accompanying thoughts, emotions, and/or the physical sensations that are aroused), while tracking the therapist's finger as it is waved back and forth or some other stimulus that moves from side to side. The sequence is repeated, each time asking the client to focus on "what comes up" during the sets of eye movements, until anxiety diminishes. The client also is instructed to consider an alternative and positive thought while imagining the trauma and tracking the bilateral stimulation.

Research on the efficacy of EMDR has progressed over the past 10 to 15 years from case reports and uncontrolled studies to larger and more rigorously conducted treatment trials. Overall, studies have shown that EMDR is an efficacious treatment for PTSD. Spates, Koch, Cusack, Pagato, and Waller (2009) described seven randomized studies that were published in the past decade, most of them comparing outcome of clients treated with EMDR to those treated with exposure therapy. These authors concluded that EMDR appeared generally as effective as exposure therapy. However, there has long been a question about the function and necessity of the eye movements or other forms of alternating bilateral stimulation. To address this important issue, some studies have been designed to dismantle EMDR treatment in order to evaluate the contribution of various components. Reviewing these studies, Spates and colleagues concluded that alternating bilateral stimulation does not influence treatment outcome. Others have come to similar conclusions and expressed concerns that EMDR simply "repackaged" CBT by adding a distinguishing but inert ingredient (Davidson & Parker, 2001). While controversies around these matters continue, current evidence suggests that the efficacy of EMDR is most likely a function of exposure to trauma-related memories and cues.

## Pharmacological Treatment

Friedman, Davidson, and Stein (2009) outlined several good reasons to utilize pharmacotherapy in treating PTSD. One, there are certain neurobiological mechanisms that may be relevant to the disorder and PTSD patients exhibit abnormalities in these systems. Two, PTSD symptoms overlap a good deal with those of depression and other anxiety disorders, and PTSD is often comorbid with these other disorders.

Friedman and colleagues (2009) reviewed the pharmacotherapy literature and summarized evidence from 34 randomized controlled trials as well as reported findings from open trials and case reports. The RCTS have been conducted primarily with selective serotonin reuptake inhibitors (SSRIs such as sertraline, paroxetine, and fluoxetine), and a serotonin-norepinephrine reuptake inhibitor (SNRI; venlafaxine, extended release). These trials have yielded both positive and negative results, but on balance they support the use of SSRIs and the SNRI venlafaxine in the treatment of PTSD (and comorbid depression and anxiety). Indeed, two of these medications have current indication by the Food and Drug Administration (FDA) as treatment for PTSD: sertraline and paroxetine. SSRIs work equally well for men and women. Some evidence suggests that there is a group of chronic, treatment-refractory male veterans who do not benefit from these medications.

Friedman et al. (2009) reported evidence from clinical trials suggesting that some people (about 30%) show complete remission of PTSD after 12 weeks of SSRI treatment, while half of those having a partial response achieve complete remission when given a continued course of treatment (i.e., 24 additional weeks). Importantly, however, discontinuation of SSRIs is often followed by relapse in those who show an initial and favorable response. Whether combining medication treatment with cognitive behavioral therapy can reduce relapse after medications are discontinued is an important area for future research.

## PROLONGED EXPOSURE THERAPY

We conclude this chapter with a more in-depth and clinically focused discussion of the essential elements of exposure therapy and a case example of the use of PE. Prolonged Exposure is delivered in an individual format and usually consists of 8 to 15 therapy sessions that are 90 minutes in length. The core components of PE are education, in vivo exposure to situations that are low risk or safe but avoided because they remind the person of the trauma, and repeated imaginal exposure to the trauma memories. Breathing retraining is taught early in treatment as a tool the client can use to help calm or reduce tension. Daily homework between sessions, including in vivo exposure exercises and listening to recordings of imaginal exposure conducted in that week's therapy session, is designed to encourage exposure practice and is an important aspect of the treatment.

It is crucial that PE be provided within the context of a strong therapeutic alliance, and supported by a clear and thorough rationale for why facing painful memories and the situations that remind one of them will be helpful in recovering from PTSD. The importance of these cornerstones or foundations of therapy are discussed in the PE manual (Foa et al., 2007). Tailoring the treatment to the individual client is also a key aspect of successful PE. Throughout the initial evaluation, psychoeducation, and exposure sessions, the therapist listens for and records the client's specific symptoms and avoidances, and weaves this information into the treatment rationales and the treatment plan.

Finally, exposure is conducted in a way that promotes *emotional engagement* with the trauma memory and with objectively safe reminders of the traumatic event, and simultaneously provides experiences that help the PTSD client to achieve all of the learning that was described earlier in the section on emotional processing. Emotional processing is facilitated when the client is fully engaged with the memory but at the same time is not overwhelmed with anxiety or unable to remain grounded in the present.

We illustrate these principals and the implementation of exposure therapy via a detailed case presentation.

## Case Example

Anne, a 45-year-old African American woman, was referred to the clinic by a victim's assistance officer. An accountant, Anne had been missing work frequently and was on the verge of losing her job. In her initial evaluation Anne disclosed a history of multiple traumatic events, but the trauma that she identified as the "worst" and clearly the most distressing at the time of her evaluation was a horrifically violent attack that she suffered five years prior to time of presentation. In this prolonged assault, Anne was raped and then beaten and stabbed. She was cut severely on her hands defending herself from the knife. She struggled valiantly with the assailant, and was left for dead when she lost consciousness. Fortunately, Anne was able to call for help when she regained consciousness. She was hospitalized and had several surgeries to repair her injuries.

Five years later, when presenting for treatment, Anne's trauma-related symptoms and problems were extremely severe. She was haunted by intrusive thoughts and images of the attack, and had frequent nightmares. Anne avoided thinking and talking about the attack. She stayed at home and avoided other people as much as possible, even friends. Crowds were intolerable and even one-on-one interactions were uncomfortable. Anne was missing work due to the avoidance, and this was beginning to threaten her job. She had trouble sleeping, poor concentration, and was hyper-alert. Mistrustful of others and of herself, Anne had no confidence in her judgment about other people. These issues were heightened because Anne's attacker had been an acquaintance with whom she socialized. Consequently, all men had become unpredictable, untrustworthy, and dangerous.

Anne decided to seek treatment when she became increasingly depressed and isolated as the anniversary week of her attack approached. Her diagnoses at intake included severe PTSD and severe major depression (recurrent). She was experiencing suicidal thoughts and feelings of hopelessness. She had not had any treatment since several sessions of counseling soon after the traumatic attack, which she described as unhelpful and even negative. This experience made her hesitate to enter treatment again, but the severity of her symptoms and the interference they were causing in her life led Anne to accept a recommendation for cognitive behavioral treatment. She subsequently received 12 sessions of prolonged exposure (PE) within a treatment outcome study. We present a detailed description of Anne's PE therapy in the following section to illustrate this leading evidence-based treatment and the aims of emotional processing.

In prolonged exposure (Foa et al., 2007), the client is encouraged to engage in exposure exercises that will help to process the traumatic experiences and reduce PTSD symptoms. It is important in PE that the client understands the rationale underlying use of exposure. Thus, treatment begins in Session 1 with a discussion of the impact of traumatic experiences and the development and maintenance of PTSD. In keeping with emotional processing theory, the client is presented with the idea that symptoms have persisted because avoidance of thinking about the trauma and avoidance of reminders, although common, have prevented the experience from being emotionally processed. Moreover, this avoidance has maintained the client's views of the world as dangerous and of herself as incompetent, by preventing the occurrence of disconfirming experiences. The therapist explains that approaching the trauma memories (imaginal revisiting) and reminders (in-vivo exposure) blocks avoidance and promotes emotional processing of the trauma. The importance of emotional engagement with these exercises, and allowing oneself to experience the feelings and thoughts that result, is emphasized.

When Anne was presented this rationale, she responded that this made sense to her: "*No one* asks you to do that. They ask you what happened, but no one asks 'How did you *feel* when he attacked you?'" The procedures of imaginal and in vivo were then briefly described. The remainder of Session 1 was spent gathering information about the trauma and its impact, and teaching Anne the breathing exercise. Homework consisted of listening to a recording of the entire session, and practicing the breathing exercise.

In Session 2, the therapist provides education about common reactions to trauma. This discussion is intended to help the client understand their problems in context: that PTSD and related symptoms (e.g. shame, guilt, sadness, disruptions in relationships, reduced sexual interest) are typical reactions in the wake of trauma. The goal is to normalize these symptoms, reduce confusion and self-blame, set the focus of treatment on PTSD, and instill hope by explaining how problems will improve through therapy. Anne, like most PTSD sufferers, found this discussion informative and relieving. She realized that she was not just "losing it," there was an explanation for her sense of feeling so out-of-control, and most importantly, she could change and feel like herself again.

Session 2 continues in PE with discussion of the rationale for in vivo exposure. The therapist explains that fears associated with the trauma are often unrealistic or excessive and lead to avoidance, which prevents opportunities for important learning to occur. Lengthy and repeated confrontation with situations, places, activities, and objects that are anxiety arousing, but not objectively and realistically dangerous, yields several benefits. First, it breaks the habit of avoiding, by blocking the reinforcement that results from this behavior. Second, it promotes differentiation of trauma reminders from the traumatic event itself, thus helping the person to better discriminate situations that actually may be dangerous or high risk from those that are actually safe. Third, in vivo exposure results in habituation or reduction of anxiety. Fourth, confronting feared situations and overcoming these fears increases sense of mastery and enhances self-esteem.

PE therapists often tell clients that in vivo exposure is how we get over our fears in daily life and how we teach our children to overcome feared situations. When Anne was asked for an example of a past situation in which she overcame her fear, she immediately thought of one. Anne described how entering the apartment where her violent assault occurred, for the first time after discharge from the hospital, triggered intense distress and disturbing images and memories of her attack. Although encouraged to move away by friends and family, Anne continued to live in her building. Now, five years later, Anne did not associate her apartment with the trauma, nor did she think about it when entering. This real-life example of the benefit of repeated exposure impressed Anne.

Following discussion of the exposure rationale, various situations, activities, and objects that trigger trauma-related anxiety are identified. In Anne's therapy, the therapist helped her generate a list of avoided and/or feared situations. These situations were arranged in a hierarchy based on Anne's anticipated distress levels if she were to confront them now. Distress was rated on a 0 to 100 Subjective Units of Discomfort Scale (SUDS). Typical situations often include things like reading about similar traumas, going to crowded places, sitting with one's back to others (e.g., in a restaurant or in the middle of a crowded movie theater), or looking at reminders of the trauma. A careful assessment of objective risk is made in developing the hierarchy, and the therapist stresses that the idea is not to confront situations that are realistically dangerous. Anne's in vivo exposure hierarchy included going out to the grocery store and staying there a long time, socializing with other people, and being in crowded places like the movie theater and the mall. Items on her hierarchy that were specific trauma reminders included watching TV shows with violent scenes, reading about sexual assaults in the newspaper, looking at scars on her body from the attack and subsequent surgeries, and looking at and handling knives.

In PE, in vivo exposure is most often done as homework between sessions, beginning after Session 2 and continuing throughout treatment. Anne was asked to choose situations to practice that week, starting with the relatively low items on her hierarchy. It was explained to Anne how she was to monitor and record her SUDS level each time she engaged in exposure practice. Anne was asked to stay in each situation for a long enough period of time so that she would have a chance to experience what was really happening, and to allow her discomfort or anxiety to decrease by at least 50%. To allow this to occur, clients are urged to stay in the exposure situation for a minimum of 30 to 45 minutes. At this point in treatment, each situation is practiced repeatedly and the client moves up their hierarchy as treatment progresses. By the end of treatment, Anne, like most PE clients, was able to comfortably confront most of the situations originally avoided.

Session 3 began with a discussion of Anne's homework. This discussion focused on what Anne experienced as she practiced in vivo exposure exercises, how her SUDs levels changed, and what she learned from the exercises. The remainder of the session was devoted to her first imaginal revisiting of the traumatic memory. The therapist explained the goals of revisiting the trauma in imagination are to: (a) emotionally process and organize the memory; (b) differentiate between "remembering" the traumatic event and "being re-traumatized" (i.e., learning that remembering the trauma is not dangerous like the trauma was); (c) lower the anxiety and discomfort that are associated with the trauma memory; and (d) promote differentiation between the traumatic event and similar events, thereby decreasing the generalization of fear from Anne's specific trauma to similar but safe situations. The therapist encouraged Anne to emotionally engage or connect with the memory and the feelings that are generated in the process.

After this discussion, Anne was asked to revisit the memory by describing aloud what happened during the trauma while visualizing it as vividly as possible. She was asked to keep her eyes closed and to use the present tense, and to also include the thoughts, emotions, and sensory experiences that occurred during the traumatic event. Throughout Anne's revisiting, the therapist monitored her SUDS level, and provided support and guidance. Anne engaged in imaginal exposure for 50 minutes, repeating the memory twice. When she finished her last repetition of the memory, the therapist discussed the experience with her, continuing to process the feelings and thoughts evoked by revisiting the memory. At the end of this session, the therapist and Anne planned homework together. In addition to continuing in vivo exposure exercises, Anne was asked to listen to a recording that had been made during the imaginal exposure. Anne was to listen to this recording at home each day, to facilitate continued emotional processing of the trauma memory.

Anne's remaining PE sessions generally followed the same agenda: homework review, 30 to 45 minutes of imaginal revisiting, processing the thoughts and feelings that emerged from the exposure, and planning of the next week's homework. As therapy sessions proceeded, the imaginal exposure progressively focused on the most distressing parts of the trauma memory, or "hot spots," in a repetitive fashion. Repeatedly revisiting those parts of the memory that are associated with the highest levels of distress facilitates emotional processing. For Anne, the most distressing moments were the rape and the times that she thought she would be killed.

In each therapy session, the therapist monitors the client's distress level (as reflected by self-reported SUDS and other non-verbal behavior) during imaginal exposure. It is important for the therapist to titrate emotional engagement as needed: prompting for more details and feelings if the client is not emotionally engaged with the memory, or helping to decrease details and feelings if the level of engagement and associated distress becomes overwhelming. While Anne never missed or canceled a therapy session, she struggled with avoiding the emotions that were activated by her exposures. Anne found it very difficult to let herself connect emotionally with the horror of the prolonged attack. Therefore, in the first three or four sessions of imaginal exposure she was underengaged. In these sessions Anne closed her eyes and described the traumatic memories, but with a flatness and intellectualization that reflected her emotional detachment. Her SUDS levels were correspondingly low to moderate. Similarly, while Anne was faithful in listening to the recordings of her imaginal exposure between sessions, and she practiced in vivo exposure exercises, she did it with the same emotional reserve.

At first, Anne and her therapist were not aware of how thoroughly and extensively she avoided trauma-related stimuli and the feelings associated with her memories. However, it began to be clear by her sixth PE session (halfway through treatment), that Anne's pervasive avoidance of emotion was reducing the effectiveness of her exposures. As is not unusual when avoidance is prominent, Anne's self-reported PTSD and depression symptoms were elevated relative to their pretreatment levels, during this phase of her treatment. The therapist discussed with Anne the concern that, as much good work as she was doing with exposure practice, both in and out of session, the work was not proving beneficial because avoidance was hindering her emotional processing of the trauma. The therapist gave Anne strong encouragement to not only listen to the tapes of imaginal exposure and to do in vivo exposures, but also to really allow herself to experience the feelings, thoughts, sensations, and memories that were evoked by this practice.

Sessions 7 and 8 were a turning point for Anne. As she began to appreciate how much she was avoiding and allowed herself to feel and process the memories and reminders of her trauma, she began to feel better. By Session 8, and for the first time, Anne's PTSD and depression symptoms dropped well below pretreatment levels. Her re-experiencing symptoms subsided and she realized that it was no longer as painful to think or talk about her experiences. She also began to appreciate for the first time how she reacted and how instrumental this was in her survival; there emerged a more realistic perspective on the attack and her behavior during it. Her comments during post-imaginal exposure processing reflected a new acceptance and awareness of the traumatic event as a terrible ordeal that had ended. Anne's hypervigilance began to subside and she started to enjoy social activities.

By the end of treatment, Anne no longer met diagnostic criteria for PTSD. Her 75% decrease in symptom severity and loss of the PTSD diagnosis is a common outcome for PTSD sufferers who receive PE. This has been demonstrated repeatedly in the treatment outcome studies described earlier (e.g., Foa et al., 1999, Foa et al., 2005).

## IMPLICATIONS FOR CLINICAL PRACTICE

Great advances have been made over the past several decades in our understanding of PTSD and how to treat it effectively. Given the pressing need for efficacious and cost-effective treatments, this is timely. For example, in the United States, the large number of military personnel and their family members affected by combat and deployment-related trauma from the conflicts in Iraq and Afghanistan will require increasing numbers of mental health providers trained to treat PTSD and other trauma-related problems. Indeed, the central office for mental health of the Veteran's Administration has mandated that all mental health clinics should be able to provide veterans an evidence-based treatment like PE or Cognitive Processing Therapy (Resick et al., 2002).

Recent research on dissemination of evidence-based treatments is critically important to the mission of making good, effective treatments widely available. Numerous studies, as well as clinical work conducted in non-research settings in the United States and in other countries, have demonstrated that prolonged exposure and other forms of cognitive behavioral therapy for PTSD can be successfully implemented by community-based clinicians who are not highly trained CBT therapists. Yet, we also know that many clinicians do not use these treatments. Becker, Zayfert, and Anderson (2004) surveyed a large group of psychologists, representing a range of theoretical orientations. The psychologists were asked whether they treated patients with PTSD and whether they were trained in and used imaginal exposure with these patients. While 63% of the psychologists reported having treated more than 11 patients with PTSD, only 27% of the sample had been trained in the use of imaginal exposure for PTSD, and only 9% of respondents reported using these methods with the majority of their PTSD patients. Becker et al. also asked respondents who did not use exposure in the treatment of PTSD to explain why they did not. The three most frequently endorsed reasons for not using exposure therapy to treat PTSD were lack of training (60%), resistance to using manualized treatments (25%), and fears that patients would decompensate from the procedures (22%). Clearly, training is important in helping clinicians feel confidant enough that they are willing to use treatments like exposure. Such training is increasingly available in VA and Department of Defense settings, academic training centers, and some trauma research centers.

## Acquiring Experience in the Use of CBT

Over the years we have trained many clinicians to use prolonged exposure to treat PTSD. These years of experience have taught us what helps clinicians to feel increased readiness to implement CBT treatment. First, be trained by knowledgeable and experienced trainers. Such instruction should include use of treatment manuals or guides; the opportunity to see treatment components implemented by skilled practitioners; and in-training practice with the use of role-plays.

Second, be well grounded in the theories underlying these treatments. Prolonged exposure and other forms of CBT are theoretically based, and understanding the underlying assumptions when implementing treatment will increase a therapist's confidence and provide a basis to guide decision-making. Thus, while this chapter has provided an overview of emotional processing theory, clinicians who train to implement PE or cognitive therapy will find it worthwhile to read the theoretical literature (e.g., Foa et al., 2006; Ehlers & Clark, 2000).

Third, if at all possible, arrange follow-up consultation or supervision with an experienced clinician, and/or work with a peer consultation group. Even after a thorough basic training, many clinicians feel continued concern about implementing evidence-based treatments effectively. Ongoing consultation is extremely useful and helps to alleviate concerns and uncertainties. Our experience has been that with increasing practice and the opportunity to see clients improve, most clinicians feel comfortable and confident using these treatments.

Finally, mental health professionals who treat PTSD patients should keep in mind that CBT treatments are not only effective, but also quite robust. Research shows that clients treated by relatively novice clinicians achieve the same positive outcomes as those treated by highly trained CBT experts. Such findings demonstrate that effective use of CBT methods is a straightforward task; mastery of these methods is a feasible goal for clinicians; and no patient diagnosed with PTSD should go without the benefit of evidenced-based treatments.

## REFERENCES

Becker, C. B., Zayfert, C., & Anderson, E. (2004). A survey of psychologists' attitudes towards and utilization of exposure therapy for PTSD. *Behaviour Research and Therapy, 42*(3), 277–292.

Breslau, N., Davis, G. C., Andreski, P., & Peterson, E. (1991). Traumatic events and posttraumatic stress disorder in an urban population of young adults. *Archives of General Psychiatry, 48*, 216–222.

Bryant, R. A., Moulds, M. L., Guthrie, R. M., Dang, S. T., Mastrodomenico, J., Nixon, R. D., et al. (2008). A randomized controlled trial of exposure therapy and cognitive restructuring for posttraumatic stress disorder. *Journal of Consulting and Clinical Psychology, 76*(4), 695–703.

Cahill, S. P., Rothbaum, B. O., Resick, P. A., & Follette, V. M. (2009). Cognitive-behavioral therapy for adults. In E. B. Foa, T. M. Keane, M. J. Friedman & J. A. Cohen (Eds.), *Effective treatments for PTSD: Practice guidelines from the International Society of Traumatic Stress Studies* (2nd ed.; pp. 139–222). New York: Guilford.

Davidson, P. R., & Parker K. C. H. (2001). Eye-movement desensitization and reprocessing (EMDR): A meta analysis. *Journal of Consulting and Clinical Psychology, 191*, 48–51.

Ehlers, A., & Clark, D. M. (2000). A cognitive model of persistent posttraumatic stress disorder. *Behaviour Research and Therapy, 38,* 319–345.

Foa, E. B., & Cahill, S. P. (2001). Psychological therapies: Emotional processing. In N. J. Smelser & P. B. Bates (Eds.), *International encyclopedia of the social and behavioral sciences* (pp. 12363–12369). Oxford: Elsevier.

Foa, E. B., Dancu, C. V., Hembree, E. A., Jaycox, L. H., Meadows, E. A., & Street, G. (1999). The efficacy of exposure therapy, stress inoculation training and their combination in ameliorating PTSD for female victims of assault. *Journal of Consulting and Clinical Psychology, 67,* 194–200.

Foa, E. B., Hembree, E. A., Cahill, S. P., Rauch, S. A., Riggs, D. S., Feeny, N. C., et al. (2005). Randomized trial of prolonged exposure for PTSD with and without cognitive restructuring: Outcome at academic and community clinics. *Journal of Consulting and Clinical Psychology, 73,* 953–964.

Foa, E. B., Hembree, E. A., & Rothbaum, B. O. (2007). *Prolonged exposure therapy for PTSD: Emotional processing of traumatic experiences.* New York: Oxford University Press.

Foa, E. B., Huppert, J. D., Cahill, S. P., & Riggs, D. S. (2006). Emotional processing theory: An update. In B. O. Rothbaum (Ed.), *The nature and treatment of pathological anxiety* (pp. 3–24). New York: Guilford.

Foa, E. B., Keane, T. M., Friedman, M. J., & Cohen, J. A. (2009). *Effective treatments for PTSD: Practice guidelines from the International Society for Traumatic Stress Studies* (2nd ed.; pp. xiii, 658). New York: Guilford.

Foa, E. B., & Kozak, M. J. (1985). Treatment of anxiety disorders: Implications for psychopathology. In Tuma, A. H., & Maser, J. D. (Eds.), *Anxiety and the anxiety disorders* (pp. 421–452). Hillsdale, NJ: Erlbaum.

Foa, E. B., & Kozak, M. J. (1986). Emotional processing of fear: Exposure to corrective information. *Psychological Bulletin, 99,* 20–35.

Foa, E. B., & Riggs, D. S. (1993). Post-traumatic stress disorder in rape victims. In J. Oldham, M. B. Riba, & A. Tasman (Eds.), *American Psychiatric Press Review of Psychiatry, Volume 12* (pp. 273–303). Washington, DC: American Psychiatric Press.

Foa, E. B., & Rothbaum, B. O. (1998). *Treating the trauma of rape.* New York: Guilford.

Foa, E. B., Rothbaum, B. O., Riggs, D. S., & Murdock, T. (1991). Treatment of post-traumatic stress disorder in rape victims: A comparison between cognitive-behavioral procedures and counseling. *Journal of Consulting and Clinical Psychology, 59,* 715–723.

Foa, E. B., Steketee, G., & Rothbaum, B. (1989). Behavioral/cognitive conceptualizations of post-traumatic stress disorder. *Behavior Therapy, 20,* 155–176.

Friedman, M. J., Davidson, J. R. T., & Stein, D. J. (2009). Pharmacotherapy for adults. In E. B. Foa, T. M. Keane, & M. J. Friedman, & J. A. Cohen (Eds.), *Effective treatments for PTSD: Practice guidelines from the International Society of Traumatic Stress Studies* (2nd ed.). New York: Guilford.

Institute of Medicine (IOM). 2008. *Treatment of posttraumatic stress disorder: An assessment of the evidence.* Washington, DC: National Academies Press.

Keane, T. M., Fairbank, J. A., Caddell, J. M., & Zimering, R. T. (1989). Implosive (flooding) therapy reduces symptoms of PTSD in Vietnam combat veterans. *Behavior Therapy, 20*(2), 245–260.

Kessler, R. C., Berglund, P., Delmer, O., Jin, R., Merikangas, K. R., & Walters, E. (2005). Lifetime prevalence and age-of-onset distributions of DSM-IV disorders in the National Comorbidity Survey replication. *Archives of General Psychiatry, 62,* 593–603.

Monson, C. M., Schnurr, P. P., Resick, P. A., Friedman, M. J., Young-Xu, Y., & Stevens, S. P. (2006). Cognitive processing therapy for veterans with military-related posttraumatic stress disorder. *Journal of Consulting and Clinical Psychology, 74,* 898–907.

Resick, P. A., Galovski, T. E., Uhlmansiek, M. O., Scher, C. D., Clum, G. A. & Young-Xu, Y. (2008). A randomized clinical trial to dismantle components of cognitive processing therapy for posttraumatic stress disorder in female victims of interpersonal violence. *Journal of Consulting and Clinical Psychology, 76,* 243–258.

Resick, P. A., Nishith, P., Weaver, T. L., Astin, M. C., & Feurer, C. A. (2002). A comparison of cognitive-processing therapy with prolonged exposure and a waiting condition for the treatment of chronic posttraumatic stress disorder in female rape victims. *Journal of Consulting and Clinical Psychology, 70,* 867–879.

Resick, P. A., & Schnicke, M. K. (1992). Cognitive processing therapy for sexual assault victims. *Journal of Consulting and Clinical Psychology, 60,* 748–756.

Schnurr, P. P., Friedman, M. J., Engel, C. C., Foa, E. B., Shea, M. T., Resick, P. A., et al. (2007). Cognitive behavioral therapy for posttraumatic stress disorder in women: A randomized controlled trial. *Journal of the American Medical Association, 297,* 820–830.

Shapiro, F. (1989). Eye movement desensitization: A new treatment for posttraumatic stress disorder. *Journal of Behavior Therapy and Experimental Psychiatry, 20*(3), 211–217.

Shapiro, F. (1995). *Eye movement desensitization and reprocessing: Basic principles, protocols, and procedures.* New York: Guilford.

Spates, R. C., Koch, E., Cusack, K., Pagato, S., & Waller, S. (2009). Eye movement desensitization and reprocessing. In E. B. Foa, T. M. Keane, M. J. Friedman, & J. A. Cohen (Eds.), *Effective treatments for PTSD: Practice guidelines from the International Society of Traumatic Stress Studies* (2nd ed.). New York: Guilford.

# Treating the Full Range of Posttraumatic Reactions

Richard A. Bryant

Despite the recognition that trauma precipitates diverse psychological outcomes, there has often been a myopic focus on posttraumatic stress disorder (ptsd). the aim of this chapter is to review the breadth of psychological problems that arise after trauma, and to provide an overview of intervention strategies. the scope of this chapter is on evidence-based approaches and their relevance to the range and course of posttraumatic reactions.

## PSYCHOLOGICAL DISORDERS FOLLOWING TRAUMA

PTSD is the most commonly identified disorder that occurs after exposure to a traumatic event. Rates of PTSD vary, but often 1 in 5 people who have been trauma exposed meet symptom criteria. Across studies, the prevalence of PTSD is higher with direct (30 to 40%), rather than indirect (10% to 20%) exposure (Neria, et al., 2007). It is important to note that other disorders also commonly occur both with, and independent of, PTSD. Depression is frequently observed among survivors of traumatic events, along with various anxiety disorders (Norris, Friedman, & Watson, 2002). For example, after the Oklahoma City

Bombing, 22% of people suffered depression, 7% suffered panic disorder, 4% had generalized anxiety disorder, 9% had alcohol use disorder, and 2% had drug use disorder. Overall, 30% of people in direct proximity of the bombing had a psychiatric disorder other than PTSD (North, et al., 1999). In another study of over 1,000 traumatic injury survivors (Bryant, et al., 2010), depression was the most common disorder (16%), followed by generalized anxiety disorder (11%), agoraphobia (9%), and only then PTSD (9%). Importantly, although 23% of this sample reported a new psychiatric disorder, the majority of these disorders occurred independent of PTSD. These data highlight that effective mental health response to traumatic events needs to be cognizant of treatment strategies that encompass the range of psychiatric disorders.

## WHEN DOES ONE PROVIDE TREATMENT?

There is consensus that it is unnecessary, and potentially harmful, to provide mental health interventions too soon after trauma exposure. Whereas many people display signs of psychiatric disturbance in the immediate aftermath of a trauma, prospective studies indicate that this distress commonly subsides within the first weeks or months postincident. For example, a survey of New York City residents following the 9/11 terrorist attacks 5 to 8 weeks post-incident, found that 7.5% of adults living south of 110th Street in Manhattan had developed PTSD (Galea, et al., 2002). In February 2002, Galea's group conducted a follow-up study on another group of adults living south of 110th Street, and found that only 1.7% of the sample met PTSD criteria at this later point in time (Galea, et al., 2003). A similar pattern was found in Thailand after the 2004 tsunami, where the rate of PTSD in displaced people was 12% two months post-incident. This rate dropped to 7% at 9 months (van Griensven, et al., 2006). This study also reported that depression decreased from 30% to 25%, and anxiety decreased from 37% to 17%.

If most people recover from a traumatic incident without formal mental health intervention, it is logical to allow them to do so. Most communities have limited mental health resources that are best allocated to the minority of people who suffer persistent psychological distress.

In deciding when to provide treatment, one should not simply consider the time that has elapsed since the traumatic event, but also the context in which survivors find themselves. Many traumatic events may be described as discrete incidents that occur in a relatively stable environment; in these cases, one may expect recovery to occur within several months. In cases when a trauma persists because of social upheaval or community destruction, then assistance is most needed to cope with the stressful environment. Following Hurricane Katrina, for example, many people's lives were massively disrupted for lengthy periods because of relocation, lack of housing, and loss of basic infrastructures.

Two critical issues for deciding the appropriateness of an intervention are (a) the extent to which threat still exists for the survivor, and (b) the extent to which the survivor has sufficient resources to manage. A disaster survivor who is homeless, unemployed, and unaware of the well-being of family members may not be appropriate for a mental health intervention. It is only when an individual has secured safety and an adequate sense of security that one considers psychological treatment.

## IMMEDIATE AFTERMATH OF TRAUMA

One of the major debates over recent years has concerned whether intervening shortly after a traumatic event limits the development of subsequent posttraumatic disorders. For several decades, psychological debriefings were employed in the hope of reducing such risk. The modern form of debriefing was popularized by Mitchell, who called the intervention Critical Incident Stress Debriefing (CISD; Mitchell, 1983). Over time, an increasing number of studies have demonstrated that people who receive CISD do not enjoy better outcomes than those who do not go through the procedures (Rose, Bisson, & Wessely, 2001). Further, some people have argued that debriefing may have a toxic impact by impairing the natural recovery that typically occurs following a traumatic event. This concern has arisen out of several studies finding poorer outcomes among people who receive CISD, especially those who are highly distressed (Hobbs, Mayou, Harrison, & Worlock, 1996). It appears that requiring people to ventilate emotions within days of trauma exposure may hasten arousal and strengthen trauma memories, thereby impeding natural recovery (McNally, Bryant, & Ehlers, 2003). It should be noted that the evidence that initial debriefing may be harmful is not strong and requires replication in properly randomized studies.

In the wake of increasing evidence that CISD does not prevent PTSD, there has been a shift in thinking about what to offer survivors in the immediate aftermath of trauma. A recent commentary has outlined five key principles that are important to facilitate adaptation after disasters and traumas (Hobfoll, et al., 2007). The first principle is promoting a sense of safety. Research has shown that one of the strongest predictors of posttraumatic problems is the sense that one is under persistent threat (Mikulincer & Solomon, 1988), while enhancing safety is associated with reductions in adverse mental health outcomes (Ozer, Best, Lipsey, & Weiss, 2003). Safety can be promoted at an individual, group, organizational, and community level. The common message across contexts is to enhance the perception that immediate threat has subsided.

The second goal outlined by Marshall et al. is to promote "calming," which aims to reduce the hyperarousal that is frequent after disaster. This principle emerges from evidence that hyperarousal in the acute aftermath of trauma is strongly predictive of subsequent PTSD (Bryant, 2006; Shalev & Freedman, 2005). In fact, one argument against the utility of CISD has been that it potentially increases arousal immediately after trauma exposure, and therefore impairs adaptation (Hobfoll, et al., 2007). Strategies that help to calm an individual include relaxation training, breathing control, problem-solving, and adaptive self-talk.

The third principle involves promoting a sense of self-efficacy, which entails the belief that one's actions will lead to positive outcomes. This perception is important as it encourages individuals and communities to regain a sense of control over their environment. Problem-solving is a core strategy in this goal, because it allows the individual to develop skills and successfully overcome their immediate problems.

The fourth goal is promoting connectedness. This goal is supported by evidence that social support is one of the strongest buffers against problems after trauma exposure (Norris, Friedman, & Watson, 2002). The fifth goal is instilling hope, because optimism can be an important predictor of successful outcomes after trauma (Antonovsky, 1979). Optimism can be achieved at an individual level by cognitive reframing of one's expectations so they are not overly negative. At a community level, optimism is promoted by public activities that focus on adaptation, recovery, and problem-solving.

"Psychological First Aid" (PFA) is an approach that builds on many of the principles highlighted by Hobfoll et al. (2007). PFA serves as an alternative to CISD and has three major goals: to facilitate adaptive coping and problem-solving; to reduce acute stress reactions; and, to guide the survivor to additional resources that enhance coping. Importantly, PFA does not encourage ventilation of the trauma experience, as prescribed in CISD. At the same time, PFA permits discussion of an event if the individual wishes to talk about the experience. In this way, PFA attempts to enhance coping skills in the immediate aftermath of disaster without causing undue distress. It should be noted that PFA has not been subjected to empirical scrutiny, and so it is premature to conclude that it is an effective response.

## INTERVENTION STRATEGIES FOR POSTTRAUMATIC DISORDERS

This section provides an overview of treatments for various disorders that can arise in the aftermath of trauma. The goal of this discussion, in addition to highlighting evidence-based treatments, is to encourage clinicians to take a broad view of diagnostic issues when they provide a case formulation.

### Overview of Treatments for PTSD

The treatment of choice for PTSD is cognitive behavior therapy (CBT; (E. B. Foa, Keane, Friedman, & Cohen, 2009). CBT for PTSD typically commences with psychoeducation about common trauma reactions. This component aims to legitimize an individual's reactions, help the individual develop a formulation of their problems, and establish a rationale for treatment. This component is critical in treating any disorder because it establishes the role of the trauma survivor as an active participant in therapy who assumes responsibility for recovery. After providing education, it is always useful to ask the survivor to explain his or her understanding of their trauma response and how treatment will work.

This effort encourages the individual to process the information that has been given to them, and provides the therapist with the opportunity to correct any misunderstandings.

Apart from formal CBT, there are several anxiety management strategies that can provide coping skills to further a sense of mastery over fear, and to reduce arousal levels. These strategies assist highly distressed individuals to perceive a degree of control over their distress. The techniques also are relatively easy to apply. Studies indicate that anxiety management strategies are generally not as effective as exposure or cognitive approaches (Bryant, Sackville, Dang, Moulds, & Guthrie, 1999; E. B. Foa, Rothbaum, Riggs, & Murdock, 1991). Nonetheless, giving the survivor some tools to increase mastery over anxiety provides both a sense of relief and a motivation to comply with more demanding therapy tasks. Anxiety management can involve progressive muscle relaxation. However, this technique is time-consuming, and it probably is more beneficial to devote therapy time to other interventions. Breathing retraining, on the other hand, is a relatively easy skill that requires little time to teach. Although these techniques are simple, therapists should be aware that focusing on breathing or other bodily sensations can trigger reminders of the trauma, because many PTSD patients suffer panic attacks during a traumatic event, such that anxiety becomes conditioned to subsequent somatic cues (Nixon & Bryant, 2003).

Cognitive restructuring strategies are employed to counteract maladaptive appraisals that can be pivotal in the development and maintenance of a range of post-traumatic adjustment problems (Ehlers & Clark, 2000; Ehlers, Mayou, & Bryant, 1998). Cognitive restructuring involves teaching individuals to identify and evaluate the evidence for negative automatic thoughts. Patients also are encouraged to evaluate their beliefs about the trauma, the self, the world, and the future (Beck, 1976).

Several points need to be noted when providing cognitive restructuring to trauma survivors. First, many beliefs that traumatized patients hold are based on very real and threatening experiences: beliefs that they are not safe or that the world is dangerous may appear valid in the context of their traumatic experience. Therefore, it is crucial that therapists emphasize that a patient's beliefs are understandable in the aftermath of trauma. At the same time, efforts to legitimize beliefs for the sake of retaining rapport and credibility, should not deter clinicians from helping patients when extreme or biased thinking contributes to impaired functioning. Also, it is important to recognize that cognitive restructuring is not simply positive thinking (e.g., using phrases such as, "Everything will be fine"). This is important to note because many survivors of trauma experience ongoing stressful or even traumatic circumstances that require realistic appraisals. This recognition is particularly important when treating people who are high risk for ongoing trauma, including military personnel, police officers, firefighters, and paramedics.

There is good reason to suggest that exposure is the most potent component in treating PTSD (Bryant et al., 2008). Prolonged imaginal exposure requires the individual to vividly imagine the trauma for prolonged periods. The therapist assists the patient to provide a narrative of their traumatic experience in a way that emphasizes all relevant details, including sensory cues and affective responses. In an attempt to maximize the sense of reliving the experience, the individual may be asked to provide the narrative in the present tense, speak in the first person, and ensure that there is focus on the most distressing aspects. Prolonged exposure typically occurs for at least 30 minutes, and is usually supplemented by daily homework exercises. Variants of imaginal exposure involve requiring clients to repeatedly write down detailed descriptions of the experience (Resick & Schnicke, 1993). Exposure also can be implemented with the assistance of virtual reality paradigms using computer-generated imagery (Rothbaum, Hodges, Ready, Graap, & Alarcon, 2001). Most exposure treatments supplement imaginal exposure with in vivo practice that involves live graded exposure to the feared trauma-related stimuli.

## Acute Stress Disorder

In addition to strong evidence that CBT is the treatment of choice for chronic PTSD, there is also increasing evidence that the same approaches are useful as a secondary prevention approach for people who appear to be high risk for PTSD shortly after a traumatic event. Acute stress disorder (ASD) was introduced in DSM-IV to discriminate between individuals who have a transient stress response (and do not need formal mental health intervention) and those who are experiencing the early stage of a psychopathological process that will result in PTSD. ASD is currently defined as dissociative (i.e., reduced awareness of surroundings, depersonalization, derealization, numbing, amnesia) re-experiencing, avoidance, and arousal symptoms between 2 and 28 days after trauma exposure (See Table 1.3 in Chapter 1 for a full listing of ASD criteria.) It should be noted that many people with elevated levels of distress do not meet the dissociative criteria of ASD, but still go on to develop PTSD (Bryant, in press). Nevertheless, numerous studies have indicated that anxiety management, cognitive restructuring, and especially exposure are efficacious in preventing PTSD in those with ASD (Bryant, Harvey, Dang, Sackville, & Basten, 1998; Bryant, et al., 2008; Bryant, Moulds, Guthrie, & Nixon, 2005). Intervening at this stage with CBT requires some modifications. First, treatment typically commences several weeks after trauma and only when the traumatic context has stabilized and the person has the resources and social support to focus on therapy. Second, in recognition of the recency of the traumatic event, a degree of avoidance is often allowed as the person adjusts to the event. Thus, the clinician may not require the patient to progress through *in vivo* exposure to all reminders because such an approach may be unrealistic so soon after an event. Third, if an individual displays extreme agitation, strong avoidance, or marked dissociative responses several weeks after an event, it may be wise to delay exposure-based therapy for several months until these reactions abate. Fourth, if an adult who has experienced a traumatic event also reports memories of prior trauma or childhood abuse it may be advisable to delay exposure therapy for these earlier memories. Although CBT is the optimal treatment for childhood trauma-related PTSD, a traumatized person may not be ready to address developmental trauma while at the same time coping with recent threat.

## Specific Phobia

Individuals can develop specific phobic reactions after a traumatic event, without evidencing the broader problems with mood regulation and hyperarousal that characterize PTSD (McNally & Saigh, 1993). On occasion, it may challenge the clinician's diagnostic skills to distinguish between presentations of phobic reactions, depression, and PTSD (Rosen, Spitzer, & McHugh, 2008). In this context, it is important to consider the full range of symptom criteria that constitutes a PTSD diagnosis, and not reflexively apply the diagnosis whenever posttraumatic anxiety presents. For cases when specific phobia is the appropriate diagnosis, then exposure-based behavioral methods are clearly the treatment of choice. In cases of specific phobia, treatment typically omits imaginal exposure techniques because the patient does not present with re-experiencing symptoms of flashbacks and intrusive memories. Instead, therapy focuses on in vivo exposure in the same way as one treats someone who is phobic of heights or animals.

## Treating Posttraumatic Depression

It has often been believed that depression develops secondarily to PTSD, and that as PTSD resolves then depression will reduce. There is indirect support for this proposition insofar as effective treatments of PTSD often find associated decreases in depression (Resick, et al., 2008). However, the finding that depression commonly occurs in the absence of PTSD (Bryant, et al., 2010) raises questions about its appropriate treatment. Although little research has been conducted on the nature of posttraumatic depression, it appears that established depression management approaches apply to these cases: antidepressant medication, cognitive restructuring, mood monitoring, and pleasant event and activity scheduling (Hollon, Stewart, & Strunk, 2006). Patients with severe depression should be considered for antidepressant medication. It is worth noting that several classes of antidepressants (most notably, the SSRIs) are indicated for treating PTSD as well (Friedman, 2003). Any patient presenting with marked suicidal intent should definitely be considered for antidepressant review.

Although many patients will only meet criteria for major depressive disorder and not PTSD, there may be subsyndromal levels of PTSD or other anxiety problems. This presentation does not preclude offering the patient CBT for PTSD symptoms, even if full criteria are not met. For example, a patient with distressing re-experiencing symptoms, who does not have associated problems with avoidance, may still benefit from exposure-based treatment. There is evidence that many patients with depression commonly suffer intrusive images of their traumatic experiences (Brewin, 1998). This finding suggests that, in combination with standard treatments for depression, exposure approaches may be useful to address the distressing memories of a traumatic experience.

## Excessive Worry and Generalized Anxiety Disorder

It is hardly surprising that many trauma survivors develop generalized anxiety disorder (GAD), as they worry about a range of possibly harmful outcomes. This scenario is heightened by potential threat that can arise after trauma; as when individuals experience terrorist attacks, live in a war zone, or reside in areas that are high risk for natural disasters, such as hurricanes, earthquakes, or bushfires. Aftershocks may occur after an earthquake, housing may collapse after a hurricane, and subsequent attacks may occur in the context of terrorist activities. Although concern about realistic threat can be adaptive, many studies have shown that people with anxiety disorders exaggerate the likelihood of harmful events. This pattern clearly impedes adequate functioning (Ehlers & Clark, 2000).

Managing concerns about potential threat after trauma has required a different approach than one brings to bear on GAD. This is because GAD often involves irrational fears about unlikely events, while fears of terrorism or disaster may be reasonably justified. Marshall and colleagues (2007) have proposed a set of principles to address risk appraisals with trauma survivors who continue to face some degree of realistic threat. The first step is to clarify a person's belief. It is essential to determine whether the belief is rational or excessive in light of available evidence. Second, one should challenge the validity of the belief by discerning between what is likely risk versus acceptable risk. We typically accept certain levels of risk on a daily basis, such as driving in traffic, because this risk results in significant benefit. A forthright discussion of risk issues can be useful in therapy because it addresses the common problem of people unrealistically seeking zero levels of risk. As an illustration of this approach, Marshall et al. (2007) provide the example of helping a person understand the risk of traveling on a subway. They calculated that an attack similar to the July 7, 2005, London subway bombings would kill 40 persons, among 4,500,000 daily riders. This results in the likelihood of 1 death in 100,000 on any particular day. On the basis that one attack occurs per year, the risk was estimated at 1 in 30 million, or essentially zero.

The third step involves pointing out the benefits and losses associated with the belief that threat is imminent. For example, a New Yorker could have decided to avoid Manhattan and any high-rise buildings after 9/11. Although this strategy might have provided short-term relief of anxiety, it could also have led to loss of job, career advancement, social interaction, and financial opportunity. Motivational interviewing about the benefits and losses that result from a particular belief can assist a disaster survivor when deciding on a reasonable level of risk that best serves the individual's interests (Miller & Rollnick, 2002). For example, a clinician can prompt the patient to consider the costs of excessive worry and avoidance (e.g., not socializing, avoiding work, inappropriate modeling to children) and the benefits of accepting a measured amount of risk (e.g., being able to fulfill family responsibilities, maintaining work functions).

The fourth step proposed by Marshall et al. is to have a patient test alternative and more adaptive beliefs by engaging in experiments that can demonstrate how previously held fears were not justified. These four steps, when taken together, encourage trauma survivors to come to terms with an acceptable level of threat that still allows them to function in a way that is reasonably safe.

## Complicated Grief

The last decade has seen an enormous amount of empirical data emerge to indicate that complicated grief is a distinct construct. Accordingly, it has been proposed as a new diagnosis for consideration in DSM-V (Lichtenthal, Cruess, & Prigerson, 2004). Complicated grief is characterized by yearning for the deceased, bitterness about the loss, inability to proceed with life, preoccupation with the loss, hopelessness about the future, and preoccupation with sorrow. When these reactions cause impairment at least six months after the death, then a patient can be considered to be experiencing psychological disorder. Many studies have demonstrated that complicated grief symptoms form a distinct syndrome that is separate from depression or anxiety (Prigerson et al., 1999). Further, complicated grief is predictive of substantial morbidity (e.g., depression, suicidal ideation, high blood pressure), adverse health behaviors (e.g., increased smoking, alcohol consumption, insomnia), and quality of life impairment, even controlling for the effects of age, gender, and depression

(Prigerson et al., 1999). In summary, there is overwhelming evidence that complicated grief is a distinct disorder that contributes uniquely to a broad range of impairment, and is not responsive to usual treatments targeted towards depression. The available research suggests that complicated grief persists in approximately 10% of bereaved people (Bonanno & Kaltman, 2001).

There has been much controversy concerning optimal treatments of complicated grief. Several meta-analyses have indicated that global counseling immediately after loss is not effective in alleviating subsequent disorder (Currier, Neimeyer, & Berman, 2008). In contrast, there are now several randomized controlled trials that have demonstrated the efficacy of CBT for this condition (Shear, Frank, Houck, & Reynolds, 2005). The available evidence suggests that treatment can include the following components: (a) emotional reliving, (b) communicating unresolved issues with the deceased, and (c) goal setting and increasing activity schedules. Emotional reliving involves having the individual relive the circumstances of the death and related memories that cause distress. This approach mimics exposure approaches used for anxiety disorders, such as PTSD. In the context of complicated grief, this technique can also involve communicating with the deceased via "empty chair" techniques that encourage the individual to express any outstanding issues that need to be resolved. This approach can be a useful means to commence cognitive restructuring. Using probabilistic reasoning, Socratic questioning, and evidence-based reasoning, the therapist can assist the patient to alter maladaptive appraisals about their relationship to the deceased and their capacity to carry on in life without the person. Therapy often devotes six to eight sessions on addressing loss-related distress, by employing reliving and cognitive approaches. Therapy can then progress to enhancing future adaptation by facilitating goals and ensuring that the patient engages in daily and social activities. This latter approach is important because complicated grief is characterized by withdrawal and the absence of positive stimuli.

## Treating Posttraumatic Agoraphobia and Panic Disorder

Agoraphobia and panic disorder are commonly reported following trauma. Further, there is increasing evidence that panic attacks play an important role in psychopathological responses to trauma. For example, many adults with panic disorder report a history of trauma, and many trauma survivors report panic attacks within the previous two weeks. Also, panic attacks are common during traumatic experiences, occurring in 53% to 90% of trauma survivors (Nixon & Bryant, 2003). Fear conditioning models propose that elevated fear at the time of trauma is conditioned to stimuli associated with the traumatic experience, with repeated exposures serving to elicit ongoing fear (Pitman, 1989). Building on this model, it has been proposed that panic reactions that occur at the time of trauma may strengthen fear conditioning. This fear conditioning, in turn, may lead to subsequent panic when reminders trigger cued pain attacks.

An intriguing question concerning the management of posttraumatic panic and agoraphobia is whether these conditions should be managed differently from similar conditions that occur in the absence of trauma. Managing panic disorder typically involves interoceptive exposure that teaches the patient that feared outcomes of somatic cues (e.g., chest pain, breathing difficulties) do not actually signify catastrophic outcomes (e.g., cardiac arrest). This is achieved by inducing aversive somatic sensations in patients (e.g., via hyperventilation), and then reinforcing the belief that there is no adverse outcome. It is questionable whether trauma-related panic requires this approach, particularly when the attacks experienced by trauma survivors are linked to trauma memories. A recent study conducted by our team demonstrated that attacks in classic panic disorder patients are associated with fear of somatic outcomes. Patients with post-traumatic panic feared both somatic outcomes and the effects of trauma memories. In our clinical experience, treating the trauma memories with prolonged exposure usually results in successful reduction of panic attacks. Thus, there usually is no need with trauma survivors to implement interoceptive exposure. The clinician wants to keep in mind, however, that if one has completed exposure to trauma memories and panic attacks persist, one should definitely administer interoceptive exposure and address catastrophic beliefs about somatic cues.

## Substance Use Disorder

There is overwhelming evidence that PTSD, and trauma exposure, are associated with substance abuse disorders (Chilcoat & Breslau, 1998).

The most common model of posttraumatic substance use disorders is that people self-medicate to minimize the distress associated with post-traumatic responses. It is proposed that this response can be highly maladaptive because substance use has both anxiety-producing and stress-response dampening effects. Substance use may be maintained by the immediate reinforcement of anxiety reduction, but it contributes to an overall worsening of anxiety and promotes further substance use. Further, findings from uncontrolled studies suggest that patients whose PTSD symptoms remain untreated, quickly relapse following substance use treatment, with the severity of PTSD symptoms related to relapse rates. Fortunately, receipt of PTSD treatment shortly after substance use treatment is related to better outcomes, with remission of substance use problems lasting through 5-year follow-up assessments (Read, Brown, & Kahler, 2004).

At this point in time, there is a dearth of well-conducted trials to shape practice for comorbid PTSD and substance use disorder. One popular approach is the Seeking Safety model, which has been subjected to controlled evaluation and shown to reduce substance use and PTSD symptoms (Najavits, Gallop, & Weiss, 2006). This approach is based on the premise that treating trauma survivors with substance use disorder requires teaching them adaptive skills to minimize risk for engaging in dangerous behaviors that result in abusing substances. This treatment package involves a very broad range of skills, tailored to the specific needs of the trauma survivor. The package may include teaching adaptive cognitions, distress tolerance, interpersonal skills, anger management, and how to cope with triggers. A potential weakness of this approach is that it does not integrate proven CBT approaches into the treatment program (i.e., exposure treatment).

There are several uncontrolled treatment studies that have adopted collaborative care approaches that integrate motivational interviewing, case management, and trauma-focused CBT (Najavits et al., 2009). At this point in time, it appears that optimal treatment for comorbid PTSD and substance use disorder involves integrating exposure and cognitive restructuring with established substance use management strategies. The sequencing of therapy typically involves ensuring that substance abuse is addressed via motivational interviewing (Miller & Rollnick, 2002), stimulus control strategies, coping skills, and case management. These steps are followed with cognitive restructuring and exposure approaches that can address the PTSD symptoms.

## The Construct of Complex Trauma

Much has been written in recent years concerning the construct of complex trauma. The defining feature of complex trauma is deficiency in regulating emotions, which occurs in the context of other PTSD reactions. This presentation often involves impulsive behaviors that occur in response to poor tolerance of extreme emotions, including substance abuse, risky sexual behavior, and self-harm. The construct of complex trauma overlaps, but is distinguished from borderline personality disorder, insofar as the former predominantly involves PTSD that is compounded by emotional regulation deficits. In contrast, whereas Borderline Personality Disorder often entails PTSD symptoms, the focus is on unstable relationships, fear of abandonment, and emotional lability. The prevailing opinion on how to manage complex trauma responses rests upon an extension of CBT. This adaptation teaches the person coping skills to manage emotions more effectively. Only after these initial interventions does the clinician want to commence standard CBT for PTSD. Cloitre has shown that this "two-stage" approach can effectively treat PTSD in adult survivors of childhood sexual abuse (Cloitre, Koenen, Cohen, & Han, 2002). In the first phase (consisting of approximately eight sessions), the clinician focuses on teaching skills for monitoring, labeling and managing emotions; identifying triggers; understanding the relationship between thoughts and emotions; tolerating distress (e.g., breathing retraining); and identification of interpersonal schema (e.g., how the individual appraises self in relation to others). The purpose of the latter strategy is to understand dysfunctional appraisals learnt during childhood and how these maladaptively impact current relationships. Through discussion, role plays, assertiveness training, and rehearsal, the person learns more adaptive ways of appraising and interacting with other people (Levitt, Malta, Martin, Davis, & Cloitre, 2007).

Some commentators have suggested other novel approaches to treating complex trauma reactions. One approach places much emphasis on the impact of severe trauma on bodily functions, and suggests that traumatization results in "somatic memories" in which traumas are relived via sensori-motor experiences (Ogden, Pain, & Fisher, 2006). The model proposes that, in addition to top-down approaches that presume cognitions influence emotions, there also are bottom-up mechanisms, in which bodily reactions directly impact psychological functioning. This approach posits that effective treatment of complex trauma can be achieved by activating somatic sensations; thereby helping the trauma survivor to identify and be aware of various sensations purportedly linked to past trauma. It is argued that this process results in greater tolerance of physical responses to trauma, and contributes to better outcomes. Despite the popularity of this approach, there is no evidence that it is effective, or that the theory upon which it is based is sound. Patients suffering complex trauma require the best treatments available, and should not be subject to interventions based on untested speculation. Clinicians are encouraged to use CBT approaches that are specifically adapted for patients with emotional dysregulation difficulties (Cloitre, Koenen, Cohen, & Han, 2002).

## Mild Traumatic Brain Injury

Although not a psychiatric disorder, another frequent complicating feature for many trauma survivors involves their sustaining a mild traumatic brain injury (MTBI). MTBI commonly occurs following motor vehicle accidents, assaults, combat, and industrial accidents. There has been enormous attention in recent years on the interplay between MTBI and posttraumatic psychiatric disorders (Bryant, 2001b), as well as a longstanding debate over the extent to which PTSD can develop after MTBI. Commentators used to argue that people who sustain a MTBI are unlikely to develop PTSD because they suffered impaired consciousness secondary to the brain injury, and accordingly did not encode the necessary mental representations of the traumatic experience to cause fear reactions (Sbordone & Liter, 1995). In more recent years, it has been shown that PTSD can occur after MTBI. This is because patients with MTBI can still have "islands" of memory for the traumatic experience; trauma can occur following resolution of posttraumatic amnesia; and, some fear conditioning can occur despite impaired consciousness (Bryant, 2001a). Curiously, there even is some evidence that MTBI may be associated with an increased risk for PTSD, as recently documented with combat troops returning from Iraq or Afghanistan (Hoge, et al., 2008; Schneiderman, Braver, & Kang, 2008). Prevailing biological models of PTSD have proposed that the disorder develops as a result of impaired functioning of the medial prefrontal cortex, which limits regulation of the amygdala (Charney et al., 1994; Rauch, Shin, & Phelps, 2006). This model is supported by neuroimaging evidence that finds PTSD is characterized by diminished recruitment of the medial prefrontal cortex during fear processing (Lanius, Bluhm, Lanius, & Pain, 2006; Rauch & Shin, 1997). It has been suggested that damage to the prefrontal networks during the course of the MTBI may compromise their functioning and contribute to PTSD (Bryant, 2008).

Treating PTSD, or other psychiatric disorders after MTBI, is only marginally different from usual methods. Thus, CBT is still the treatment of choice for PTSD that occurs with MTBI (Bryant, Moulds, Guthrie, & Nixon, 2003). Two minor adjustments are required in treating patients. First, as MTBI often results in islands of amnesia, prolonged exposure needs to focus on those aspects of the memory that can be recalled. Alternately, more focus may be placed on *in vivo* exposure to activate fear networks, with less reliance on retrieving memories.

## Sequencing the Treatment of Comorbid Conditions

When a patient presents with comorbid conditions, it is important to sequence treatment components in a way that allows for optimal benefit. Several principles can be applied to treatment planning. First, it is imperative that the patient's safety be addressed. This requires that any factors threatening the patient's immediate well-being should be addressed. Suicidal intent, substance dependence, or self-harm tendencies should be managed with appropriate strategies to ensure that the patient is safe and stabilized. Second, it is necessary to consider any presentation that is likely to interfere with other forms of therapy. If a patient is likely to engage in substance abuse during exposure therapy, this must be addressed prior to commencing exposure. Similarly, if a patient has marked problems with emotional regulation, it is advisable to first teach necessary skills before commencing other forms of therapy that invoke memories of the trauma. Third, it is useful to address aspects of the clinical presentation that will lead to generalized benefit. For example, if a patient presents with PTSD and insomnia, it is very likely that sleeping difficulties will be reduced once nightmares and associated PTSD issues are reduced. Finally, it is important to focus treatment on those core issues that address the major concerns of the patient. Providing general anxiety management skills to a patient with severe PTSD symptoms (e.g., breathing techniques), may offer some relief, but such efforts do not address the core problem. More to the point, clinicians should focus as quickly as possible on exposure and cognitive restructuring. Evidence shows that these approaches correct the major symptoms of PTSD.

## CASE STUDY

Maggie is a 36-year-old police officer who presented at a Traumatic Stress Clinic. She reported a range of psychological difficulties, including anxiety, depression, and the tendency to self-harm. Maggie reported that she had served as a police officer for 13 years, but had retired a year earlier because of her psychological difficulties. She initially worked in criminal scene investigation, in which she was exposed to many scenes of violence, homicide, and suicide. She subsequently transferred to a child sexual assault investigation unit. Maggie stated that this work was highly stressful because of daily interactions with children who were being abused. Maggie stated that for many years she had suffered nightmares and intrusive images of grotesque scenes that she had witnessed as a crime scene investigator. Her situation deteriorated after she transferred to child sexual assault duties, because she felt it increasingly difficult to deal with the problems reported by children in abusive families.

At the time of presentation, Maggie reported several problems. She stated that she suffered frequent intrusive images and nightmares of approximately a dozen homicide scenes that she attended, as well as several cases of childhood abuse in which she relived abusive events that children had related to her. She engaged in pervasive avoidance of any reminders, including not watching television or reading newspapers that might contain police matters. She rarely left her house because she reported marked panic attacks when she was in public. Maggie also reported significant depression, including suicidal intent, dysphoria, withdrawal, very low motivation, and a strong sense of guilt for not assisting abused children more effectively. Maggie reported that she had been abusing alcohol for seven years; she reported drinking approximately 1 to 1 1/2 bottles of wine per night to lessen her distress. Maggie also reported that she had been self-harming for the last two years. She stated that she felt urges to inflict pain on herself by cutting her arms or placing lit cigarettes on her skin. On presentation, Maggie was able to display cut and burn marks on her arms and legs. Interestingly, Maggie also reported that she often was unaware of things people were saying or things she had done. She stated that she was unaware of these periods at the time, but subsequently people would remind her of conversations that she could not recall. Maggie disclosed during the assessment that she had consulted the Internet and wondered if she had a dissociative disorder.

A comprehensive assessment of a trauma patient should map that person's history of prior traumatic events, and the ways they responded. In Maggie's case, she reported that she suffered childhood abuse (including digital penetration and rape) between the ages of 7 and 10 years of age. When she was 10, the father's abuse was discovered, and he was removed from the family home. Maggie reported that she had experienced nightmares about these experiences for years during adolescence, and she had avoided sexual activity during later years. She recalled that during her adolescence she had great difficulty regulating emotions, and periodically engaged in cutting behavior, binge eating, and abusing alcohol. Further, Maggie's memories of abuse became more frequent and distressing when she began working on the child sexual assault investigations.

## Case Formulation

This case requires a multifactorial formulation because of the complex interaction of factors apparently contributing to Maggie's presentation. There is little doubt that Maggie suffers PTSD, with comorbid Major Depressive Disorder and Substance Use Disorder. Complicating her presentation, however, is the apparent difficulty in regulating emotions, resulting in self-harm and substance use. This aspect is consistent with current conceptualizations of complex trauma. One useful model for framing a therapeutic approach to this case is that proposed by Cloitre and colleagues (2006). This model posits that PTSD secondary to an abusive childhood can result in a complex clinical presentation that is characterized by emotional dysregulation and maladaptive behaviors. The diagnosis of Borderline Personality Disorder was not made because Maggie did not report fears of abandonment, a history of unstable relationships, or identity disturbance. As described above, the therapeutic implication of this model is that CBT approaches to treating PTSD should be preceded by skills training. This approach would provide Maggie with a better capacity to manage emotional reactions. These skills would hopefully stabilize her self-harm and alcohol abuse, which would allow her to more constructively utilize exposure therapy.

A second model that has direct application to Maggie is the cognitive model of PTSD (Ehlers & Clark, 2000). This theory holds that people with PTSD have intrusive and distressing memories of past experiences that are triggered by current stimuli, during which time the individual confuses the past event with present circumstances. Additionally, this theory posits that catastrophic perceptions about oneself, others, and the world lead to exaggerated estimates of likely harm and negative outcomes in the future. This framework suggests that resolution of PTSD requires that trauma memories are emotionally processed in a way that permits constructive interpretation of the past experiences. This approach has much in common with fear network models that posit the need to process trauma memories, so the individual can accept their experience is in the past (Foa, 1997). In Maggie's case, her images of blood and decomposed bodies were a vivid and intrusive part of her autobiographical memory. Further, it was apparent that PTSD and depression symptoms, and particularly feelings of guilt, were strongly based in her maladaptive appraisals about not protecting the abused children with whom she worked.

Importantly, Maggie's appraisals appear to have furthered maladaptive behavioral strategies. For example, in the assessment it was apparent that Maggie feared that her emotional responses were so intense that she could not cope. Specifically, she feared that she would "go crazy" if she allowed the emotions to persist. This belief led to her frequently engaging in other behaviors to distract herself from feelings of guilt and anxiety. Maggie reported that she remained at home because she feared that if she suffered a panic attack, she could not cope with the associated emotions and memories. The effect of this behavioral avoidance was that it reinforced Maggie's belief that she could only maintain emotional safety by avoiding all reminders of past traumas. This pattern resulted in further withdrawal and social isolation.

## Treatment Plan

A treatment plan for Maggie would be multi-pronged—following cognitive behavioral principles but also accommodating her individual presentation. The initial phase of treatment would involve providing Maggie with psychoeducation that explained the reasons for her presenting symptoms. This rationale would explain to Maggie that her PTSD reactions were an understandable response to her range of experiences, and that her police experiences had compounded lessons learned as a child. Specifically, Maggie would need to learn that she never had a chance to adequately learn how to regulate her changing emotions, and this had resulted in years of alcohol abuse and self-harm. Further, she had responded to work stress with avoidance and maladaptive distracting activities because she had not learned how to address these issues. It would be important to normalize Maggie's responses, while ensuring that she perceived her self-destructive behaviors as poor problem-solving strategies. It would be clarified that a goal of therapy was to learn better skills so as to manage emotional changes more adaptively. Maggie also would need to be informed that her symptoms of hyperarousal and re-experiencing were a function of elevated responses to threat. She would need to understand that flashbacks, nightmares, and panic were a function of her body still being in alert mode and hypervigilant to threat. Maggie would need to learn that these reminders are not actually threatening anymore, and that she can have memories of past events without catastrophic outcomes.

The educational phase for Maggie's treatment would also emphasize that she did not have a dissociative disorder. Instead, her reports of poor concentration and memory were entirely consistent with someone with very elevated arousal. This level of distress often causes cognitive overload to the point that an individual does not encode or consolidate information, and accordingly does not recall it. It could be detrimental to Maggie to believe that she suffers a dissociative disorder because it might reduce her sense of mastery and lead her to believe that her personality is fragmented. One goal of all interactions with trauma survivors is to ensure that they perceive a sense of control over their condition and their future, feelings that trauma typically diminishes. Each of Maggie's presentations can be treated with evidence-based approaches, and nothing would be gained by providing her with a framework of dissociative disorder that might only confuse an understanding of her condition. This is particularly the case as there was no evidence that Maggie suffered any form of dissociation, other than expected impaired cognitive processes secondary to panic and hyperarousal.

## Course of Treatment

Following Cloitre's model (Cloitre, et al., 2002), Maggie's treatment commenced with eight sessions of skills training that aimed to curb her alcohol abuse, self-harm, and emotional dysregulation. Specifically, Maggie was taught to identify and label her feelings, and then to monitor them on a daily basis to determine the triggers responsible for different reactions she experienced during the course of a day. She was taught basic distress tolerance skills, including breathing retraining, distraction, and self-talk. Sessions were devoted to helping Maggie identify the link between her thoughts and her intense emotional reactions. Fundamentally, Maggie expressed the fear that she was incapable of tolerating strong emotions. She learned that this thought was a major factor in her engaging in alcohol abuse and self-harm. She was encouraged to rehearse other strategies to tolerate emotional reactions, and to conduct behavioral experiments to establish whether these emotional responses would be as catastrophic as she feared. Maggie devoted weeks exposing herself to triggers of emotional response while trying to tolerate her reactions through breathing retraining, distraction, mindfulness techniques, and reassuring herself that the emotions were transient and she could cope. Therapy also focused on Maggie's understanding that a major cause of her guilt about the children she worked with was rooted in her own experiences about not protecting herself from an abusive father. Through cognitive restructuring approaches, Maggie was able to learn that she had blamed herself for the abuse she was subjected to, and this was transferred onto her inability to assist the children she dealt with as a police officer. Maggie was able to learn that her actions were in fact exemplary, and she did everything a good police officer would have done. By the completion of the skills training program, Maggie reported feeling less guilt about her actions, and she was better able to manage her distress. During these sessions, Maggie also engaged in alcohol use management strategies, which involved considerable motivational interviewing. This approach encouraged Maggie to consider the problems caused by her drinking, and to compare these against any short-term benefits.

Following these sessions, Maggie commenced her trauma-focused therapy. This initially involved prolonged exposure, in which she was required to provide a narrative to her memories. As Maggie had experienced many traumatic experiences, and these formed the images of many of her intrusions, it was decided that she select the three most distressing memories. Prolonged exposure commenced with her providing a narrative of a scene in which there were strong images of blood. Although at this point she was unaware of the context or the narrative surrounding this image, Maggie nominated this as one of her most distressing memories. Maggie simply focused on this image and experienced extreme distress. This continued for 30 minutes in which she remained distressed; at the conclusion of this exercise, the therapist and Maggie discussed at length her emotional reactions and emphasized her capacity to tolerate the distress. Given Maggie's level of distress and history of poor emotional regulation, it was decided that she would not commence exposure for homework at this stage. Instead, she attended another therapy session three days later, in which the exposure was continued. Not surprisingly, she experienced a marked increase in nightmares and intrusions in the days following the initial exposure session. To her credit, Maggie was able to employ the distress tolerance skills learned previously to manage her distress without engaging in maladaptive or self-destructive behaviors. At the next exposure session, Maggie continued with her focus of the blood image, and was encouraged to contextualize it with other details. Despite considerable distress, she was able to recall that the scene came from a homicide that she attended in her work as a police officer, at which time she had to photograph the dismembered body of a child. As Maggie retrieved more details of this scene, she was asked to narrate to the therapist the entire scene and each of her actions, while focusing specifically on her thoughts and emotional responses. Maggie was asked to relive this scene in the first person and present tense to heighten her engagement with her emotional responses. When Maggie initially relived this entire scene she chose to skip over certain aspects of the memory because she did not feel she could cope with them. This was allowed because Maggie was achieving the major goal of engaging with her trauma memories and not avoiding them. This narration lasted approximately 15 minutes, during which time she was extremely distressed. At the completion, Maggie was asked to repeat the scene twice, providing a sequence of 45 minutes of exposure. During subsequent exposure sessions, Maggie agreed to focus on the aspects of the trauma that she skipped previously; these involved documenting the nature of the sexual abuse that the girl had been subjected to. Exposure on this scene continued for a further four sessions, at which point Maggie decided it was time to repeat the procedure with a second nominated memory. In each of these sessions, Maggie continued to discuss her guilt-oriented cognitions about the abused children. Through these discussions, Maggie realized that her guilt about not better assisting the children was unrealistic, and was actually an extension of her unfounded guilt about not protecting herself from her father's abuse.

Halfway through the prolonged exposure, an *in vivo* exposure program was also initiated. This involved Maggie gradually leaving her house and going to the local department store; this was chosen because of the abundance of children and other reminders that were available. A hierarchy was established in which Maggie initially left her house for short distances, but for lengthy periods of time (1 hour), while accompanied by a friend. Maggie's practice was subsequently increased to include further distances and going out on her own. Despite her history of panic attacks, interoceptive exposure was not necessary because Maggie ceased to have panic attacks following the prolonged imaginal exposure.

Therapy was concluded after 15 sessions. Maggie reported markedly reduced PTSD symptoms, controlled alcohol use, absence of panic attacks, and the ability to leave her house with relative confidence. It is noteworthy that at the completion of therapy, Maggie did not report any lapses in attention or memory; this response validates the therapist's decision to not reinforce the notion of dissociative disorder, but rather to normalize these alterations in awareness as a function of elevated arousal.

Given the complexity of Maggie's condition, it was agreed that she would attend booster sessions to remind her of the emotion regulation strategies, especially during periods of stress.

## CONCLUDING COMMENT

As research continues to expand our clinical insights beyond the scope of PTSD, there is increasing awareness that traumatic events lead to a broad array of mental health problems. Fortunately, there is a comprehensive evidence-based literature to guide a clinician's choice of treatment for PTSD, specific phobia, depression, and other posttraumatic conditions. Clinicians will best serve their patients if they adopt a broad view toward case formulations, do not limit their focus on a PTSD diagnosis, and implement empirically supported treatments.

## REFERENCES

Antonovsky, A. (1979). *Health, stress, and coping.* San Francisco: Jossey-Bass.

Beck, A. T. (1976). *Cognitive therapy and the emotional disorders.* New York: International Universities Press.

Bonanno, G. A., & Kaltman, S. (2001). The varieties of grief experience. *Clinical Psychology Review, 21*(5), 705–734.

Brewin, C. R. (1998). Intrusive memories, depression and PTSD. *Psychologist, 11*(6), 281–283.

Bryant, R. A. (2001a). Posttraumatic stress disorder and mild brain injury: Controversies, causes and consequences. *Journal of Clinical and Experimental Neuropsychology, 23*(6), 718–728.

Bryant, R. A. (2001b). Posttraumatic stress disorder and traumatic brain injury: Can they co-exist? *Clinical Psychology Review, 21*(6), 931–948.

Bryant, R. A. (2006). Longitudinal psychophysiological studies of heart rate: Mediating effects and implications for treatment. *Annals of the New York Academy of Sciences, 1071,* 19–26.

Bryant, R. A. (2008). Disentangling mild traumatic brain injury and stress reactions. *New England Journal of Medicine, 358*(5), 525–527.

Bryant, R. A. (in press). Acute stress disorder as a predictor of posttraumatic stress disorder: A systematic review. *Journal of Clinical Psychiatry.*

Bryant, R. A., Creamer, M., O'Donnell, M., Silove, D., Clark, C. R., & McFarlane, A. C. (2010). The psychiatric sequelae of traumatic injury. *American Journal of Psychiatry, 167,* 312–320.

Bryant, R. A., Harvey, A. G., Dang, S. T., Sackville, T., & Basten, C. (1998). Treatment of acute stress disorder: A comparison of cognitive-behavioral therapy and supportive counseling. *Journal of Consulting and Clinical Psychology, 66*(5), 862–866.

Bryant, R. A., Mastrodomenico, J., Felmingham, K. L., Hopwood, S., Kenny, L., Kandris, E., et al. (2008). Treatment of acute stress disorder: A randomized controlled trial. *Archives General Psychiatry, 65*(6), 659–667.

Bryant, R. A., Moulds, M., Guthrie, R., & Nixon, R. D. (2003). Treating acute stress disorder following mild traumatic brain injury. *American Journal of Psychiatry, 160*(3), 585–587.

Bryant, R. A., Moulds, M. L., Guthrie, R. M., & Nixon, R. D. (2005). The additive benefit of hypnosis and cognitive-behavioral therapy in treating acute stress disorder. *Journal of Consulting and Clinical Psychology, 73*(2), 334–340.

Bryant, R. A., Sackville, T., Dang, S. T., Moulds, M., & Guthrie, R. (1999). Treating acute stress disorder: An evaluation of cognitive behavior therapy and supporting counseling techniques. *American Journal of Psychiatry, 156*(11), 1780–1786.

Charney, D. S., Southwick, S. M., Krystal, J. H., Deutch, A. Y., Murburg, M. M., & Davis, M. (1994). Neurobiological mechanisms of PTSD. In M.M. Murburg (Ed.), *Catecholamine function in posttraumatic stress disorder: Emerging concepts* (pp. 131–158). Washington, DC.: American Psychiatric Press, Inc.

Chilcoat, H. D., & Breslau, N. (1998). Investigations of causal pathways between PTSD and drug use disorders. *Addictive Behaviors, 23*(6), 827–840.

Cloitre, M., Cohen, L., & Kownen, K. (2006). *Treating survivors of childhood abuse: Psychotherapy for the interrupted life.* New York: Guilford.

Cloitre, M., Koenen, K. C., Cohen, L. R., & Han, H. (2002). Skills training in affective and interpersonal regulation followed by exposure: A phase-based treatment for PTSD related to childhood abuse. *Journal of Consulting and Clinical Psychology, 70*(5), 1067–1074.

Currier, J. M., Neimeyer, R. A., & Berman, J. S. (2008). The effectiveness of psychotherapeutic interventions for bereaved persons: A comprehensive quantitative review. *Psychological Bulletin, 134*(5), 648–661.

Ehlers, A., & Clark, D. M. (2000). A cognitive model of posttraumatic stress disorder. *Behaviour Research and Therapy, 38*(4), 319–345.

Ehlers, A., Mayou, R. A., & Bryant, B. (1998). Psychological predictors of chronic posttraumatic stress disorder after motor vehicle accidents. *Journal of Abnormal Psychology, 107*(3), 508–519.

Foa, E. B. (1997). Psychological processes related to recovery from a trauma and an effective treatment for PTSD. *Annals of the New York Academy of Science, 821,* 410–424.

Foa, E. B., Keane, T. M., Friedman, M. J., & Cohen, J. A. (Eds.). (2009). *Effective treatments for PTSD: Practice guidelines from the International Society of Traumatic Stress Studies* (2nd ed.). New York: Guilford.

Foa, E. B., Rothbaum, B. O., Riggs, D. S., & Murdock, T. B. (1991). Treatment of posttraumatic stress disorder in rape victims: A comparison between cognitive-behavioral procedures and counseling. *Journal of Consulting and Clinical Psychology, 59*(5), 715–723.

Friedman, M. J. (2003). Pharmacologic Management of Posttraumatic Stress Disorder. *Primary Psychiatry, 10*(8), 66–68, 71–73.

Galea, S., Resnick, H., Ahern, J., Gold, J., Bucuvalas, M., Kilpatrick, D., et al. (2002). Posttraumatic stress disorder in Manhattan, New York City, after the September 11th terrorist attacks. *Journal of Urban Health, 79*(3), 340–353.

Galea, S., Vlahov, D., Resnick, H., Ahern, J., Susser, E., Gold, J., et al. (2003). Trends of probable post-traumatic stress disorder in New York City after the September 11 terrorist attacks. *American Journal of Epidemiology, 158*(6), 514–524.

Hobbs, M., Mayou, R., Harrison, B., & Worlock, P. (1996). A randomised controlled trial of psychological debriefing for victims of road traffic accidents. *British Medical Journal, 313,* 1438–1439.

Hobfoll, S. E., Watson, P., Bell, C. C., Bryant, R. A., Brymer, M. J., Friedman, M. J., et al. (2007). Five essential elements of immediate and mid-term mass trauma intervention: Empirical evidence. *Psychiatry, 70*(4), 283–315; discussion 316–269.

Hoge, C. W., McGurk, D., Thomas, J. L., Cox, A. L., Engel, C. C., & Castro, C. A. (2008). Mild traumatic brain injury in US soldiers returning from Iraq. *New England Journal of Medicine, 358*(5), 453–463.

Hollon, S. D., Stewart, M. O., & Strunk, D. (2006). Enduring effects for cognitive behavior therapy in the treatment of depression and anxiety. *Annual Review of Psychology, 57,* 285–315.

Lanius, R. A., Bluhm, R., Lanius, U., & Pain, C. (2006). A review of neuroimaging studies in PTSD: Heterogeneity of response to symptom provocation. *Journal of Psychiatric Research, 40*(8), 709–729.

Levitt, J. T., Malta, L. S., Martin, A., Davis, L., & Cloitre, M. (2007). The flexible application of a manualized treatment for PTSD symptoms and functional impairment related to the 9/11 World Trade Center attack. *Behaviour Research and Therapy, 45*(7), 1419–1433.

Lichtenthal, W. G., Cruess, D. G., & Prigerson, H. G. (2004). A case for establishing complicated grief as a distinct mental disorder in DSM-V. *Clinical Psychology Review, 24*(6), 637–662.

Marshall, R. D., Bryant, R. A., Amsel, L., Suh, E. J., Cook, J. M., & Neria, Y. (2007). The psychology of ongoing threat - Relative risk appraisal, the September 11 attacks, and terrorism-related fears. *American Psychologist, 62*(4), 304–316.

McNally, R. J., Bryant, R. A., & Ehlers, A. (2003). Does early psychological intervention promote recovery from posttraumatic stress? *Psychological Science,* 45–79.

McNally, R. J., & Saugh, P. A. (1993). On the distinction between traumatic simple phobia and posttraumatic stress disorder. In J. R. T. Davidson & E. B. Foa (Eds.), *Posttraumatic stress disorder: DSM-IV and beyond.* Washington, DC: American Psychiatric Press, Inc.

Mikulincer, M., & Solomon, Z. (1988). Attributional style and combat-related posttraumatic stress disorder. *Journal of Abnormal Psychology, 97*(3), 308–313.

Miller, W. R., & Rollnick, S. (2002). *Motivational interviewing: Preparing people for change.* New York: Guilford.

Mitchell, J. T. (1983). When disaster strikes: The critical incident stress debriefing process. *Journal of Emergency Medical Services, 8,* 36–39.

Najavits, L. M., Gallop, R. J., & Weiss, R. D. (2006). Seeking safety therapy for adolescent girls with PTSD and substance use disorder: A randomized controlled trial. *Journal of Behavioral Health Services Research, 33*(4), 453–463.

Najavits, L. M., Ryngala, D., Back, S. E., Bolton, E., Mueser, K. T., & Brady, K. T. (2009). Treatment of PTSD and comorbid disorders. In E. B. Foa, T. M. Keane, M. J. Friedman & J. A. Cohen (Eds.), *Effective treatments for PTSD* (2nd ed.; pp. 508–535). New York: Guilford.

Neria, Y., Olfson, M., Gross, R., Gamerrof, M., Manetti-Cusa, J., & Weissman, M. (2007). 9/11 PTSD among urban primary care patients in NYC: A longitudinal examination. *European Psychiatry, 22,* S283–S284.

Nixon, R. D., & Bryant, R. A. (2003). Peritraumatic and persistent panic attacks in acute stress disorder. *Behaviour Research and Therapy, 41*(10), 1237–1242.

Norris, F. H., Friedman, M. J., & Watson, P. J. (2002). 60,000 disaster victims speak: Part I. An emirical review of the empirical literature, 1981–2001. *Psychiatry, 65,* 207–239.

North, C. S., Nixon, S. J., Shariat, S., Mallonee, S., McMillen, J. C., Spitznagel, E. L., et al. (1999). Psychiatric disorders among survivors of the Oklahoma City bombing. *Journal of the American Medical Association, 282*(8), 755–762.

Ogden, P., Pain, C., & Fisher, J. (2006). A sensorimotor approach to the treatment of trauma and dissociation. *Psychiatric Clinics of North America, 29*(1), 263–279.

Ozer, E. J., Best, S. R., Lipsey, T. L., & Weiss, D. S. (2003). Predictors of posttraumatic stress disorder and symptoms in adults: A meta-analysis. *Psychological Bulletin, 129*(1), 52–73.

Pitman, R. K. (1989). Post–traumatic stress disorder, hormones, and memory. *Biological Psychiatry, 26*(3), 221–223.

Prigerson, H. G., Shear, M. K., Jacobs, S. C., Reynolds, C. F., Maciejewski, P. K., & Davidson, J. et al. (1999). Consensus criteria for traumatic grief. *British Journal of Psychiatry, 174*, 67–73.

Rauch, S. L., & Shin, L. M. (1997). Functional neuroimaging studies in posttraumatic stress disorder. In R. Yehuda & A. C. McFarlane (Eds.), Psychobiology of posttraumatic stress disorder (pp. 83–98). New York: New York Academy of Sciences

Rauch, S. L., Shin, L. M., & Phelps, E. A. (2006). Neurocircuitry models of posttraumatic stress disorder and extinction: Human neuroimaging research–past, present, and future. *Biological Psychiatry, 60*(4), 376–382.

Read, J. P., Brown, P. J., & Kahler, C. W. (2004). Substance use and posttraumatic stress disorders: Symptom interplay and effects on outcome. *Addictive Behaviors, 29*(8), 1665–1672.

Resick, P. A., Galovski, T. E., O'Brien Uhlmansiek, M., Scher, C. D., Clum, G. A., & Young-Xu, Y. (2008). A randomized clinical trial to dismantle components of cognitive processing therapy for posttraumatic stress disorder in female victims of interpersonal violence. *Journal of Consulting and Clinical Psychology, 76*(2), 243–258.

Resick, P. A., & Schnicke, M. K. (1993). *Cognitive processing therapy for sexual assault victims: A treatment manual.* Newbury Park, CA: Sage Publications.

Rose, S., Bisson, J., & Wessely, S. (2001). Psychological debriefing for preventing posttraumatic stress disorder (PTSD) (Cochrane Review) *The Cochrane Library* (Issue 3 ed.). Oxford: Update Software.

Rosen, G. M., Spitzer, R. L., & McHugh, P. R. (2008). Problems with the PTSD diagnosis and its future in DSM-V. *British Journal of Psychiatry, 192*, 3–4.

Rothbaum, B. O., Hodges, L. F., Ready, D., Graap, K., & Alarcon, R. D. (2001). Virtual reality exposure therapy for Vietnam veterans with posttraumatic stress disorder. *Journal of Clinical Psychiatry, 62*(8), 617–622.

Sbordone, R. J., & Liter, J. C. (1995). Mild traumatic brain injury does not produce post-traumatic stress disorder. *Brain Injury, 9*(4), 405–412.

Schneiderman, A. I., Braver, E. R., & Kang, H. K. (2008). Understanding sequelae of injury mechanisms and mild traumatic brain injury incurred during the conflicts in Iraq and Afghanistan: Persistent postconcussive symptoms and posttraumatic stress disorder. *American Journal of Epidemiology, 167*(12), 1446–1452.

Shalev, A. Y., & Freedman, S. (2005). PTSD following terrorist attacks: A prospective evaluation. *American Journal of Psychiatry, 162*(6), 1188–1191.

Shear, K., Frank, E., Houck, P. R., & Reynolds, C. F., III. (2005). Treatment of complicated grief: A randomized controlled trial. *Journal of the American Medical Association, 293*(21), 2601–2608.

van Griensven, F., Chakkraband, M. L. S., Thienkrua, W., Pengjuntr, W., Cardozo, B. L., Tantipiwatanaskul, P., et al. (2006). Mental health problems among adults in tsunami-affected areas in southern Thailand. *Journal of the American Medical Association, 296*(5), 537–548.

CHAPTER

# 10

# Cross-Cultural Perspectives on Posttraumatic Stress

JAMES D. HERBERT
EVAN M. FORMAN

Most cultures have historically framed reactions to trauma within the context of religion, with priests and shamans offering interpretation of the causes or meanings of traumatic events, while also serving in the role of healer. Within Western cultures, beginning in the mid-19th century, physicians gradually began to expand their purview to include psychological reactions to trauma. This process culminated in the creation of the medical diagnosis of posttraumatic stress disorder (PTSD) in 1980, which completed the transformation of reactions to trauma from the religious domain to a biomedical framework. This transformation, led by American psychiatry, clinical psychology, and related fields, has exerted widespread influence. The resulting "positivistic paradigm," in which human suffering and psychopathology are thought to exist independent of local theories, has resulted in a loss of recognition that cultural factors play an important role in the development and treatment of posttraumatic reactions. Despite such concerns, Western biomedical models of trauma and associated interventions are increasingly exported throughout the world. According to the United Nations, there are currently over 12.8 million internally displaced persons, 9.8 million refugees, and an additional 10.3 million "people of concern" worldwide

(UNHCR, 2006). Many of these individuals have experienced traumatic events per modern diagnostic standards, and clinicians have increasingly targeted Western interventions toward them.

Our central thesis is twofold. First, a variety of social and psychological factors, including factors typically associated with culture, invariably shape reactions to traumatic events, and the likelihood they will be viewed as pathological. While such cultural effects impact many forms of psychopathology, they appear especially important in the case of posttraumatic reactions. Second, an understanding of cultural factors is critical when assessing and treating individuals posttrauma. We begin our discussion of these concerns by briefly considering what is meant by "culture." We then review the predominant biomedical model of posttraumatic reactions, focusing on the diagnostic construct of PTSD. We examine the many ways in which psychological, environmental, and cultural factors shape reactions to trauma, including the prevalence and nature of pathological reactions. We observe that cultural effects can be studied cross-sectionally (by comparing different groups at a given point in time), as well as historically across time (within a continuously evolving culture across time). We explore what insights a historical perspective yields on the question of cultural factors in posttraumatic reactions. Finally, we consider the assessment and treatment of posttraumatic stress, including PTSD, within a culture-sensitive framework.

## WHAT IS CULTURE?

Derivation of the word "culture" reflects the idea of fostering and nurturing commonalities among individuals. While cultural anthropologists have not reached consensus on a single definition of the term, the United Nations Educational, Scientific and Cultural Organization provides a useful description: "Culture should be regarded as the set of distinctive spiritual, material, intellectual and emotional features of society or a social group . . . in addition to art and literature, lifestyles, ways of living together, value systems, traditions and beliefs" (UNESCO, 2002).

The term "culture" can refer to broad groups that share certain beliefs and practices, extending across several nations (e.g., "Western culture"), to groups defined by national boundaries (e.g., "French culture"), to areas within a country (e.g., "Canadian maritime culture"), all the way down to local communities such as social, vocational, religious, or even familial groups. When examining cultural factors that shape reactions to trauma, it is important to keep in mind the wide range of levels that make up such factors. Also, at whatever level one examines, no culture is static. Therefore, in addition to a cross-sectional comparison of cultures at a given time point, one can compare the impact of cultures across historical periods.

## POSTTRAUMATIC STRESS DISORDER

In terms of the conceptualization, classification, and treatment of psychopathology, American beliefs and practices have become the dominant perspective worldwide. Since publication of the third edition of the *Diagnostic and Statistical Manual of Mental Disorders* in 1980 (*DSM*; APA, 1980), and with respect to psychological reactions to trauma, the prevailing perspective has viewed posttraumatic reactions within a biomedical context—specifically as the medical condition of PTSD.

Since its introduction in the DSM-III (APA, 1980), interest in PTSD has grown rapidly among scholars, clinicians, and the public at large. Further, the definition of what constitutes trauma, and therefore risk for PTSD, has expanded in subsequent editions of the DSM (e.g., *DSM-IV*; APA, 1994). Qualifying traumatic events have been extended to include learning about or witnessing another person's exposure to a life-threatening event. Traumatic events no longer need to be outside the range of normal experience, nor do they need to be defined by objective standards external to the individual. Within this definition, the majority of Americans have experienced at least one event that qualifies as a traumatic stressor (Breslau & Kessler, 2001). This gradual and ongoing expansion of trauma has led PTSD to become the dominant framework by which reactions to a wide range of adverse events are understood. Accompanying this development is the ever-increasing medicalization of human suffering (Summerfield, 2004).

There are a variety of consequences when we adopt a biomedical model to understand posttraumatic suffering. First, PTSD is understood as a "natural kind," that exists independent of our theories. As with other medical conditions, PTSD is assumed to be universal, manifesting itself consistently with a unique symptom profile and etiology across cultures, both at any given time point as well as transhistorically. This is the way biomedical diseases work. However, unlike bone fractures or viral infections that may entail the same causal agents regardless of time or place, conditions such as PTSD are presumably socially constructed and therefore culture-bound.

## POSTTRAUMATIC RESPONSES ACROSS CULTURES

An often overlooked aspect of PTSD is the fact that exactly what constitutes traumatic events, and the perceived severity of such events, varies by culture. Summerfield (2004) observed:

> There is nothing quintessential about a particular traumatic experience. The attitudes of wider society (which may change over time) shape what individual victims feel has been done to them, and shape the vocabulary they use to describe this, whether or how they seek help, and their expectations of recovery. The more a society sees a traumatic event (rape, for example) as a serious risk to the present or future health and well-being of the victim the more it may turn out to be. In other words, societally constructed ideas about outcomes, which include the pronouncements of the mental health field, carry a measure of self-fulfilling prophecy (p. 232).

Many events considered traumatic within one culture are not so perceived by others. Consider childhood sexual abuse, which has received intense focus in Western societies as a common traumatic event leading to PTSD. An act of fellatio between a pubescent boy and an older man would be universally condemned as childhood sexual abuse by Western standards. However, such acts are a common rite of passage among traditional Melanesian cultures (Bohn, 1996). Even within American culture, the assumption of inevitable lasting traumatic effects of childhood sexual abuse has been questioned (Rind, Tromovitch, and Bauserman, 1998). Outside the sexual realm, cultural differences continue to be found. Terheggen, Stroebe, and Kleber (2001) documented that Tibetans ranked destruction of religious symbols as the most traumatic event possible, ahead of other events such as death of a friend or even being tortured.

A biomedical perspective suggests that rates of PTSD might be consistent across populations exposed to similar traumatic events. Contrary to this prediction, prevalence estimates of PTSD vary widely, both within and between cultures. For example, studies of recent immigrants to industrialized countries as well as of nationals within developing countries reveal widely variable rates of PTSD (see Yeomans and Forman, 2009). Similarly, estimates of the prevalence of PTSD within a culture are highly variable depending on factors such as gender and ethnicity. The National Comorbidity Survey found an overall rate of PTSD among American men of 8.2%, as compared to 20.4% among women (Kessler, Sonnega, Bromet, Hughes, & Nelson, 1995). Pole, Best, Metzler, and Marmar (2005) reviewed evidence that Latinos in the United States demonstrate higher rates of PTSD than white or black counterparts.

The observation that posttraumatic reactions in other cultures do not necessarily conform to Western expectations is consistent with emerging culturally sensitive research. Yeomans, Herbert and Forman (2008) used a combination of qualitative interviews by native speakers and standardized instruments to assess posttraumatic reactions among internally displaced people in the central African nation of Burundi. In order to avoid response contamination resulting from expectancies, open-ended interviews by trained native interviewers preceded the assessment of specific symptoms. All of the interviewees had experienced at least one, and typically several, traumatic events. Content analysis of the interview data revealed that the most common reactions concerned material complaints rather than psychological symptoms. Assessment of psychopathology revealed symptoms of somatization, anxiety, and depression, with relatively few specific symptoms of PTSD per se. Similarly, Baron (2002) found that the distress of Sudanese refugees in Northern Uganda focused more on material concerns such as lack of food, poor health care, and the ongoing threat of violence rather than psychological symptoms. The majority did not develop distressing symptoms, and for those who did, these tended to take the form of anxiety, somatic complaints, and depressive symptoms.

In their review of cross-cultural studies, Marsella and colleagues (1996; Marsella & Christopher, 2004) observed that, among the minority of individuals who respond with persistent symptoms, posttraumatic reactions tend to differ across cultures. They noted that the intrusive symptoms of PTSD tended to occur across cultures, while avoidance/ numbing symptoms were not consistently observed. Marsella suggested that PTSD symptoms may be highest in cultures in which avoidance and numbing are more common, because these symptoms are key in maintaining other aspects of the disorder.

## Culture and Resilience

Western journalists and health professionals who visit survivors of severe natural disasters in pre-industrialized, developing countries are often struck by the resilience of the native population. Writing in the *New York Times*, journalist David Brooks (2008) described his experience visiting the Sichuan Province in Western China following a magnitude 7.9 earthquake that killed approximately 70,000 people on May 12, 2008. Despite scenes of horrific devastation, the local villagers were generally upbeat and optimistic, displaying few signs of psychopathology. Brooks was puzzled by the reactions of the survivors he interviewed, writing:

> These were weird, unnerving interviews, and I don't pretend to understand what's going on in the minds of people who have suffered such blows and remained so optimistic. All I can imagine is that the history of this province has given these people a stripped-down, pragmatic mentality: Move on or go crazy. Don't dwell. Look to the positive. Fix what needs fixing. Work together.

Similar observations were made by researchers studying survivors of the 2004 Asian tsunami (Rakjumar, Premkumar & Tharyan, 2008), responsible for 280,000 deaths and more than one million displacements. These researchers obtained PTSD prevalence rates of only 6.4% among those from a devastated Indian coastal village. They concluded that "coping mechanisms exist at individual and community levels that enhance resilience in the face of adversity and enable normal functioning in the majority of those affected, without requiring professional intervention" (p. 853).

Sometimes social support and other cultural factors can be more important than the actual traumatic event. Wang et al. (2000) compared the reactions of inhabitants in two villages, both hit by the previously mentioned severe earthquake in northern China. Wang found that the village with the higher level of initial exposure to the earthquake also had a higher level of post-earthquake support. Rather than experiencing higher rates of PTSD in accord with a dose-response model of trauma, the town residents with greater exposure actually had lower rates of PTSD. Evidently, social support factors act as a strong buffer to promote resilience and natural recovery after trauma.

## POSTTRAUMATIC RESPONSES ACROSS HISTORY

As discussed above, historical analysis provides another means by which to study cultures. Traumatologists sometimes point to historical descriptions of PTSD-like symptoms to support the universality of PTSD (Parry-Jones & Parry-Jones, 1994). However, a careful reading of the historical literature actually supports the opposite perspective. That is, the normative reactions to trauma vary widely over time, and reflect the dominant cultural theories about the impact of trauma (Herbert & Sageman, 2002). Consider for example, various trauma-related conditions that were diagnosed among railroad workers during the mid-19th century. These conditions, known as "railway spine" and "neurasthenia," were characterized by paralysis of the legs and emotional instability. Originally thought to result from spinal compression during injuries, both epidemiological and anatomical data soon revealed that the condition was actually psychological in nature. Jean-Martin Charcot (1889) went so far as to induce symptoms of railway spine using hypnosis. Analogous to current biomedical theories of PTSD (e.g., Bremner, 2001), Charcot believed his hypnotic inductions produced anatomical brain lesions that resulted in the symptoms of railway spine. Subsequent investigators, however, demonstrated that hypnotic effects were due to expectancies conveyed by the popular culture and the examining physician (Bernheim, 1889; Delboeuf, 1890). When care was taken to avoid conveying expectations of any particular symptoms, Charcot's hypnotic demonstrations could not be replicated. This led Hippolyte Bernheim and Joseph Delboeuf to emphasize the importance of fostering positive expectancies by means of an intervention they termed "psychotherapy." By the turn of the 20th century, railway spine was widely viewed as a posttraumatic psychological condition rather than a result of physical insult. Nevertheless, the specific symptoms of railway spine, particularly hysterical paralysis, stand in stark contrast to the symptom picture of modern PTSD.

Similar lessons have been learned in military settings (Jones & Wessely, 2005; Shephard, 2000). During the First World War, for example, a large number of psychiatric causalities were evaluated as a consequence of the relentless trench warfare that took place. The most common symptom presentation among psychiatric casualties in that war included mutism, hysterical crying, and intractable trembling (termed *Kriegszitterer* or "war trembling" by the Germans). Strong contrasts were noted between British soldiers' lack of improvement from "shell-shock" and French soldiers' swift recovery. This difference has been attributed to the fact that French soldiers were treated near the front without excessive messages of the seriousness of the condition, whereas British soldiers were evacuated to hospitals in England. During the last two years of the war, the British also adopted a program of rapid psychotherapeutic intervention near the front lines, resulting in dramatic reductions in psychiatric casualties (Shephard, 2000). In anticipation of the entrance of the United States into the war, the American physician Thomas Salmon (1917) further developed the French and English program into a strategy that came to be known by the acronym "PIE," for proximity, immediacy, and expectancy. Posttraumatic casualties were treated immediately and as close as possible to the front, with clear expectancies for full improvement. After a brief rest period, soldiers were given meaningful work, and returned to their units as quickly as possible.

Following the First World War, psychoanalysis became the dominant model of psychopathology in both Europe and the United States, and the powerful role of suggestion in posttraumatic reactions was all but forgotten. The initial campaigns of the Second World War brought alarming psychiatric casualty rates, which at one point even exceeded the rate of troop mobilization (Glass, 1973). When Salmon's PIE was reintroduced, casualty rates fell dramatically. Shephard (1999) has termed these approaches "Pitiless Psychology," characterized by avoidance of pathological diagnostic terms, initial periods of rest with an expectation of rapid return to battle, and elimination of pensions for war-related neuroses. The lessons of the two World Wars were applied by American military psychology and psychiatry in subsequent conflicts, with significant decreases in combat-related psychological casualties.

The popularity of current biomedical models of psychopathology, combined with a Western ethnocentric bias and a lack of historical perspective, has led to the widespread belief that PTSD constitutes a natural kind—a disorder that is universally observed throughout time and across cultures. To the contrary, our brief historical overview has shown that manifestations of posttraumatic symptoms have changed substantially over time. The lessons of the past century, and in particular of the two World Wars, highlight the critical importance of expectancies in the immediate aftermath of trauma in shaping subsequent pathology or recovery. Such findings call into question the prevailing conventional wisdom regarding the nature of PTSD.

## ASSESSMENT OF POSTTRAUMATIC REACTIONS

With an appreciation for the variations that occur in posttraumatic reactions, we can now turn our attention to issues of assessment and treatment. A summary of key points for clinicians to consider is presented in Table 10.1 on the following page.

Assessment of posttraumatic reactions almost always begins with a discussion of the nature, intensity, and duration of a traumatic event. When approaching this task, clinicians understand that some individuals may be reluctant to discuss their traumatic experience. There may be a variety of reasons for such reluctance, including shame, avoidance of painful memories or affect, or the belief that such discussions are irrelevant to the individual's current problems. Clinicians should be aware that a reluctance to discuss difficult topics can be more likely in some cultural groups (for example, Chinese and Latino men) than others (Norris, Weisshar, Conrad, Diaz, Murphy, & Ibanez, 2001; Wang et al., 2000).

**Table 10.1  Recommendations for a Culturally Informed Approach to Posttraumatic Stress**

| Assessment | • Assume neither vulnerability nor resilience.<br>• Avoid framing questions in such a way as to lead the respondent to conform to Western expectations of responses to trauma.<br>• Be aware that some individuals are culturally normed to minimize symptoms.<br>• Cast a broad net in the assessment of symptoms.<br>• Beware of assessment tools that are not carefully translated and validated into indigent languages. |
|---|---|
| Formulation | • Understand the impact of a traumatic event within the context of the meaning ascribed by an individual's culture. Don't assume that events have the same impact across individuals/cultures.<br>• Acknowledge that the way people cope with traumatic stress may vary depending on a number of factors, including cultural background.<br>• Be aware of unconscious and conscious motivations to present with posttraumatic symptoms, especially of PTSD. |
| Treatment | • Utilize a phased approach to intervention, with treatment depending on the acute, subacute, or chronic posttraumatic phase.<br>• Do not suggest directly or indirectly that an individual will exhibit chronic symptoms or will develop PTSD. Avoid psychoeducation, or administer only with extreme caution.<br>• Utilize culturally consistent sources of recovery (e.g., community-building and extended social support).<br>• Utilize CBT treatments across cultures, with sensitivity to cultural differences and incorporating relevant cultural practices.<br>• Work to reduce clinician-client power imbalance that may be exacerbated by cultural differences. |

When conducting an assessment interview, clinicians must avoid suggestive questions that could shape an individual's memory of the traumatic event (Loftus, 1997) and/or establish morbid expectancies. This requires keen interviewing skills and sensitivity to the individual's current state of mind. In addition, the clinician must be mindful of relevant cultural norms and mores. Resources such as the classic book *Ethnicity and Family Therapy* (McGoldrick, Giordano, & Garcia-Preto, 2005) are useful guides to typical cultural patterns associated with various ethnic groups.

A trusting therapeutic rapport is critical, and questions should be posed in an open-ended manner, especially initially. It is also critical for the clinician to suspend his or her own beliefs about how individuals "should" respond to traumatic events. In fact, it is helpful to go out of one's way to seek evidence that might contradict one's beliefs. Otherwise it is far too easy to succumb to what is known as "confirmation bias" (the highlighting and remembering of belief-congruent information over data that contradicts expectations).

A variety of clinician-rated interviews and self-report questionnaires have been developed to assess posttraumatic symptoms. Although such measures can provide useful quantitative symptom indices, they are not without limitations. All currently popular questionnaires and interview-based measures were developed in English, and few have been translated and validated into other languages. Some attempts at translation have revealed linguistic difficulties, as some common English concepts do not exist in other cultures. For example, there is no word for "trauma" in Kurundi (the language of Burundi, Africa). We are aware of one particular trauma workshop in Burundi that spent hours attempting to translate the word, and finally chose a phrase that means "having one's heart turned upside down" (A. Niyongabo, personal communication, March 15, 2005).

More fundamentally, there is the question of whether the concept of PTSD best reflects the experience of individuals in non-Western cultures. Consider that the most common approach to studying PTSD in non-Western countries typically involves these steps: translate PTSD symptoms into a native language checklist; approach an indigent population; assess the listed symptoms; find the extent to which they are endorsed by traumatized groups; report PTSD rates; and conclude that PTSD exists in that culture. This exercise and the findings that result are then used to support PTSD's presumed universality. An example of such a study was conducted by McCall and Resick (2003). They approached the Ju'hoansi tribe of Kalahari Bushmen, and with the help of village elders, identified individuals who had experienced domestic violence and who were symptomatic. They then presented these individuals with a translation of the DSM symptoms of PTSD. Not surprisingly, 35% of the sample endorsed symptoms of PTSD.

A critical problem with such an approach is that any constellation of symptoms among distressed individuals will inevitably lead to a certain number of positive cases. Consequently, the endorsement of distress symptoms tells us little to nothing about the actual validity of a proposed taxonomic entity. For example, suppose that we claim to have discovered a new diagnostic category, which we will call "post-amputee neurosis" (PAN). We claim that individuals who have lost a limb, especially as the result of trauma, will display a specific symptom pattern consisting of hypersomnia, joint pain (outside of the affected limb), anger outbursts, dissociative episodes, and intermittent periods of deflated self-esteem. Now, we translate a list of these symptoms into local dialects, and approach victims of the civil war in the Darfur region of Sudan. We seek out amputees in particular, read off our checklist, and ask if they have experienced these symptoms. We would not be surprised to find that a significant number endorse some of the symptoms. Moreover, we find that amputees endorse symptoms at a higher rate than non-amputees, and double-amputees endorse more symptoms than single amputees. Would these results validate the existence of PAN? Obviously not. Note that the more distressed the group, the more likely they will endorse symptoms of any form of pathology. And of course, amputees are likely to be more distressed than non-amputees (and double amputees more distressed than single amputees). Consequently, amputees will endorse more symptoms of PAN, or of most anything else on a psychiatric checklist, for that matter.

In order to assess how individuals from different cultures actually respond to trauma, one must avoid decontextualized checklists and instead cast a broader net. As the example of PAN illustrates, the nature of posttraumatic responses assessed in research is largely a function of the methods used. Mackowiak and Batten (2008) recently used the symptom checklist method in an analysis of the lives of four major historical figures (Alexander the Great, Captain James Cook, Emily Dickinson, and Florence Nightingale), and concluded that each likely suffered from PTSD. Of course, an examination of checklists for many different disorders might very possibly have resulted in the conclusion that these individuals fulfilled criteria in each instance. Thus, a depression checklist could lead to a diagnosis of depression, a panic checklist to a diagnosis of panic disorder, and so on. In fact, if one totally ignored historical and cultural contexts, it is possible that Alexander the Great could be retrospectively diagnosed with severe narcissistic personality disorder for wanting to conquer the world, and a possible psychotic disorder for believing in multiple gods, including one who periodically sent lightning bolts to Earth and another who created love with shooting arrows.

Additional issues may influence the assessment of posttraumatic responses, especially in non-Western cultures (Yeomans & Forman, 2009). Individuals may be motivated to respond with socially desirable responses according to their perceptions of what an appropriate or favorable response might be. Such effects are particularly problematic given the power imbalance that typically exists between Western researchers and indigent populations. Western knowledge is often tacitly held to be superior to local knowledge, regardless of its applicability in a particular context (Wessels, 1999; Peddle, Monteiro, Guluma, & Macauley, 1999). This can result in individuals modifying their reports, and perhaps even their actual experience, to match the perceived expectations of researchers. One example of this effect was found by Yeomans, Herbert, and Forman (2008). In this study, indigent rural Africans with greater exposure to Western PTSD psychoeducation reported more symptoms of PTSD relative to those with less or no exposure.

Actual or anticipated secondary gain can also shape reports of traumatic reactions. Individuals in poverty-stricken societies may be motivated to report symptoms of psychological distress in hopes of obtaining resources directed toward those determined to be most needy (Kagee & Naidoo, 2004). Similarly, resources for individuals in industrialized societies are sometimes contingent upon ongoing manifestation of symptoms. For example, current policy of the American Veterans Administration provides considerable compensation for PTSD-related disability, but payment ceases if symptoms remit (Frueh, Smith, & Barker, 1996). Such contingencies can create powerful incentives to develop, maintain, and report symptoms. This is not to suggest that individuals are necessarily malingering, although deliberate exaggeration of symptoms undoubtedly sometimes occurs. Rather secondary gain may reinforce the actual experience of posttraumatic symptoms. A parallel example exists among petitioners for political asylum for whom success sometimes hinges on the extent to which PTSD symptoms convince a judge of the veracity of their trauma history. It is important to recognize that these incentives exist for the clinician as well, if for no other reason than wanting to "help" their clients. These concerns have been discussed by Derek Summerfield, a British psychiatrist who views PTSD as a Western "invention" that has been improperly imposed on non-Western cultures (Summerfield, 2001; 2002; 2004; 2005).

Problems with research methods that rely on decontextualized checklists, combined with issues related to perceived social desirability, power differential between researcher and subject, and possible secondary gain, highlight the importance of research methods that strive to avoid these factors in order to provide the most accurate picture of responses to trauma. Examples of good practices include so-called "ethnosemantic" interviews by native interviewers that precede queries about specific symptoms in order to avoid contamination.

## CULTURALLY SENSITIVE TREATMENT

Before discussing culturally sensitive treatment guidelines, it is important to review several basic findings that pertain to posttraumatic reactions. First, contrary to the prevailing conventional wisdom among many mental health clinicians, the majority of people who experience traumatic events are actually quite resilient (Agaibi & Wilson, 2005). Most will be initially upset immediately following the trauma, and may experience a variety of symptoms, but will recover within a matter of days to weeks. It is therefore important that interventions acknowledge and address the short-term distress that most people experience, while simultaneously supporting factors that encourage resilience. Second, it is becoming increasingly clear that, in the immediate aftermath of trauma, people are acutely sensitive to suggestions regarding expectations of how one should be responding. Although such messages may come from the culture at large, they are especially powerful when delivered by health care professionals. If one conveys expectations that the trauma is likely to result in persistent symptoms, the likelihood of such symptoms increases. If, on the other hand, a clinician normalizes the traumatized individual's experience as temporary, transient reactions to extraordinary circumstances, with the clear expectation of full recovery, then the likelihood of recovery increases.

Despite this overall pattern of resilience, a minority of individuals continue to experience persistent and clinically significant symptoms. These individuals can benefit from scientifically supported treatments. Yet, even this group should not be subjected to interventions that convey that drawn-out posttraumatic symptoms are the normative reaction to trauma. Clinicians should avoid over-pathologizing an individual's reactions to adversity. Simply framing a reaction as a "symptom" of mental disorder can lead to iatrogenic effects. As an illustration, in our study of Burundian war trauma survivors, those who were randomly assigned to attend an intervention workshop that contained a standard psychoeducational component about PTSD had *worse* outcomes than those assigned to an equivalent intervention without the psychoeducational component (Yeomans, Forman, & Herbert, in press).

Taken together, these facts suggest that a phased approach to intervention is most appropriate, with interventions linked to the stage an individual finds him- or herself in relation to the traumatic event. Therefore, we discuss intervention efforts in three stages: the acute posttraumatic phase, the subacute phase, and the chronic phase (Herbert & Forman, 2006; Herbert & Sageman, 2002).

## Acute Phase

The most important priority immediately following a traumatic event is attending to the material needs of the traumatized individual, including safety, food, and medical intervention, as needed. Psychological interventions should focus on restorative and recuperative measures, in the context of supportive, encouraging, and optimistic messages regarding full recovery. The individual's reactions should be normalized, without undue attention. This is not the time for introspective analysis of the meaning behind one's symptoms. Adequate rest is essential and medication can be prescribed as a sleep aid if necessary.

It is important to encourage meaningful activities to minimize morbid preoccupation with the trauma and one's symptoms. This is not to suggest that individuals should be encouraged to avoid thoughts of the trauma or distressing feelings associated with it, or from speaking about it if they wish. Indeed, a growing body of evidence suggests that psychological avoidance can be quite problematic (e.g., Hayes et al., 2004). Rather, the idea is to encourage an individual to engage in meaningful activities to avoid morbid preoccupation with the traumatic event, to encourage a sense of self-efficacy, and, as much as possible, to restore a sense of normalcy. In this regard, indigenous cultural practices and rituals can be especially helpful. Thus, in certain Native American and Southeast Asian cultures, a specific set of post-trauma rituals has developed to cleanse the spirit and restore the soul (Wilson, 2006). In more collectivist cultures in particular, community-building efforts can be especially relevant. For example, after the 2008 Chinese earthquake, survivors quickly set about burying the dead, clearing rubble, and reconstructing schools and other communal buildings. Such community-building efforts have been empirically demonstrated to powerfully mitigate the effects of trauma in collectivist societies (Wang et al., 2000). More generally, clinicians should promote culturally appropriate forces of emotional and social support, and remain mindful that traumatic experiences and the responses that follow take place within a cultural context.

As important as what to do in the immediate aftermath of a trauma is what *not* to do. There is growing evidence that certain common posttraumatic intervention programs (e.g., Critical Incident Stress Debriefing) are at best ineffective, and at worse can be harmful. Indeed, professional treatment guidelines, such as the United Kingdom's National Institute for Clinical Excellence guidelines, explicitly caution against the use of posttraumatic psychological debriefing (Mayor, 2005). Certainly, clinicians do not want to export to non-Western cultures a treatment model that has failed in its own milieu.

## Subacute Phase

Even if morbid suggestions and expectations are carefully avoided, some individuals develop persistent symptoms and require treatment. There is no clear consensus on exactly when normal, transient reactions cross the line to become "symptoms" of a disorder. As a general rule, we suggest that clinicians consider treatment within weeks of a traumatic event if reactions remain highly distressing and cause impairment in functioning, as judged within the context of the individual's social group and culture.

With regard to what treatment is advised during the subacute phase, several studies in Western countries have supported the use of short-term cognitive behavior therapy. This type of intervention can be delivered a few weeks following a traumatic event to those whose symptoms have not resolved on their own. Research has shown that short-term CBT in the aftermath of trauma can be effective in preventing the development of chronic problems (Bryant et al., 1998, 1999, 2003; Foa, Hearst-Ikeda, & Perry, 1995). It is important to emphasize that this type of intervention should only be used with individuals having significant distress and dysfunction as a result of their symptoms. Thus, unlike debriefing programs that are improperly recommended for all survivors, short-term CBT programs are targeted only for individuals with clinically significant symptoms that have persisted weeks following the event. As in the acute posttraumatic phase, it is important that morbid expectations be avoided, and that indigent cultural practices be respected and incorporated into treatment.

## Chronic Phase

In the aftermath of trauma, some individuals continue to experience a chronic symptom picture, with impairment in functioning. A growing research literature supports the effectiveness of several specific, cognitive-behavioral therapy (CBT) interventions for chronic posttraumatic symptoms. However, nearly all of this research has been conducted with Western populations. Thus, the generalizability of these approaches across cultures is uncertain. Nevertheless, there are several promising indicators that the effects of CBT may generalize across cultures. First, the samples of trauma victims in a number of Western effectiveness studies were diverse ethnically and, presumably, culturally. Second, a few studies have specifically evaluated the effectiveness of exposure-based therapy for PTSD with racial minority populations. For instance, Zoellner, Feeny, Fitzgibbons and Foa (1999) compared the responses of African Americans and Caucasians to exposure treatment and found equivalent dropout and improvement rates. Similarly, a published series of uncontrolled case studies concluded that exposure treatment significantly reduced PTSD symptoms among low-income African American women (Feske, 2001). Third, the specific techniques of CBT appear to be based on sound, universal principles concerning anxiety reduction that might be expected to cut across cultural lines (Rosen & Davison, 2003). Fourth, there are a limited, but growing, set of studies of CBT-based interventions

for non-Western trauma victims that echo findings with Western populations (e.g., Paunovic & Öst, 2001). In one study, 43 Sudanese refugees in
Northern Uganda were randomly assigned to receive either psychoeducation, psychoeducation plus supportive counseling, or psychoeducation
plus narrative exposure therapy. Only those receiving exposure therapy
experienced decreases in PTSD symptoms (Neuner, Schauer, Klaschik,
Karunakara, & Elbert, 2004).

On the basis of the above, we suggest that clinicians operate on the
assumption that standard CBT interventions, especially exposure-based
interventions, should be the treatment of choice for chronic posttraumatic
symptoms in persons of varying cultural backgrounds. One important caveat
is that the intervention program, while retaining its core components, must
be adapted to be culturally respectful, sensitive, and appropriate.

## ADDITIONAL STRATEGIES AND CONCERNS

*Stress inoculation training:* Closely related to cognitive restructuring
is Stress Inoculation Training (SIT; Meichenbaum, 1993), a multicom-
ponent intervention comprised of relaxation, guided self-dialogue, covert
modeling (visualizing the successful confrontation of an anxiety-provoking
situation), role-playing, and thought stopping (e.g. subvocally saying the
word "stop!" to interrupt distressing ruminative thoughts). Although SIT
appears to be effective, some evidence suggests it is not as powerful as prolonged exposure and provides no incremental benefits (Foa, Rothbaum,
Riggs & Murdock, 1991; Foa et al., 1999). Moreover, growing evidence
suggests that attempting to suppress trauma-related cognitions through
such techniques as thought stopping may, in fact, paradoxically increase
the frequency and intensity of the thoughts (Harvey & Bryant, 1998).

*Acceptance-based therapies:* The paradoxical effects of thought stopping
point to the more general role of psychological avoidance (i.e. the avoidance of aversive thoughts, memories, images, emotions, etc.; Herbert,
Forman, & England, 2009) in the development and maintenance of
PTSD. Several models of cognitive behavior therapy such as Acceptance
and Commitment Therapy (ACT; Hayes, Strosahl, & Wilson, 1999)
directly address psychological avoidance and can be applied in the treatment of PTSD (Orsillo & Batten, 2005; Walser & Hayes, 1998; Walser

& Westrup, 2007). Although promising, little research has yet investigated ACT for posttraumatic disorders.

*Imagery rehearsal therapy:* Imagery rehearsal therapy (IRT; Davis, 2009; Krakow et al., 2001) is a specific cognitive behavioral intervention that can target nightmares and sleep disturbances associated with PTSD. In addition to standard sleep hygiene interventions, IRT involves having the patient write down a disturbing dream. The patient then modifies the dream however he or she desires, and the modified version is then rehearsed daily in imagination. Initial studies of IRT are promising (Maher, Rego, & Asnis, 2006). At the same time, clinicians should be sensitive to culture views regarding dreams and dream content (e.g., when dreams are thought to involve spiritual messages).

## Treatments to Avoid

When clinicians work with patients, it is as important to know what treatments to avoid as what treatments to offer. For example, there is little evidence to suggest that traditional psychoanalytic or supportive psychotherapy are effective treatments for chronic posttraumatic symptoms. Another approach lacking support is that of "psychoeducation," at least as it has been applied during debriefings in Western settings. As previously noted, there is, in fact, some initial evidence that psychoeducation about Western conceptions of PTSD is *harmful* rather than helpful. Recently, concerns with psychoeducation have been extended to a non-Western culture. In this study (Yeomans, Forman, & Herbert, in press), Burundians with severe and multiple trauma histories were randomly assigned to one of two versions of a four-day workshop, or a waitlist control. The two workshops differed only in that one intervention included a psychoeducational component. Results indicated that the psychoeducational component reduced the beneficial aspects of the intervention program, presumably by creating a morbid expectation on the part of the participants.

A number of so-called "power" or "energy" therapies have been aggressively promoted over the past decade for PTSD and related conditions, both in the United States and throughout the developed and developing world (Rosen, Lohr, McNally, & Herbert, 1998). The most prominent of these are eye movement desensitization (EMDR; Shapiro, 2001) and thought field therapy (TFT; Callahan, 1985). These programs claim to operate via unusual mechanisms, and promise much more rapid and effective treatment than standard therapies, including state-of-the-art exposure-based treatments. The evidence, however, does not support this claim. EMDR has been shown to be effective, but no more so than existing treatments, and in some cases somewhat less so (Davidson & Parker, 2001; Devilly, 2002; Devilly & Spence, 1999). Importantly, the distinguishing feature of EMDR—eye movements or other bilateral, therapist-induced stimulation—does not contribute to its effects, suggesting that EMDR is but a variant of cognitive-behavior and exposure-based techniques (Herbert et al., 2000). Similarly, there is no scientific support for the miraculous claims made regarding TFT and its variants. Despite these negative findings, power therapies have been exported to Third World countries in curious forms and for all manner of afflictions. The interested clinician can do an Internet search for these methods to find various examples (e.g., work in Africa by the Association for Thought Field Therapy). We strongly recommend that therapists avoid the power therapies, in favor of more scientifically supported treatments whose claims are consistent with the available evidence.

By far the most potentially damaging treatment approaches for posttraumatic reactions are programs aimed at "recovering" repressed memories of traumatic events. Such therapies may involve any number of techniques, including hypnosis, age regression, and guided imagery, that are designed to uncover "repressed" traumatic memories, often of childhood sexual abuse. Research has now convincingly demonstrated that traumatic repression is inconsistent with the way memory actually works (Schacter, 1996), and that these highly suggestive techniques can actually create memories of abuse that never actually occurred, which are then experienced as veridical (Loftus, 2003). Therapists should avoid such approaches, and should be especially mindful of the risk of inadvertently creating memories through suggestive techniques.

## CONCLUDING POINTS

In the past three decades, a tremendous interest in the psychological effects of traumatic experiences has developed. Creation of the diagnostic construct of PTSD in 1980 served as a catalyst to jump-start research and clinical innovations into posttraumatic reactions. Such work has yielded important fruit. We have gained a clearer picture of normative reactions to aversive events and factors that impede or promote recovery. Effective treatments have been developed for those with persistent symptoms. And importantly, we have an increasingly clear sense of what *not* to do.

The picture is not entirely positive, however. Despite these achievements, the construct of PTSD has become reified, commonly viewed as a "natural kind" that exists relatively independent of its sociocultural context. The results of cross-cultural and historical studies argue against this perspective. There is mounting evidence that posttraumatic reactions are shaped by a variety of factors. Among the most critical of these factors is the cultural context, which largely determines not only which events are experienced as traumatic, but the nature and degree of pathology of subsequent reactions. History demonstrates that normative posttraumatic symptoms have changed over time, while cross cultural research shows that despite some commonalities, symptoms appear to differ across cultures even today. In addition, the popularity of PTSD tends to draw attention away from one of the most striking facts about posttraumatic reactions: Most individuals show remarkable resilience even following severe traumatic events. It is critical that mental health professionals focus on promoting such resilience, rather than inadvertently undercutting it through well-intentioned but misguided efforts.

Rather than subsuming all posttraumatic reactions under the rubric of a single biomedical diagnostic label (e.g., PTSD), there is growing evidence that such reactions are best understood in their cultural context. Clinicians will find that their assessment and intervention efforts are most effective when infused with culturally sensitive practices.

## REFERENCES

Agaibi, C. E., & Wilson, J. P. (2005). Trauma, PTSD, and resilience: A review of the literature. *Trauma, Violence & Abuse, 6,* 195–216.

American Psychiatric Association (1980). *Diagnostic and statistical manual of mental disorders* (3rd ed.). Washington, DC: Author.

American Psychiatric Association (1994). *Diagnostic and statistical manual of mental disorders* (4th ed.). Washington, DC: Author.

Baron, N. (2002). Community based psychosocial and mental health services for southern Sudanese refugees in long term exile in Uganda. In J. de Jong (Ed.), *Trauma in war and peace: Prevention, practice, and policy* (pp. 157–203). New York: Kluwer Academic/ Plenum.

Bernheim, H. (1889). *Suggestive therapeutics: A treatise on the nature and uses of hypnotism.* New York: G. P. Putnam's Sons.

Bohn, A. (1996). Festivals and sex. In E. J. Haeberle (Ed.), *Human sexuality: An encyclopedia.* Berlin, Germany: Humboldt-Universität zu Berlin.

Bremner, J. D. (2001). Hypotheses and controversies related to effects of stress on the hippocampus: An argument for stress-induced damage to the hippocampus in patients with posttraumatic stress disorder. *Hippocampus, 11,* 75–81.

Breslau, N., & Kessler, R. C. (2001). The stressor criterion in DSM-IV posttraumatic stress disorder: An empirical investigation. *Biological Psychiatry, 50,* 699–704.

Brooks, D. (2008, Aug. 14). Where's the trauma and the grief? *New York Times.*

Bryant, R. A., Harvey, A. G., Dang, S. T., Sackville, T., & Basten, C. (1998). Treatment of acute stress disorder: A comparison of cognitive-behavioral therapy and supportive counseling. *Journal of Consulting and Clinical Psychology, 66,* 862–866.

Bryant, R. A., Moulds, M. L., & Nixon, R. V. D. (2003). Cognitive behaviour therapy of acute stress disorder: A four-year follow-up. *Behaviour Research and Therapy, 41,* 489–494.

Bryant, R. A., Sackville, T., Dang, S. T., Moulds, M., & Guthrie, R. (1999). Treating acute stress disorder: An evaluation of cognitive behavior therapy and supportive counseling techniques. *American Journal of Psychiatry, 156,* 1780–1786.

Callahan, R. (1985). *Five minute phobia cure.* Wilmington, DE: Enterprise.

Charcot, J. M. (1889). *Clinical lectures on diseases of the nervous system, Vol. III.* Trans. T. Savill. London: The New Sydenham Society.

Davidson, P. R., & Parker, K. C. H. (2001). Eye movement desensitization and reprocessing (EMDR): A meta-analysis. *Journal of Consulting & Clinical Psychology, 69,* 305–316.

Davis, J. L. (2009). *Treating post-trauma nightmares: A cognitive behavioral approach.*, New York: Springer Publishing Co.

Delboeuf, J. (1890). *Le magnétisme animal.* Paris: Félix Alcan.

Devilly, G. J. (2002). Eye movement desensitization and reprocessing: A chronology of its development and scientific standing. *Scientific Review of Mental Health Practice, 1,* 113–138.

Devilly, G. J., & Spence, S. H. (1999). The relative efficacy and treatment distress of EMDR and a cognitive behavioral trauma treatment protocol in the amelioration of posttraumatic stress disorder. *Journal of Anxiety Disorders, 13,* 131–157.

Feske, U. (2001). Treating low income Mexican-American women with posttraumatic stress disorder: A case series. *Behavior Therapy, 32,* 585–601.

Foa, E. B., Dancu, C. V., Hembree, E. A, Jaycox, L. H., Meadows, E. A., & Street, G. P. (1999). A comparison of exposure therapy, stress inoculation training, and their combination for reducing posttraumatic stress disorder in female assault victims. *Journal of Consulting and Clinical Psychology, 67,* 194–200.

Foa, E. B., Hearst-Ikeda, D., & Perry, K. J. (1995). Evaluation of a brief cognitive-behavioral program for the prevention of chronic PTSD in recent assault victims. *Journal of Consulting and Clinical Psychology, 63,* 948–955.

Foa, E. B., Rothbaum, B. O., Riggs, D. S., & Murdock, T. B. (1991). Treatment of posttraumatic stress disorder in rape victims: A comparison between cognitive–behavioral procedures and counseling. *Journal of Consulting and Clinical Psychology, 59,* 715–723.

Frueh, B. C., Smith, D. W., & Barker, S. E. (1996). Compensation seeking status and psychometric assessment of combat veterans seeking treatment for PTSD. *Journal of Traumatic Stress, 9,* 427–439.

Glass, A. (1973). *Neuropsychiatry in World War II. Vol. II: Overseas theaters.* Washington, DC: Office of the Surgeon General, Department of the Army.

Harvey, A. G., & Bryant, R. A. (1998). The role of valence in attempted thought suppression. *Behaviour Research & Therapy, 36,* 757–763.

Hayes, S. C., Strosahl, K., & Wilson, K.G. (1999). *Acceptance and commitment therapy: An experiential approach to behavior change.* New York: Guilford.

Hayes, S. C., Strosahl, K., Wilson, K. G., Bissett, R. T., Pistorello, J., & Toarmino, D. et al. (2004). Measuring experiential avoidance: A preliminary test of a working model. *The Psychological Record, 54,* 553–578.

Herbert, J. D., & Forman, E. M. (2006). Posttraumatic stress disorder. In J. E. Fisher & W. O'Donohue (Eds.), *Practitioner's guide to evidence based psychotherapy* (pp. 555–566). New York: Springer.

Herbert, J. D., Forman, E. M., & England, E. E. (2009). Psychological acceptance. In W. O'Donohue & J. E. Fisher (Eds.), *General principles and empirically supported techniques of cognitive behavior therapy* (pp. 102–114). New York: John Wiley & Sons.

Herbert, J. D., Lilienfeld, S. O., Lohr, J. M., Montgomery, R. W., O'Donohue, W. T., & Rosen, G. M. (2000). Science and pseudoscience in the development of eye movement desensitization and reprocessing: Implications for clinical psychology. *Clinical Psychology Review, 20,* 945–971.

Herbert, J. D., & Sageman, M. (2002). "First do no harm:" Emerging guidelines in the treatment of posttraumatic reactions. In G. M. Rosen (Ed.), *Posttraumatic stress disorder: Issues and controversies.* Chichester, England: John Wiley & Sons.

Jones, E., & Wessely, S. (2005). *Shell shock to PTSD: Military psychiatry from 1900 to the Gulf War.* New York: Psychology Press.

Kagee, A., & Naidoo, A. V. (2004). Reconceptualizing the sequelae of political torture: Limitations of a psychiatric paradigm. *Transcultural Psychiatry, 41,* 46–61.

Kessler, R. C., Sonnega, A., Bromet, E., Hughes, M., & Nelson, C. B. (1995). Posttraumatic stress disorder in the National Comorbidity Survey. *Archives of General Psychiatry, 52,* 1048–1060.

Krakow B., Hollifield M., Johnston L., Koss, M., Schrader, R., & Warner, T. D. et al. (2001). Imagery rehearsal therapy for chronic nightmares in sexual assault survivors with posttraumatic stress disorder: A randomized controlled trial. *Journal of the American Medical Association, 286,* 537–545.

Loftus, E. F. (1997). Creating false memories. *Scientific American, 277,* 70–75.

Loftus, E. F. (2003). Make-believe memories. *American Psychologist, 58,* 867–873.

Mackowiak, P. A., & Batten, S. V. (2008). Post-traumatic stress reactions before the advent of post-traumatic stress disorder: Potential effects on the lives and legacies of Alexander the Great, Captain James Cook, Emily Dickinson, and Florence Nightingale. *Military Medicine, 173,* 1158–1163.

Maher, M. J., Rego, S. A., & Asnis, G. M. (2006). Sleep disturbances in patients with post-traumatic stress disorder: Epidemiology, impact and approaches to management. *CNS Drugs, 20,* 567–590.

Marsella, A. J., & Christopher, M. A. (2004). Ethnocultural considerations in disasters: An overview of research, issues, and directions. *Psychiatric Clinics of North America, 27,* 521–539.

Marsella, A. J., Friedman, M. J., & Spain, E. H. (1996). Ethnocultural aspects of PTSD: An overview of issues and research directions. In A. J. Marsella, M. J. Friedman, E. T. Gerrity, & R. M. Scurfield (Eds.), *Ethnocultural aspects of posttraumatic stress disorder: Issues, research, and clinical applications.* Washington, DC: American Psychological Association.

Mayor, S. (2005). Psychological therapy is better than debriefing for PTSD. *British Medical Journal, 330,* 689.

McCall, G., & Resick, P. (2003). A pilot study of PTSD symptoms among Kalahari Bushmen. *Journal of Traumatic Stress, 16,* 445–450.

McGoldrick, M., Giordano, J., & Garcia-Preto, N. (2005). *Ethnicity and family therapy* (3rd ed.). New York: Guilford.

Meichenbaum, D. (1993). Stress inoculation training: A 20-year update. In P. M. Lehrer & R. L. Woolfolk (Eds.), *Principles and practice of stress management* (pp. 373–406). New York: Guilford.

Neuner, F., Schauer, M., Klaschik, C., Karunakara, U., & Elbert, T. (2004). A comparison of Narrative Exposure Therapy, supportive counseling, and psychoeducation for treating Posttraumatic Stress Disorder in an African refugee settlement. *Journal of Counseling and Clinical Psychology, 72,* 579–587.

Norris, F. H., Weisshar, D. L., Conrad, M. L., Diaz, E. M., Murphy, A. D., & Ibanez, G. E. (2001). A qualitative analysis of posttraumatic stress among Mexican victims of disaster. *Journal of Traumatic Stress, 14,* 741–756.

Orsillo, S. M., & Batten, S. V. (2005). Acceptance and commitment therapy for PTSD. *Behavior Modification, 29,* 95–129.

Parry-Jones, B., & Parry-Jones, W. L. L. (1994). Post-traumatic stress disorder: Supportive evidence from an eighteenth century natural disaster. *Psychological Medicine, 24,* 15–27.

Paunovic, N., & Öst, L. (2001). Cognitive-behavior therapy vs. exposure therapy in the treatment of PTSD in refugees. *Behaviour Research and Therapy 39,* 1183–1197.

Peddle, N., Monteiro, C., Guluma, V., & Macauley, T. (1999). Trauma, loss, resilience in Africa: A psychosocial community based approach to culturally sensitive healing. In K. Nader, N. Dubrow, & B. H. Stamm (Eds.), *Honoring differences: Cultural issues in the treatment of trauma and loss.* Philadelphia: Brunner/Mazel.

Pole, N., Best, S. R., Metzler, T., & Marmar, C. R. (2005). Why are Hispanics at greater risk for PTSD? *Cultural Diversity and Ethnic Minority Psychology, 11,* 144–161.

Rajkumar, A. P., Premkumar, T. S., & Tharyan, P. (2008). Coping with the Asian tsunami: Perspectives from Tamil Nadu, India on the determinants of resilience in the face of adversity. *Social Science & Medicine, 67,* 844–853.

Rind, B., Tromovitch, P., & Bauserman, R. (1998). A meta-analytic examination of assumed properties of child sexual abuse using college samples. *Psychological Bulletin, 124,* 22–53.

Rosen, G. M., & Davison, G. C. (2003). Psychology should identify empirically supported principles of change (ESPs) and not credential trademarked therapies or other treatment packages. *Behavior Modification, 27*, 300–312.

Rosen, G. M., Lohr, J. M., McNally, R. J., & Herbert, J. D. (1998). Power therapies, miraculous claims, and the cures that fail. *Behavioural and Cognitive Psychotherapy, 26*, 99–101.

Salmon, T. (1917). *The care and treatment of mental diseases and war neuroses ("shell shock") in the British army.* New York: War Work Committee of the National Committee for Mental Hygiene, Inc.

Schacter, D. L. (1996). *Searching for memory: The brain, the mind, and the past.* New York: Basic Books.

Shapiro, F. (2001). *Eye movement desensitization and reprocessing: Basic principles, protocols, and procedures* (2nd ed.). New York: Guilford.

Shephard, B. (1999). Pitiless psychology: The role of prevention in British military psychiatry in the Second World War. *History of Psychiatry, 10*, 491–510.

Shephard, B. (2000). *A war of nerves: Soldiers and psychiatrists 1914–1994.* London: Jonathan Cape.

Summerfield, D. (2001). The invention of post-traumatic stress disorder and the social usefulness of a psychiatric category. *British Medical Journal, 322*, 95–98.

Summerfield, D. (2002). Effects of war: Moral knowledge, revenge, reconciliation, and medicalized concepts of "recovery." *British Medical Journal, 325*, 1105–1107.

Summerfield, D. (2004). Cross-cultural perspectives on the medicalization of human suffering (pp. 233–244). In G. M. Rosen (Ed.), *Posttraumatic stress disorder: Issues and controversies.* Chichester, England: John Wiley & Sons.

Summerfield, D. (2005). "My whole body is sick . . . My life is not good": A Rwandan asylum seeker attends a psychiatric clinic in London. In D. Ingleby (Ed.), *Forced migration and mental health: Rethinking the care of refugees and displaced persons* (pp. 95–113). New York: Springer.

Terheggen, M., Stroebe, M., & Kleber R. (2001). Western conceptualization and Eastern experience: A Cross-cultural study of traumatic stress reactions among Tibetan refugees in India. *Journal of Traumatic Stress, 14*, 391–403.

UNESCO (2002). *Universal declaration on cultural diversity.* Downloaded from http://www.unesco.org/education/imld_2002/universal_decla.shtml

United Nations High Commission on Refugees (UNHCR) (2006). *2006 Global trends: Refugees, asylum seekers, returnees, internally displaced and stateless persons.* New York: Author.

Walser, R. D., & Hayes, S. C. (1998). Acceptance and trauma survivors: Applied issues and problems. In V. M. Follette & J. I. Ruzek (Eds.), *Cognitive-behavioral therapies for trauma* (pp. 256–277). New York: Guilford.

Walser, R. D., & Westrup, D. (2007). *Acceptance & commitment therapy for the treatment of post-traumatic stress disorder and trauma-related problems: A practitioner's guide to using mindfulness and acceptance strategies.* Oakland, CA: New Harbinger.

Wang, X., Gao, L., Shinfuku, N., Zhang, H., Zhao, C., & Shen, Y. (2000). Longitudinal study of earthquake-related PTSD in a randomly selected community sample in north China. *The American Journal of Psychiatry, 157,* 1260–1266.

Wessels, M. (1999). Culture, power, and community: Intercultural approaches to psychosocial assistance and healing. In K. Nader, N. Dubrow, & B. H. Stamm (Eds.), *Honoring differences: Cultural issues in the treatment of trauma and loss* (pp. 267–280). Philadelphia: Brunner/Mazel.

Wilson, J. P. (2006). *The posttraumatic self: Restoring meaning and wholeness to personality.* New York: Brunner-Routledge.

Yeomans, P. D., & Forman, E. M. (2009). Cultural factors in traumatic stress. In S. Eshun & R. Gurung (Eds.), *Sociocultural influences on mental health* (pp. 221–244). Boston: Blackwell.

Yeomans, P. D., Forman, E. F., & Herbert, J. D. (in press). A randomized trial of a reconciliation workshop with and without PTSD psychoeducation in Burundian sample. *Journal of Traumatic Stress.*

Yeomans, P., Herbert, J. D., & Forman, E. M. (2008). Symptom comparison across multiple solicitation methods among Burundians with traumatic event histories. *Journal of Traumatic Stress, 21,* 231–234.

Zoellner, L. A., Feeny, N. C., Fitzgibbons, L. A., & Foa, E. B. (1999). Response of African American and Caucasian women to cognitive behavioral therapy for PTSD. *Behavior Therapy, 30,* 581–595.

AFTERWORD

# PTSD's Future in the DSM: Implications for Clinical Practice

GERALD M. ROSEN
B. CHRISTOPHER FRUEH
SCOTT O. LILIENFELD
PAUL R. McHUGH
ROBERT L. SPITZER

Contributions to this book have shown the reader how three decades of research on PTSD and other posttraumatic reactions have advanced our ability to assess and treat individuals in the aftermath of adverse events. At the same time, this body of research has brought us full circle in thinking about posttraumatic psychiatric morbidity. When introduced in the DSM-III, PTSD rested on the hypothesis that a distinct subset of "traumatic" stressors (Criterion A) reliably led to a distinct clinical syndrome (Criteria B through D). With some irony, research spurred by PTSD's introduction has come to challenge most every aspect of the construct's originating assumptions (Rosen & Frueh, 2007; Rosen & Lilienfeld, 2008). This undermining of PTSD's ostensibly essential features (e.g., specific etiology, distinct clinical syndrome) is just one of many developments in a field filled with more than its share of issues and controversy. Chapters in this text have dealt with these issues, and provided recommendations and guidance for the practicing clinician. This leaves us to focus on PTSD's future in forthcoming editions of the DSM, and whether changing its criteria will impact clinical practice. These concerns go to the heart of how clinicians conceptualize their patients' problems, construct case formulations, and plan treatment interventions in the aftermath of trauma.

## PTSD'S UNCERTAIN FUTURE IN THE DSM

Several authors in this volume have discussed the origins of PTSD, its introduction into the DSM-III, and revisions that occurred in the DSM-IV. Now, leading figures in the field of traumatology are turning their attention to PTSD's future in the DSM-V and beyond. With an expected publication date of DSM-V in 2013, debate on whether and how to redefine PTSD's symptom criteria and conceptual foundations has increased in volume and intensity.

### Traumatic Events and Criterion A

A key issue in PTSD's uncertain future is the matter of Criterion A, and the assumption of a specific etiology. In the face of numerous publications that document PTSD symptoms without the occurrence of a Criterion A event, Weathers and Keane (2007) discussed the "Criterion A problem." After reviewing the literature, Weathers and Keane concluded that Criterion A still served a useful "gatekeeper" function and provided "a reasonable, viable definition of a trauma" (p. 115). They proposed that both elements of Criterion A (the objective life-threatening component, A1, and the subjective emotional experiencing component, A2) be retained. North, Suris, Davis, and Smith (2009) reached a similar conclusion while recommending wording changes for greater conceptual precision.

A different approach to the Criterion A problem was proposed by Kilpatrick, Resnick, and Acierno (2009). They concluded that Criterion A1 should be retained largely in its current form, but that changes in Criterion A2 were needed. One change to Criterion A2, requiring further research, would be to expand the range of emotional reactions beyond "fear, helplessness, or horror," thereby including a broader spectrum of subjective distress. Kilpatrick et al. also considered the advisability of changing Criterion A to include *either* A1 or A2, rather than requiring A1 *and* A2.

Spitzer, First, and Wakefield (2007) proposed that trauma should include only events that have been "directly experienced." McNally (2009) similarly suggested that Criterion A's definition be tightened, such that indirect, informational exposure to someone else's misfortune would not qualify as a traumatic stressor. McNally also proposed the elimination of Criterion A2. He noted that subjective emotions, such as fear and helplessness, confounded the concept of a response with the concept of a stimulus.

In contrast to proposals on redefining Criterion A, Maier (2006) has suggested that the gatekeeper requirement of a traumatic event should be eliminated entirely. Brewin, Lanius, Novac, Schnyder, and Galea (2009) evaluated the literature on Criterion A and came to a similar conclusion: "If Criterion A does not assist in making a diagnosis, and the attempt to define it simply creates controversy, it is hard to argue that it is worth retaining" (p. 4).

Perhaps most illustrative of the current situation, Long and Elhai (2009) reviewed the history of Criterion A and observed: "This issue's controversial nature and subjectivity in opinion can be demonstrated by the fact that the present study's authors disagree on it" (p. 175). In other words, even co-authors of the same article held differing views on how to resolve problems inherent in Criterion A and PTSD's assumption of a specific etiology. As noted by Dohrenwend (in press), recent data challenge the bedrock assumption on which the PTSD diagnosis is based, namely, that exposure to life-threatening stressors is the primary cause of a distinctive stress syndrome.

## Symptom Criteria B through D

Without a coherent position on the question of specific etiology, the validity of PTSD largely rests on the distinctiveness of its clinical syndrome. Yet PTSD's symptom criteria and their overlap with other disorders remain as controversial as the Criterion A problem (Rosen, Spitzer, & McHugh, 2008; Spitzer et al., 2007). Reflecting on this basic diagnostic concern, Asmundson and Taylor (2009) observed:

An important step in validating PTSD is to demonstrate that it has incremental validity over specific phobia and depression—that is, to show that the diagnosis of PTSD conveys important information relevant to understanding the etiology and treatment of trauma-related psychopathology that is not conveyed by a combination of these other diagnoses (p. 726).

Spitzer et al. (2007) discussed this "non-specificity" of the PTSD syndrome. Concurring with an analysis by McHugh and Treisman (2007) that PTSD had "redefined and overextended the reach" of long-recognized reactions to adversity, Spitzer et al. recommended a tightening of PTSD's symptom criteria. They proposed that only symptoms directly related to trauma exposure be retained. Thus, symptoms overlapping with other diagnoses (e.g., depression), including irritability, insomnia, difficulty concentrating, and markedly diminished interests, would be removed. McNally (2009) agreed with the possible elimination of nonspecific symptoms, while recommending that Criterion C3 (traumatic amnesia) be dropped. McNally also viewed several reexperiencing symptoms (Cluster B) as core to the PTSD construct, because these reactions (e.g., intrusive thoughts, nightmares) directly involve the traumatic event. North and colleagues (2009), in contrast, concluded that Cluster C symptoms (e.g., avoidance and emotional numbing) serve as the true markers of psychopathology. Within this framework, intrusion and hyperarousal symptoms (Clusters B and D) are thought to indicate emotional distress only. Empirical examination of PTSD's symptom criteria in adolescents and adults has yielded findings that further call into question the defining or core symptoms of the disorder (Elhai, Grubaugh, Kashdan, & Frueh, 2008; Ford, Elhai, Ruggiero, & Frueh, 2009).

Adopting a totally different approach to the issue of PTSD's symptom criteria, Resick and Miller (2009) observed that emotions other than fear or anxiety play a prominent role in maintenance of the disorder. They reviewed a body of research, leading them to conclude that fear is not necessary for the development of PTSD. As proposed by Resick and Miller, the symptom criteria for PTSD should be expanded to include other significant emotions, such as guilt, shame, and anger. Further, because fear and anxiety are not central to the development of PTSD, the diagnosis should no longer appear among the anxiety disorders, as is the case in DSM-IV. Instead, Resick and Miller proposed that the

DSM-V should contain an entirely new class of disorders, a "spectrum of traumatic stress disorders," which could include PTSD, acute stress disorder, adjustment disorder, and possibly such categories as "complex PTSD, complicated or traumatic grief disorder," and other "clinically significant trauma-related externalizing reactions not currently captured by any existing diagnostic category."

Rosen and Lilienfeld (2008) expressed concern that proposals to expand the symptom criteria and various new versions of stress-related disorders have led to a new form of "criterion creep." They echoed a point expressed by others (e.g., McHugh & Treisman, 2007; Shephard, 2004; Spitzer, et al., 2007; Summerfield, 2001, 2004) that PTSD was becoming a cultural narrative that medicalized an ever-expanding range of human reactions to adversity. They observed that peer review journals have published articles on yet another stress syndrome, "Posttraumatic Embitterment Disorder," and questioned if this development raised the specter of future proposals for posttraumatic anger disorder, posttraumatic shame disorder, and so on. Such extensions of the "PTSD model" and other unforeseen consequences caution against the adoption of new but inadequately tested criteria.

Debates on the future of PTSD in the DSM-V leave little doubt that most every assumption underlying this diagnosis has come under scientific scrutiny. Rosen and Lilienfeld (2008) even suggested that PTSD might best be listed in an appendix of the DSM that accommodates experimental criteria sets that remain in dispute and require further research.

## Working Proposal of the DSM-V Committee

In the midst of varied and competing suggestions on how to define PTSD's criteria, committee members for the DSM-V recently posted their current proposals (APA, 2010). At the time of this writing, the proposed criteria can be found at www.dsm5.org, under "Anxiety Disorders," and then "Posttraumatic Stress Disorder."

The direction that appears to have been taken by DSM-V committee members, is to maintain the stressor and symptom criteria with some modification. Criterion A is redefined in accordance with those who proposed dropping the subjective element (A2). If the current proposal holds, then traumatic stressors in the next edition of the DSM will be defined in the following manner:

The person was exposed to the following event(s): death or threatened death, actual or threatened serious injury, or actual or threatened sexual violation, in one or more of the following ways:

> Experiencing the event(s) him or herself
>
> Witnessing the event(s) as they occurred to others
>
> Learning that the event(s) occurred to a close relative or close friend
>
> Experiencing repeated or extreme exposure to aversive details of the event(s) (e.g., first responders collecting body parts; police officers repeatedly exposed to details of child abuse)

Committee members added a qualifier to exclude the possibility of PTSD being diagnosed after watching television or movies, "unless this is part of a person's vocational role." In some ways, this is a rather remarkable qualifying condition. One can ask if at any time in the history of medicine it was necessary to clarify whether a *new* psychiatric disorder might result from exposure to an entertainment medium. That such a statement is perceived to be needed is itself testament to the state of PTSD specifically, and trauma studies in general.

Further, the new working proposal for Criterion A does not resolve any of the core issues that constitute the "Criterion A problem" (Weathers & Keane, 2007). This same state of affairs applies to current recommendations by DSM-V committee members to redefine PTSD's symptom criteria. Based on findings from multiple factor analytic studies (Asmundson, Stapleton, & Taylor, 2004), the current working proposal is to group PTSD's symptom criteria into four clusters (intrusion symptoms, avoidance, negative alterations in cognitions and mood, and, alterations in arousal and reactivity), rather than the current three. Within these four clusters are listed 21 symptoms, as compared with the current 17. The new proposal, while vastly increasing the number of combinations by which a PTSD diagnosis can be obtained, does nothing to address the core issues of symptom overlap and co-morbidity with other diagnostic entities.

## Systemic Issues

Issues concerning PTSD and the DSM-V extend to matters that are systemic to the broader field of psychiatric nosology. Although a great deal has been written on these basic concerns, and how mental disorder should be defined (e.g., Beutler & Malik, 2002; Houts & Follette, 1998; Kirmayer & Young, 1999; Lilienfeld & Marino, 1995; Spitzer, 1999; Wakefield, 1992, 1999; Zachar & Kendler, 2007), these discussions are beyond the scope and purpose of the present text. Nevertheless, one central issue needs to be addressed, as it bears direct implications for the practicing clinician.

Within the DSM, psychiatric diagnoses generally are descriptive categories. In other words, clinicians classify, think, and treat their patients according to the presenting signs and symptoms. One benefit of this "atheoretical" framework is that it allowed for reliable diagnostic definitions that invigorated research and promoted uniform standards of practice. At the same time, the DSM employs a classificatory and diagnostic method that distinguishes disorders on the basis of manifest appearance, rather than on potentially etiological distinctions. In effect, the DSM approaches the task of diagnosing psychiatric disorder in a manner similar to the practice of internal medicine in the 19th century. At that time, possibly distinct disorders that induced fever, pain, or swelling were classified and separated according to those objective features, rather than on the basis of their underlying pathology and/or etiology.

Several commentators have discussed how diagnostic categories within the DSM identify subjects using a "top down" method (e.g., McHugh, 2005; McHugh & Treisman, 2007). This approach, in which patients are diagnosed in checklist fashion, is graphically demonstrated in the diagnostic "trees" appended to the DSM. Within this framework, if a shared symptom is given diagnostic priority, patients who may actually suffer from distinct disorders can be drawn into what becomes an over-inclusive category. Ideally, and contrary to the top-down approach, clinicians want to understand their patients by considering psychiatric disorders within the full context of individuals and their situational circumstances. By this method, a psychiatrist draws diagnostic formulations from a "bottom-up" approach that evaluates an individual's full biography and takes into account his or her previous psychological problems, temperament, mental state, and situational contexts. When thinking "bottom up," a diagnostician considers all forms of psychological maladjustments that people can experience and express with mental symptoms.

Although all may agree that a classification system based ultimately on greater understanding of pathology and etiology is desirable, psychiatry may not be ready to make such wholesale changes in the next edition of the DSM. With regard to PTSD, there have been recent efforts to understand the "nature" of the disorder as a stress-induced, fear circuitry problem (Shin & Handwerger, 2009). Yet, as previously discussed, Resick and Miller (2009) argued that PTSD should no longer be conceptualized as an anxiety disorder. These and other authors view PTSD as a disorder that conflates loss, grief, changed beliefs in self and others, and other reactions that occur in the aftermath of the traumatic event. And so, even with attempts to resolve systemic problems with the DSM, there are conflicting views of what should be done. There also are concerns that psychiatry is not yet ready for a paradigm shift in how it classifies disorder. As observed by Fyer and Brown (2009):

> Plans to make major modifications in the classification should probably be undertaken with some degree of caution. Although many patients have symptoms that do not fit neatly into the DSM categories, the use of these categories has clearly been helpful, both in describing variation in patients' subjective experiences and in enabling research that has improved both the efficacy and, at least in some areas, the specificity of treatment (p. 132).

Whatever takes place in the DSM-V, it appears that a genuine solution to the current state of affairs will not be found by adding more qualifiers to the diagnostic manual, or by debating what checklist of symptoms is best. Rather, a major modification in practice and thought is needed—one that encourages a thorough assessment of individual patients in terms of disorders that are distinguished on the basis of their pathology and etiology. When psychiatric nosology will be ready to institute such a change remains a matter of intense debate.

## SOCIOPOLITICAL CONSIDERATIONS

One other important contextual consideration is the sociopolitical background from which the diagnosis of PTSD emerged. Formal recognition of the diagnosis occurred in the United States in the late 1970s as the plight of returning Vietnam veterans received growing attention from the media and veterans advocates. Anti-Vietnam war voices joined with other groups concerned about rates of domestic violence, and together pushed for the creation of a new diagnosis that had both clinical and political utility (Satel & Frueh, 2009; Shephard, 2004; Summerfield, 2001). Perhaps more than any other diagnosis in the DSM, PTSD originated as much a political as a clinical construct.

PTSD's inclusion of a specific etiological event also opened the door for disability, workman's compensation, or other civil suit claims. Consider for example that 94% of treatment-seeking veterans also seek compensation. At the same time, a major portion of research on PTSD has been conducted within the Veterans Affairs (VA) system. Other samples of traumatized individuals (e.g., accident victims with personal injury claims) have entered the data pool as well (Rosen, 2006). The problem here is that individuals who seek disability payments may present with exaggerated symptoms that are unresponsive to otherwise effective therapies. In this way, social and economic factors can influence data and our supposed understanding of posttraumatic morbidity. That this is occurring was recently demonstrated in an analysis showing that VA disability policies were counter-therapeutic and hindering research efforts (Frueh, Grubaugh, Elhai, & Buckley, 2007). Other analyses have shown how financial incentives can undermine the integrity of the PTSD knowledge base (Frueh et al., 2005). Such findings raise additional concerns regarding how clinicians view the victims of trauma and apply the diagnosis of PTSD.

## CLINICAL IMPLICATIONS FOR UNDERSTANDING POSTTRAUMATIC DISORDERS

Issues covered in this book's chapters, and debates on the future of PTSD in the DSM, bear important implications for clinical practice.

Most important, the creation of the PTSD diagnosis in 1980 has shaped how we conceptualize an individual's reactions in the aftermath of trauma. On the one hand, the diagnosis offers several advantages over opposing frameworks, foremost of which is that the diagnosis is parsimonious. With the use of a single diagnostic construct, an individual's presenting problems are accounted for, an etiological model is provided, and treatment goals can be defined. On the other hand, the diagnosis is not without its limitations. Of greatest concern, the PTSD diagnosis encourages a "top-down" assessment model that lumps most posttraumatic reactions under the rubric of a single term. Essentially normal reactions are joined with more severe symptoms of disorder, contributing to confusion as to what is adaptive and what is maladaptive. Multiple processes (e.g., conditioned fear, grief, family dynamics) are conceptualized as largely "caused" by a singular event that is hypothesized to contribute to an underlying pathogenesis, such as fragmented memory or deregulated stress hormones. Finally, the diagnosis of PTSD creates the illusion that a disorder in nature has been identified: a disorder that accounts for and even "explains" an individual's problems. A clinician is then apt to apply the PTSD diagnosis to an ever-expanding array of events and emotions. In this way, human reactions to adversity become widely medicalized and the "PTSD model" increasingly becomes an overused narrative. Such an unmindful approach can mislead the therapeutic, rehabilitative, and prognostic proposals offered to patients.

Despite the level of controversy surrounding PTSD and the suggestion that it be placed in an appendix for experimental criterion sets, the diagnosis is unlikely to disappear from psychiatric classification in the foreseeable future. As observed by Shephard (2004), the construct has become too embedded in our professional and cultural narratives. Also, the diagnosis has a certain level of utility for the practicing clinician. Nevertheless, we urge clinicians to take into account the serious limitations of the PTSD diagnosis. McHugh (2008) argued, persuasively in our view, that PTSD is merely a descriptive label for a broad spectrum of states of mind that can follow horrific events, as opposed to a coherent and homogeneous mental disorder. Perhaps one day it will be shown that PTSD, in some revised form, reflects a distinctive disorder in nature that occurs among a *subset* of individuals exposed to trauma.

But for now, PTSD remains a label that reflects multiple concerns: the biology of human emotions, the psychological status of the individual, and the significance of the situation (both personal and social). Within this framework, the goal of assessment is to achieve an understanding of each of these themes on a case-to-case basis, employing all that we know about human reactions to adversity and the range of disorders that can follow. The essential take-home message from all we have learned is that clinicians should not reflexively apply the diagnosis of PTSD to all post-traumatic reactions.

Rather than conceptualizing PTSD as a genuine and unitary disorder in nature, we should consider the broad range of reactions that people experience in response to adverse events, and the complex contexts in which these reactions occur (e.g., an individual's pre-incident risk characteristics; life circumstances; adjustment issues required by losses and injuries; family and social contexts). This framework can be applied regardless of any changes made in forthcoming editions of the DSM. Interestingly, this broad view toward stress reactions was characteristic of thinking in the field of general stress studies decades before the PTSD construct was created. If anything has been learned from the long history of that field, and the far shorter history of PTSD, it is that multiple dispositional and environmental factors combine in complex ways to produce variable outcomes. It is difficult to imagine that the enormous complexity of human reactions to adversity will ever be explained by a single disorder in nature.

## REFERENCES

American Psychiatric Association. (2010, February). http://www.dsm5.org

Asmundson, G. J. G., Stapleton, J. A., & Taylor, S. (2004). Are avoidance and numbing distinct PTSD symptom clusters? *Journal of Traumatic Stress, 17,* 467–475.

Asmundson, G. J. G., & Taylor, S. (2009). PTSD diagnostic criteria: Understanding etiology and treatment [Letter to the editor]. *American Journal of Psychiatry, 166,* 726.

Beutler, L. E., & Malik, M. L. (2002) (Eds.). *Rethinking the DSM: A psychological perspective*. Washington, D.C.: American Psychological Association.

Brewin, C. R., Lanius, R. A., Novac, A., Schnyder, U, & Galea, S. (2009). Reformulating PTSD for DSM-V: Life after Criterion A. *Journal of Traumatic Stress, 22*, 366–373.

Dohrenwend, B. P. (in press). Toward a typology of high risk major stressful events and situations in posttraumatic stress disorder and related psychopathology. *Psychological Injury and Law.*

Elhai, J. D., Grubaugh, A. L., Kashdan, T. B., & Frueh, B. C. (2008). Empirical examination of a proposed refinement to posttraumatic stress disorder's symptom criteria using the National Comorbidity Survey Replication data. *Journal of Clinical Psychiatry, 69*, 597–602.

Ford, J. D., Elhai, J. D., Ruggiero, K. J., & Frueh, B. C. (2009). Refining posttraumatic stress disorder diagnosis: Evaluation of symptom criteria with the National Survey of Adolescents. *Journal of Clinical Psychiatry, 70*, 748–755.

Frueh, B. C., Elhai, J. D., Grubaugh, A. L., Monnier, J., Kashdan, T., Sauvageot, J.A., et al. (2005). Documented combat exposure of U.S. veterans seeking treatment for combat-related post-traumatic stress disorder. *British Journal of Psychiatry, 186*, 467–472.

Frueh, B. C., Grubaugh, A. L., Elhai, J. D., & Buckley, T.C. (2007). U.S. Department of Veterans Affairs disability policies for PTSD: Administrative trends and implications for treatment, rehabilitation, and research. *American Journal of Public Health, 97*, 2143–2145.

Fyer, A. J., & Brown, T. A. (2009). Stress-induced and fear circuitry anxiety disorders. In G. Andrews, D.S. Charney, P.J. Sirovatka, & D.S. Regier (Eds). *Stress-induced and fear circuitry disorders: Refining the research agenda for DSM-V.* Arlington, VA: American Psychiatric Association.

Houts, A. C., & Follette, W. C. (1998). Mentalism, mechanisms, and medical analogues: Reply to Wakefield (1998). *Journal of Consulting and Clinical Psychology, 66*, 853–855.

Kilpatrick, D. G., Resnick, H. S., & Acierno, R. (2009). Should PTSD Criterion A be retained? *Journal of Traumatic Stress, 22*, 374–383.

Kirmayer, L. J., & Young, A. (1999). Culture and context in the evolutionary concept of mental disorder. *Journal of Abnormal Psychology, 108*, 446–452.

Lilienfeld, S. O., & Marino, L. (1995). Mental disorder as a Roschian concept: A critique of Wakefield's "Harmful Dysfunction" Analysis. *Journal of Abnormal Psychology, 104*, 411–420.

Long, M. E., & Elhai, J. D. (2009). Posttraumatic stress disorder's traumatic stressor criterion: History, controversy, clinical and legal implications. *Psychological Injury and Law, 2*, 167–178.

Maier, T. (2006). Post-traumatic stress disorder revisited: Deconstructing the A-criterion. *Medical Hypotheses, 66,* 103–106.

McHugh, P. R. (2005). Striving for coherence: Psychiatry's efforts over classification. *Journal of the American Medical Association (JAMA), 293,* 2526–2528.

McHugh, P. R. (2008). *Try to remember: Psychiatry's clash over meaning, memory, and mind.* New York, Dana Press.

McHugh, P. R., & Treisman, G. (2007). PTSD: A problematic diagnostic category. *Journal of Anxiety Disorders, 21,* 211–222.

McNally, R. J. (2009). Can we fix PTSD in DSM-V? *Depression and Anxiety, 26,* 597–600.

North, C. S., Suris, A. M., Davis, M., & Smith, R. P. (2009). Toward validation of the diagnosis of posttraumatic stress disorder. *American Journal of Psychiatry, 166,* 34–41.

Resick, P. A., & Miller, M. W. (2009). Posttraumatic stress disorder: Anxiety or traumatic stress disorder? *Journal of Traumatic Stress, 22,* 384–390.

Rosen G. M. (2006). DSM's cautionary guideline to rule out malingering can protect the PTSD data base. *Journal of Anxiety Disorders, 20,* 530–535.

Rosen, G. M., & Frueh, B. C. (2007). Challenges to the PTSD construct and its database: The importance of scientific debate. *Journal of Anxiety Disorders, 21,* 161–163.

Rosen, G. M., & Lilienfeld, S. O. (2008). Posttraumatic stress disorder: An empirical analysis of core assumptions. *Clinical Psychology Review, 28,* 837–868.

Rosen, G. M., Spitzer, R. L., & McHugh, P. R. (2008). Problems with the posttraumatic stress disorder diagnosis and its future in DSM-V. *British Journal of Psychiatry, 192,* 3–4.

Satel, S. L., & Frueh, B. C. (2009). Sociopolitical aspects of psychiatry: Posttraumatic stress disorder (pp. 728–733). In B. J. Sadock, V. A. Sadock, P. Ruiz (Eds.). *Comprehensive textbook of Psychiatry* (9th *edition).* Baltimore, MD: Lippincott, Williams, & Wilkins.

Shephard, B. (2004). Risk factors and PTSD: A historian's perspective. In G. M. Rosen (Ed.) *Posttraumatic stress disorder: Issues and controversies* (pp. 39–61). Chichester: John Wiley & Sons.

Shin, L. M., & Handwerger, K. (2009). Is posttraumatic stress disorder a stress-induced fear circuitry disorder? *Journal of Traumatic Stress, 22,* 409–415.

Spitzer, R. L. (1999). Harmful dysfunction and the DSM definition of mental disorder. *Journal of Abnormal Psychology, 108,* 430–432.

Spitzer, R. L., First, M. B., & Wakefield, J. C. (2007). Saving PTSD from itself in DSM-V. *Journal of Anxiety Disorders, 21,* 233–241.

Summerfield, D. (2001). The invention of post-traumatic stress disorder and the social usefulness of a psychiatric category. *British Medical Journal, 322*, 95–98.

Summerfield, D. (2004). Cross-cultural perspectives on the medicalization of human suffering (pp. 233–244). In G. M. Rosen (Ed.), *Posttraumatic stress disorder: Issues and controversies*. Chichester, England: John Wiley & Sons.

Wakefield, J. C. (1992). Disorder as harmful dysfunction: A conceptual critique of DSM-III-R's definition of mental disorder. *Psychological Review, 99*, 232–247.

Wakefield, J. C. (1999). Mental disorder as a black box essentialist concept. *Journal of Abnormal Psychology, 108*, 465–472.

Weathers, F.W., & Keane, T. M. (2007), The criterion A problem revisited: Controversies and challenges in defining and measuring psychological trauma. *Journal of Traumatic Stress, 20*, 107–121.

Zachar, P., & Kendler, K. S. (2007). Psychiatric disorders: A conceptual taxonomy. *American Journal of Psychiatry, 164*, 557–565.

# Author Index

# Subject Index

# STUDY PACKAGE
# CONTINUING EDUCATION
# CREDIT INFORMATION

## A Clinician's Guide to Posttraumatic Stress Disorder

Our goal is to provide you with current, accurate and practical information from the most experienced and knowledgeable speakers and authors.

Listed below are the continuing education credit(s) currently available for this self-study package. *Please note: Your state licensing board dictates whether self study is an acceptable form of continuing education. Please refer to your state rules and regulations.*

**SOCIAL WORKERS:** PESI, LLC, 1030, is approved as a provider for social work continuing education by the Association of Social Work Boards (ASWB), (1-800-225-6880) through the Approved Continuing Education (ACE) program. PESI maintains responsibility for the program. Licensed Social Workers should contact their individual state boards to review continuing education requirements for licensure renewal. Social Workers will receive **4.25** continuing education clock hours for completing this self-study package.

**PSYCHOLOGISTS:** PESI, LLC is approved by the American Psychological Association to sponsor continuing education for psychologists. PESI, LLC maintains responsibility for these materials and their content. PESI is offering these self- study materials for **4.0** hours of continuing education credit.

**COUNSELORS:** PESI, LLC is recognized by the National Board for Certified Counselors to offer continuing education for National Certified Counselors. Provider #: 5896. We adhere to NBCC Continuing Education Guidelines. This self-study package qualifies for **4.25** contact hours.

**ADDICTION COUNSELORS**: PESI, LLC is a Provider approved by NAADAC Approved Education Provider Program. Provider #: 366. This self-study package qualifies for **5.0** contact hours.

**Procedures:**

1. Review the material and read the book.

2. If seeking credit, complete the posttest/evaluation form:

-Complete posttest/evaluation in entirety; including your email address to receive your certificate much faster versus by mail.

-Upon completion, mail to the address listed on the form along with the CE fee stated on the test. Tests will not be processed without the CE fee included.

-Completed posttests must be received 6 months from the date printed on the packing slip.

Your completed posttest/evaluation will be graded. If you receive a passing score (70% and above), you will be emailed/faxed/mailed a certificate of successful completion with earned continuing education credits. (Please write your email address on the posttest/evaluation form for fastest response) If you do not pass the posttest, you will be sent a letter indicating areas of deficiency, and another posttest to complete. The posttest must be resubmitted and receive a passing grade before credit can be awarded. We will allow you to re-take as many times as necessary to receive a certificate.

If you have any questions, please feel free to contact our customer service department at 1.800.844.8260.

PESI LLC
PO BOX 1000
Eau Claire, WI 54702-1000

# A Clinician's Guide to Posttraumatic Stress Disorder

**PESI**

PO BOX 1000
Eau Claire, WI 54702
800-844-8260

| For office use only |
| --- |
| Rcvd. _____ |
| Graded _____ |
| Cert. sent _____ |

Any persons interested in receiving credit may photocopy this form, complete and return with a payment of $15.00 per person CE fee. A certificate of successful completion will be sent to you. To receive your certificate sooner than two weeks, rush processing is available for a fee of $10. Please attach check or include credit card information below.

**Mail to: PESI, PO Box 1000, Eau Claire, WI 54702 or fax to PESI (800) 554-9775 (both sides)**

**CE Fee: $15: (Rush processing fee: $10)**       **Total to be charged** _____

**Credit Card #:** _____   **Exp Date:** _____ **V-Code*:** _____
(*MC/VISA/Discover: last 3-digit # on signature panel on back of card.) (*American Express: 4-digit # above account # on face of card.)

|  | LAST | FIRST | M.I. |
| --- | --- | --- | --- |

Name (please print): _____   _____   _____

Address: _____ Daytime Phone: _____

City: _____ State: _____ Zip Code: _____

Signature: _____ Email: _____

Date Completed: _____ Actual time (# of hours) taken to complete this offering: _____ hours

**Program Objectives**  After completing this publication, I have been able to achieve these objectives:

1. Recognize assumptions that separate PTSD from the more general field of stress studies.  1. Yes  No

2. Discuss major issues and controversies surrounding the PTSD diagnosis.  2. Yes  No

3. Distinguish between symptoms of disorder and normal reactions when assessing patients for PTSD.  3. Yes  No

4. Define "Criterion A" and explain why it is crucial to the PTSD diagnosis.  4. Yes  No

5. Analyze assumptions that underlie the concept of "traumatic memory."  5. Yes  No

6. Appraise the status of various attempts to identify a biological signature for PTSD.  6. Yes  No

7. Identify assessment strategies and instruments for assessing posttraumatic reactions.  7. Yes  No

8. Appreciate major clinical concerns when planning interventions in the immediate aftermath of trauma.  8. Yes  No

9. List components of the major evidence-based treatments for PTSD.  9. Yes  No

10. Understand the importance of cross-cultural perspectives and sensitivity to special populations when dealing with trauma victims.  10. Yes  No

PESI LLC
PO BOX 1000
Eau Claire, WI 54702-1000

ZNT042445                                CE Release Date: 5/27/2010

Participant Profile:
1. Job Title: _____ Employment setting: _____

1. Which of the following statements about the PTSD diagnosis are true:
(a) Numerous issues and controversies surround the diagnosis of PTSD
(b) PTSD has clearly been established as a disorder in nature
(c) Most individuals develop PTSD after a traumatic event
(d) PTSD's criteria have not changed since the diagnosis was first introduced in DSM-III

2. When a patient presents with loss of interest, anger, and tension after a traumatic event, the clinician should:
(a) Diagnosis the patient as having PTSD
(b) Diagnosis both PTSD and Depression
(c) Diagnosis the presence of a general Stress Adaptation Syndrome
(d) Distinguish between normal reactions to adversity and symptoms of disorder before providing any diagnosis

3. Which of the following statements is not true about the occurrence of PTSD symptoms:
(a) they only occur after a traumatic (Criterion A) events
(b) they have been reported in people watching scary television programs
(c) they have been found among depressed patients who have not even experienced trauma
(d) they can present among individuals who have no risk factors

4. Research has shown that traumatic memories are:
(a) Badly fragmented as compared to normal memories
(b) Often forgotten due to traumatic repression
(c) Accurately stored as if a "flashbulb" photograph
(d) Not unlike memories of non-traumatic events

5. Attempts to identify a biological signature have demonstrated:
(a) PTSD diagnosed patients have smaller than normal hippocampal volumes
(b) PTSD patients are often physiologically reactive when confronted by trauma relevant stimuli
(c) PTSD patients have abnormally low cortisol levels
(d) PTSD patients have abnormally high cortisol levels

6. Which of the following is an important issue when assessing patients for PTSD:
(a) Establish the occurrence of a traumatic event
(b) Consider the full range of disorders that can follow trauma
(c) Rule out malingering when issues of compensation apply
(d) All of the above

7. Which of the following statements apply to early interventions in the immediate aftermath of trauma:
(a) Clinicians should be cautious because early interventions can be harmful
(b) Involvement of mental health professionals is clearly needed to prevent future PTSD
(c) Trauma victims benefit from participating in critical incident debriefings
(d) Both a and b are true

8. The most effective component contributing to the effectiveness of Cognitive-Behavioral Therapy is:
(a) Alteration of the patient's cognitions
(b) Bilateral stimulation with alternating eye movements
(c) Planned exposure practice
(d) Psychodynamic analysis

9. Which of the following statements about PTSD are true:
(a) Posttraumatic reactions present the same across all cultures
(b) Posttraumatic reactions are universal throughout history
(c) Posttraumatic reactions can be specific to ethnicity and culture
(d) Both a and b are true

PESI LLC
PO BOX 1000
Eau Claire, WI 54702-1000